APPROACHING
THEATRE

Advances in Semiotics
Thomas A. Sebeok, General Editor

APPROACHING THEATRE

under the direction of
André Helbo, J. Dines Johansen,
Patrice Pavis, Anne Ubersfeld

with the collaboration of
Marvin Carlson, Marco De Marinis,
Svend Erik Larsen, Ane Grethe Østergaard,
Franco Ruffini, Lars Seeberg

INDIANA UNIVERSITY PRESS
Bloomington and Indianapolis

The paper used in this publication meets the minimum requirements of American
National Standard for Information Sciences—Permanence of Paper for Printed
Library Materials, ANSI Z39.48-1984.
♾™

Manufactured in the United States of America

Library of Congress Cataloging-in-Publication Data

Théâtre, modes d'approche. English
Approaching theatre / under the direction of André Helbo . . . [et
al.] ; with the collaboration of Marvin Carlson . . . [et al.].
p.   cm. — (Advances in semiotics)
Translation of: Théâtre, modes d'approche.
ISBN 0-253-32723-7
1. Theater—Philosophy.   2. Theater—Production and direction.
I. Helbo, André.   II. Series.
PN2039.T5413   1991
792'.01—dc20   90-43691

1 2 3 4 5 95 94 93 92 91

Contents

Foreword

In terms of its interpenetration with the rest of our lives, theatre should be the most approachable of the arts. Every child knows the pleasure of pretending to be something one is not, of acting a role in a world of the imagination, and countless modern studies in sociology and anthropology have emphasized how pervasive elements of theatricalization and performance are in our social and psychological actions and interactions. At the same time, the very ubiquity of the theatrical in human life and culture—and, conversely, the apparent ability of theatre, as a human activity, to absorb all other human activities into itself—make it so varied and complex a phenomenon as to test the limits of any mode of critical understanding.

How then can we approach the theatre critically, with any hope of gaining some useful insights into it? The first and by no means the easiest task is to determine, despite inevitable ambiguities, the object of investigation. What is the theatre object? Although elements of theatricalization and, even more broadly, of performance can be traced throughout our social and cultural structures, this study focuses upon the still very broad field of theatre in its traditional interpretation as a specific sociocultural phenomenon involving physical enactment, normally of a pre-existing text, before a group of spectators. Even so broad and general a definition suggests a variety of complex theoretical concerns. What are the psychological, phenomenological, and semiotic implications of enactment? What is the actual relationship between enactors and spectators? What is the contribution of each to the "meaning" or "understanding" of the theatrical event? And, perhaps most debated in discussions of the theatrical object, what is, or should be the relationship between the enactment and any pre-existing written text?

Traditional theatre scholarship has privileged the written dramatic text, and the many tools developed for literary analysis have been applied to it with considerable success. The theatrical performance, on the other hand, has been frequently neglected, or thought of as a mere illustration of the literary text. Although what semioticians have called the "performance text" has received much more critical attention in recent times, tools for its analysis are still far less developed than those for literary analysis, and the critical relationship between literary and performance text remains an area of much controversy. This is not only because the performance, operating on so many more channels than the written text, provides a more complicated object for analysis, but also because the performance is so much more clearly an unique event, and thus less accessible to the sort of analysis designed for the more stable written text. When one adds to this theoretical complexity the further problems of how to relate the theatre meaningfully to other media or to the broader concept of performance, the question of how to approach "the theatre" becomes a difficult one indeed.

The present volume attempts to provide an overview of some of the most promising recent work in this area. Its assumption is that so complex a phenomenon as theatre is best approached from a variety of directions, differing methodologies offering insights that will both complement and supplement each other. This is therefore a multinational and multidisciplinary endeavor, assembled by some of Europe's leading theatre scholars, and offering a general introduction to theatre study by combining recent insights from a variety of methodologies. It has a general orientation toward semiotic analysis, but complementary approaches—historical, sociological, and anthropological, for example—are utilized as well. The central concern is with analysis of the theatrical event as constructed on the stage and in the auditorium, with attention to the contributing elements of this event—the text, the actor, the space, the spectator, the social circumstances, and so on.

A number of features in addition to its wide range of critical methodologies distinguish this work from other recent theoretical studies of the theatre as a phenomenon. One is the concern with placing the theatre within the overarching world of the related media—radio, television, cinema, video. The interdependence and interaction of the various media is discussed and the media are compared across a broad spectrum of distinguishing features in subject, material, and function.

Another important feature of this study is a detailed application of critical analysis to a variety of specific recent performance events, both in theatre and in dance. Despite the great interest in theoretical analysis of performance in recent years, such analysis has tended to be abstract and general or, if focussed, has tended to focus upon the dramatic script rather than its stage realization. In Saussurian terms, *langue* has been almost always privileged over *parole*. The reasons for this are obvious. The script provides an accessible and relatively stable artifact for analysis, and has moreover been the traditionally privileged part of theatre, the authenticating basis for both performance and performance analysis.

This study directly confronts this problem, not only with a discussion of the complex relationships between written text and performance, but with a specific analytic strategy for the elusive "performance text." A detailed questionnaire for the guiding of performance analysis is proposed, and its usefulness demonstrated by its application to a variety of productions by major figures in the modern theatre, such as Peter Brook, Antoine Vitez, Pina Bausch, and the Royal Shakespeare Company. The resulting analyses are unique case studies suggesting how the range of theoretical approaches offered in this book might be profitably applied to specific studies of theatrical performance. Perhaps the most challenging single problem in developing a working methodology for theatrical analysis is the combined complexity and fugacity of the individual theatrical event that must remain at the heart of such study. The production analyses in this book should provide useful models for the further development of such a methodology.

Marvin Carlson

Preface

Whether theatre is viewed as textual product or performance event, it has today become the object of new types of enquiry and investigation. Sociologists explore the theatricality of everyday life, linguists remind us of the force of theatrical metaphors in verbal structures, neurochemists refer to theatrical functions, which they see as the new universals of behavior. Theatre practitioners write books describing their art, collaborate with researchers and academics, and add to the flow of scholarly studies on opera, dance, circus, and performance art.

This renewal of interest makes even more painfully obvious the lack of a good scholarly introduction to performance studies, but the task of developing appropriate pedagogical methods poses formidable problems. The challenge has now been taken up by four scholars, each involved in a specific university tradition, and in this joint work they have attempted to achieve two things: an introduction to the major scholarly theories that are being applied to the analysis of performance; and a multidisciplinary approach that through the very multiplicity of methods utilized will reveal something of the complexity of contemporary theatrical production.

This book is the result of an initiative taken by the Free University of Brussels, which in 1983 and 1984 was awarded a grant by the European Office for Cooperation in Education to coordinate a joint study program in the performing arts; thanks to the participation of the Institute of Theatre Studies (University of Paris III) and the University of Odense (Denmark), units of this educational program have been reviewed and assessed and tried out in practice with 600 students a year. The results of these trials, together with additional input from colleagues at the Universities of Bologna and the City University of New York, appear in this book in a variety of forms: surveys of current research, presentation of analytical methods and concepts, definition of technical terms, questionnaires, and case studies. Publication of this textbook provides evidence of both international collaboration and cultural pluralism; it is evidence, too, of an accord at the institutional level which has already led to exchange schemes for students in the participating universities. It is hoped that the directions indicated in the book will make it a useful contribution to all those interested in the study of theatre practice.

A. H.

APPROACHING THEATRE

I.
Performance studies

1. The field

The performing arts have become a subject of interest in a number of disciplines, each of which—in accordance with its own priorities—emphasizes different aspects of performance practice. The ensuing range of approaches is indicated in the following list.

a) *Empirical research* is concerned with collecting information about specific performance traditions. Ignoring theoretical hypotheses, it concentrates essentially on *notation* (of gesture, movement, facial expressivity, stage spaces, declamatory styles), the work of the actor, and the physical organization of the stage. This type of study finds its inspiration in the work of theatre practitioners themselves and for this reason may be unduly constrained by the metaphysical presuppositions inherent in notions such as the eighteenth-century codes of emotion and the performance conventions derived from them (including Lessing's *Hamburg Dramaturgy* and the writings of Goethe and Schiller). The tendency in some contemporary work (such as Eugenio Barba's theatrical anthropology) is to combine theatre practice and analysis: here the focus is no longer particular forms of theatrical expression but more general models of theatricality. Furthermore, twentieth-century dramatists have tended to undertake activities which one might have assumed to be more the preserve of other disciplines. Sociological concerns are one such example: the attempts to attract a working-class audience, to move theatres out of the big city centers, the choice of new types of performance space, community cultural-development activities. Semiotic analysis is evident in the claims of many directors: work on levels of meaning, rethinking the notion of character, physical performance styles, direct appeals to the audience. There is also the increasingly frequent tendency in modern productions for the stage to present its own functioning as part of the show. In addition to all this, the development of new stage technologies involving specialized knowledge (set construction, lighting design) has in turn inspired works which exploit the new technology in architecture, electronics (new types of color filter; remote control; programmed, automatically focused lights; lasers), and computer controls (microprocessors, etc).

b) *The social sciences* provide specialized methods and approaches which take dramatic text analysis into new domains.

Historical studies examine the conditions determining the theatrical production of a given period, and assist in distinguishing and identifying significant features. This sort of study emphasizes the extent to which stage practices, audiences, objects, and techniques are historically *marked,* exemplifying the social and ideological structures and "codes" of their time.

Philosophy approaches the representational arts from several perspectives in relation to time and truth (e.g., deception, Sartrean inauthenticity). Henri Gouhier's study of theatre aesthetics inspired a number of attempts to define the essence of theatricality. More recently, broadly based general studies such as T. Kowzan's *Littérature et spectacle* have attempted to situate the theatre in relation to other art forms, and this work is leading to the development of a poetics of theatre types (utopian, comic, etc.) which relates to genre theory. This is the goal that André Veinstein is pursuing.

Interpretative criticism, which derives from both philology and literary criticism, offers a number of theoretical options which facilitate recognition of operative features in the play or performance text (staging, acting, costume, etc.) and allow these to be "read" so as to produce an overall meaning, which may or may not be compatible with the initial interpretative hypothesis.

Dramaturgy, in the contemporary meaning of the word, is concerned with the relation between the means of expression (the narrative material, stage space and time, formal organization) and the vision of the world to be expressed.

Psychology provides a means to examine in greater depth the work of the actor (the more rigorous analysis of the notion of "doubling" and of the "natural" which practitioners have hitherto discussed in intuitive terms) and the experience of the spectator. The means of investigation in this area have been significantly improved (see Maryvonne Saison, *Imaginaire imaginable*) with the development of psychodrama. The therapeutic value of theatre has been acknowledged, and this has opened the way for both creative work and critical analysis (in theatre, dance, and puppetry). Psychoanalysts have undertaken a number of substantial studies in the field of theatre, especially on acting and on the play.

Sociological methods (interviews, surveys, statistical analyses) are being applied to audience reception: conditions of perception, audience composition (preferences, needs, patterns of cultural consumption), and to the relation between audience and theatre locale. More broadly, these studies situate the socio-cultural role of the theatre in the perspective of the leisure industry and in terms of cultural politics, as well as exploring the connection between the theatrical and daily life (Duvignaud, Goffman, Debord, Bourdieu). Demand analysis (box-office percentages, audience patterns) can be related to economic parameters (size of potential audience in a given area at a given time, the social and economic factors determining demand). The growing body of work in the economic domain can be related to Bourdieu's theory of *habitus.*

Semiotics looks at performance activity as a structure made up of sign systems organized into particular meaning-bearing ensembles, and its ambit includes the production process, reception, and performance models. Its aim is double: the study of both how the object of interest functions, and how the sign systems operate within the socio-cultural network. Theatre semiotics can thus be seen as essentially initiatory, encouraging interaction with a number of disciplines and providing a basis for assessing the relevance of their contribution.

c) Some of the "hard" sciences are also expressing interest in the study of performance. Biologists and neurochemists perceive performance as a "behavioral function" (Laborit) which corresponds to genetic programs shaped by environmental factors (simulacrum, ritual, and parade all share comparable rhythmical structures). Mathematicians such as René Thom have shown how these biological systems can be modeled; physics and acoustics—which in the work of Pradier designate theatre a "living science"—have also made notable contributions to knowledge in the last few years.

2. Means of investigation

The means of investigation at our disposal today are constantly being improved; nevertheless they remain constrained by the theoretical hypotheses which underpin them.

a) Questionnaires and other survey methods are geared to study from outside such things as the spectator's decoding processes. This book will, however, propose some new approaches in this field.

b) Visual recording methods pose the problem of what has been recorded and, more fundamentally, of whether to analyze code by code or within a global perspective. The *photograph* was historically the first such recording method, but we are now well aware that photography is itself a form of creative expression (*écriture*) whose "grammar" consists of such things as camera angle, lens type, light intensity, and depth of field. Rather than presenting an objective record of performance, it offers the possibility of re-creation. The same can be said of *slides*. Taking into account the above-mentioned constraints, still photography nevertheless makes it possible to analyze cross sections or slices of the performance and can also provide evidence of atmosphere or audience mood. *Film* brings with it the dynamism of the moving image, but this introduces the risk of distortion in the case of a very static performance, as some of Bablet's experiments have shown. The perception of the theatrical event through the lens of one or more movie cameras and the impossibility of presenting simultaneously both performance stimulus and audience response limit the value of this kind of documentation. On the other hand, the preservation of some trace of the performance can make analysis far more precise; documentation of rehearsals (for example, Vitez's record of the rehearsals of *Vendredi*) provides a great deal of insight into the creative process. *Video recording* is subject to the same limitations as film although the flexibility of the medium makes it more appropriate for precise documentation. Taken together, all these techniques constitute an improvement in documentary capacity in the domain of theatre. Theatre records have been substantially refined as can be seen in some of the collaborative ventures undertaken by libraries and theatre museums (e.g., the establishment by the International Association of Libraries and Museums of the Performing Arts (SIBMAS) of the pertinent features of theatrical productions, details of which are to be collected and preserved in a computer index). All of this provides the possibility of much more accurate and rigorous studies.

3. Terminology

The terminology used by theatre specialists is far from having clear, universally accepted meanings. It would therefore be useful to take an overall look at the theatrical lexicon and to describe the semantic field involved.

The word *theatre* (from the Greek *theatron*, a place for viewing, the amphitheatre surrounding the orchestra) designates a social space (theatre building or performance space). In French the word can also be used to refer to the audience (*amuser le théâtre*) but while the Oxford English Dictionary gives a similar seventeenth-century definition ("A theatreful of spectators, the audience at a theatre"—1602), this is not in current English usage.

The word *spectacle* (from the Latin *spectare*, to look) has two definitions. Strictly defined, it designates the visible aspects of the performance; more broadly it evokes symbolically an aspect of the general theatricality which is fundamental to our culture. [Translator's note: In English the term "spectacle" is used to refer to theatrical productions in which visual display is a dominant feature. A range of terms is needed in English (show, production, and —most frequently—performance) to indicate the semantic field covered by current French usage of the word *spectacle*.]

The term *representation* (from the Latin *repraesentatio*, the action of placing before the eyes, making a picture) is often considered in relation to the Platonic opposition between mimesis and diegesis. It accentuates the notion of performance as a physical event intended to make something present by substituting one thing for another; this paradox leads to consideration of both illusion and convention, and reminds us that theatre constructs meaning without denying the presence of the representing object. In addition, representation obliges us to think of theatre, not as a story told by a narrator, but in terms of a narrative communicated to the spectator through specifically dramatic languages.

The word *actor* (or the Greek *hypokrinomai*, to answer on cue, to explain, to play a part) brings in the notion of *role* and by derivation that of *ruse*. The word thus bears the mark of the actor's social status, alternately reviled and rehabilitated over succeeding historical periods. The lexical field associated with the actor introduces both play and theatrical code; today this correlation is seen as indicative of the social function of the actor, that of imitating a role that is not his own, theatricalizing a social role which activates codes other than his own. Like the jester, magician, and madman, the actor confronts society with an unknown "Imaginary" and reveals the codes underpinning this. From the perspective of writing, aesthetics, and ideology, the actor is a kind of freak, defined through play (which may or may not express genuine personal emotion), by social codes, and by the transfer of identity.

4. Methods

A. Means of expression

The physical means of expression, the actual substance of performance, are to a large extent the preferred object of reflection for theatre practitioners; besides reflection on the aesthetic message and the function of the performance, theatre directors tend to concentrate discussion on the following areas.

THE TEXT

For some, the text is seen as a written score which precedes the performance; for others the text exists only in its spoken form and in relation to the other performance codes. Repeatable and enduring, the text is transformed by the performance into voice, an ephemeral phenomenon. This transformation justi-fies the distinction between (written) dramatic text designed to be read, produc-tion text (stage direction, didascalia), and theatre text (the ensemble designed to be performed). While theatre history provides many extreme examples of a production text that has a dramatic function (Beckett's *Act without Words,* Cocteau's *The Human Voice*), it is now normally accepted that a production is composed of the interweaving of dramatic text and what may be called the text of tradition (the corpus produced by earlier directors).

SPEECH

The spoken word poses the problematical question of the power of language, and it therefore has to be approached through its intermeshing with other performance codes:

a) *Gesture:* either autonomous or as support to the verbal, preceding speech (Marivaux's *lazzi*) or following it, on occasion replacing decor. Movement can be symbolic (coded), a visual translation of relationships (Beckett), or a means of constructing place (Meyerhold).

b) *Facial expression*, basis of focalization, must be seen in terms of the overall aesthetic of the production.

c) *Props* (objects, costume, make up, hair styles, masks) have to be situated both in terms of the narrative content and of the style of staging (verism, symbolism, neutrality), and they contribute to the building up of layers of meaning.

STAGE DESIGN

a) Lighting can be used to assist focalization, to include or exclude the auditorium in relation to the playing space. From oil lamps to projectors, electric light to lasers, technological progress has profoundly modified the contribution of lighting to theatrical expression.

b) The same can be said of sound effects and incidental music. Creating a mood (Antoine) or imposing a rhythm on the action (Wagner) or on a character (Beckett), music can also be used to structure space (Arrabal) and to punctuate the performance.

c) The set poses the problem of the overall scenographic organization: it can be mimetic or symbolic, it can have a dynamic function (Craig) or a static one (Antoine), it can be used to display the plasticity of the human body (Appia), or it can be dispensed with entirely (Copeau, Vilar, Grotowski). Twentieth-century theatre has sometimes been dubbed a "progression toward emptiness."

STAGE/AUDITORIUM RELATIONSHIP

The relation between stage and auditorium raises questions concerning theatre aesthetics and actor training. The performance may or may not demand an active response from the audience. (Vilar aimed for communion; others seek provocation, guilt, the questioning of received wisdom, identification, demand for intervention or verification.) The emphasis in actor training varies greatly as a consequence of the performance functions desired: elucidation through theatre of the mechanics of everyday life, translation of universal myths, arousal of emotion, exploration of self, improvisation, acceptance or refusal of chance occurrences, and so forth.

The table below indicates a number of key moments in the development of performance theory as exemplified in the work of some major theatre practitioners.

The preceding description has utilised an empirical selection/listing of detail: it was concerned with the material substance of performance (staging, color, form) rather than the object of knowledge. Simply listing the component elements of theatrical performance in this way omits the signifying relationship —it ignores the work of the spectator constructing meaning by making connections across the spatio-temporal axis of the performance and elaborating structures of coherence. A further problem with this approach is that it suggests that the theatrical sign is constructed and defined exclusively through the prior existence of the performance tradition. Uncritical acceptance of the categories and reductive definitions (which are essentially the product of the directorial vision) would result in failure to confront the question of how the performance-object is constructed and indeed at what level it can be said to exist. While Artaud touched on the problematic involved in these questions, it is worth devoting a little more attention to the aesthetic and semiological dimension underpinning the accompanying table.

This table recapitulates a number of modes of theatrical presentation: pure performance, means of acquiring knowledge, place of fantasy and the fictional Imaginary. At the same time, it renders explicit a number of the variables governing access to meaning:

- interpretative rules derived from the work of the actor
- rules of translation of performance into fiction
- rules imposed by the spectators and governing the other rules.

Theoretical thinking about the theatre revolves around hypotheses of the kind mentioned above. While the concerns may be in essence philosophical or aesthetic, they manifest a number of preoccupations that have recurred throughout the history of Western thought. Lessing (in his *Hamburg Dramaturgy*) focuses on the intentionality of the actor's performance even when it falls clearly within the category of mimesis. Diderot's *Paradox of the Actor* emphasizes the theatrical nature of identification; his two other essays tackle the visual components (*tableaux*) of theatrical performance and its relationship to the spectator. Jacob Engel's *Ideas on Gesture and Theatrical Action* make explicit the connection between the actor's emotion and the rhetorical strategies employed. In similar vein, Gomperz situates the actor's performance in a "semasiology." We should also mention Valéry (whose essays on dance deal with the question of aesthetic function), Hegel (the actor as material support for the representation), and Rötscher (the relationship between actor and character). There is indeed a fairly direct intellectual line of descent (Diderot and Honzl, Valéry, and Mukařovský) through to the theory developed by the Prague School. Notable contributions made by the latter in 1931 include *Aesthetics of Art and Drama* (Zich) and *Structural Analysis of the Phenomenon of the Actor* (Mukařovský).

B. Sign systems

Members of the Prague Circle were the first to attempt any systematic theorization of the performance phenomenon. J. Honzl, for example, in his exploration of the way theatrical signs function (and in particular their mobility and transformability), rejected approaches restricted to the material reality of the stage: "total art can be seen to negate theatrical expression; the latter is ultimately no more than the sum, the juxtaposition, the 'coordinated presentation' of a number of material forms: music, text, actor, decor, props, lighting. The principle of total art, however, involves recognition that the impact of theatrical expression, in other words the strength of the impression received by the spectator, is a direct function of the number of perceptions flowing simultaneously to the mind and senses of the spectator."

a) The Prague Circle, in the work of Veltruský, drew attention for the first time to the semiotization inherent in the theatrical phenomenon. The process whereby all stage signs are rendered *artificial* is the basis for the transformation into intentional signs of all phenomena marked by theatrical convention. In the theatre all events, even chance occurrences, are necessarily resemanticized by the spectator: the unintentional sign (Jouvet's stutter, a chance scratch or blemish) is perceived as meaningful by the spectator. Bogatyrev reinforced the idea of the semiotization of the stage through his notion of the excess or supplement of meaning inherent in theatrical signs as what distinguishes them from the signs of everyday life. Mukařovský, too, explored the structure of the theatrical sign: for him the performance signifier or "text" was associated with a signifier established by the collective mind of the audience.

b) The system of stage meaning was also considered and it was claimed that the denotative/connotative network was activated dialectically by the actor.

c) The overdetermination of the stage signifier—even on the denotative level (Mephisto's cloak indicating alternatively his submission to Faust and his power over the forces of evil)—led to the study of theatrical codes. Honzl noted the interchangeability of signifiers (human body replacing an object) and the lack of limitations on the class of signifiers to which they can refer. The distinction between static (fixed meanings) and dynamic codes (open range of symbolic meanings) was thus introduced.

d) The Prague scholars were also interested in the hierarchy of codes: the way meanings are generated, the shifting between verbal and non-verbal communication during the performance, led to the notion of a layering of codes.

C. Descendants of the Prague School

A) COMMUNICATION

In the wake of concepts derived from linguistics, Georges Mounin attempted the analysis of theatrical phenomena in terms of *communication*. Mounin used the word in its linguistic sense (the intentional transmission of a message from emitter to receiver, perceived as such and entailing a response through the same channel); this was thus applicable only to the fictional world on stage, for the stage/auditorium relationship, seen in this perspective, excludes any response from the spectators (who are reduced merely to applauding, booing, or hissing). This radical linguistic position has since been largely abandoned by those who wish to study the theatre *sub specie communicationis*. The idealist notion of the gap between pre-production (author, written play) and production (involvement of director, actor, spectator) has been replaced by a materialist approach *in praesentia* to the performance event. Scholars are exploring the recognition of intention, aberrant decoding (Eco), and the delegation of pleasure (Helbo), and have thus emphasized the reciprocal functions of actor and spectator in the theatrical event. The stage/auditorium relationship having been established as socially marked (linked to a particular audience and its socio-cultural context), studies are currently focusing on the language of theatre perceived in its production or reception functions within the context of a shared social experience. It is in this sense that we now speak of *performance codes* (conventions specifically applicable to performance, genre, historical period), *general codes* (linguistic, ideological/cultural, perceptual), or *mixed codes* (general codes functioning in a specific performance context). The notion of an enunciating collective is a more accurate means of designating the process of communication in the theatre, which can be seen to consist of two elements:

• a *discourse* or combination of communicative acts (theatrical discourse constitutes a specific genre in that it displays its own rules of operation, renders them explicitly "readable" in their own context while dissociating them from their everyday functions);

• a situation of enunciation which evokes a dynamic set of relationships and contracts (pre-existing or constructed by the performance) determined by the prevailing ideology.

B) SEGMENTATION

The hypothesis of the minimal unit, dear to narratologists and film analysts, has been examined critically by theatre specialists.

• We will mention for the record the works on dramatic text by Souriau, which derive from the first wave narratological studies (Brémond, Propp, etc.).

• Others have suggested a segmentation based on text/performance correlation. One group in the Italian school (Serpieri) sees performance as an intermeshing of different discourses, the play text itself containing a performative/deictic articulation which provides the basis for performance segmentation and thus determines the structure of the *mise-en-scène*. The stage space in this view is organized according to the deictic markers contained in virtual form in the text.

• Rumanian scholars (Marcus, Dinu) have approached the question of segmentation with the assistance of mathematical models. Statistical analyses of actors' movements (relative frequency and appearance on stage of characters) enable them to reduce the performance continuum to a number of "hyper-syllables" or basic units of dramatic action.

• The Paris school (based on the work of Greimas) considers that the problem of defining the theatrical sign (performance units) has not yet been resolved, and is exploring both form of expression and form of content. Whatever the substance of expression (lighting, gesture, movement, visual detail), signification is studied as an autonomous entity. For example, a light/dark contrast associated with a day/night temporal segmentation would be taken into account if it played a structural role in ordering the text of a given segment of the theatrical discourse, in particular that of signaling a narrative progression in the story.

• Peircean semiotics, too, has attempted to regroup the dispersed theatrical signs into a number of functions (iconic, indexical, symbolic) which are applicable to both written text and performance.

	Repertoire/status of the text	Function of the actor	Concept of space	Aesthetic philosophy of production	Relationship to spectator	Relationship to other art forms	Theatrical activity/descendants	Principal theoretical works
Diderot (1713–1784)	score (plot)	relationship between emotion and expression	mimetic	theory concerning the condition of passion	contemplation (no participation)	connection with poetry	Le fils naturel, Le père de famille; Lessing, Engel, Morelli, Stanislavsky	*Entretiens sur Le fils naturel* (1757) *De la poésie dramatique* (1758) *Paradoxe sur le comédien* (1773)
Antoine (1858–1943)	Naturalistic repertoire (Ibsen, Strindberg)	member of ensemble, renewal of acting (direct style)	mimetic: detailed reconstruction of everyday reality	historical realism, verism, rejection of convention	fixed price, cheap seats; darkened, comfortable auditorium; contemplation of the production	importance of mood, atmosphere, lighting effects; unity of stage effects	Théâtre libre (1887) Théâtre Antoine (1896) Odéon (1906)	*Causerie sur la mise en scène* (1903)
Fort (1872–1960)	symbolist and poetic repertoire	symbol	symbolic; pure performance	idealism, symbolism	object of suggestion	use of dance and plastic arts in theatrical performance	Théâtre d'Art (1890) Lugné-Poe Rouché	
Stanislavski (1863–1938)	naturalistic repertoire; text to be lived	crucial importance of acting (psycho-physical and specific techniques)	mimetic and pure performance; naturalism heightened by stylized elements	synthetic realism to serve needs of the actor	emotional appeal	dominance of the actor	Moscow Arts Theatre (1898); Strasberg, Grotowski	*An Actor Prepares* (1926) *Building a Character*
Meyerhold (1874–1942)	symbolist repertoire	acting techniques derived from historical styles; biomechanics	importance of the forestage	constructivism, return to convention	social and political function of theatre, creative role of spectator	influence of pantomime and fairground theatre	Theatre-Studio Director of TEO (1919)	*Theatre writings* (1907, 1912, 1922)
Craig (1872–1966)	text replaced/dominated by *mise en scène*	Ubermarionnette, suppression of feeling	schematic decor, stylized perspective	symbolism, art of suggestion	symbolic awareness, intellectual response	Wagnerian synthesis: dance, music, lighting	productions of Marivaux, Shakespeare, Ibsen	*On the Art of the Theatre* (1905–1907) *The Mask* (periodical)

Appia (1862–1928)	text conveyed by actor's body	patterns and rhythm of moving bodies	set design to enhance actor's presence	rejection of realism	shared experience of beauty	fusion of means of expression	few productions (Wagner, Claudel)	*La mise en scène du drame wagnérien* (1895) *La musique et la mise en scène* (1899) *L'Oeuvre d'art vivant* (1921)
Copeau (1879–1949)	dominance of text	actor as professional; team work	bare platform	"illustrate the truth of the work"	educate the audience (*Cahiers du Vieux Colombier*)	synthesis of all arts	Vieux Colombier (1913) Les Copiaus The Cartel of 4 Vilar	*Notebooks* (1917–1930)
Brecht (1898–1956)	new style of playwriting; narration, fable, montage	dialectician, mediator, new acting style	historicized, stage presentation of contradictions in contemporary reality	epic theatre, rejection of illusion and empathy	social didacticism, alienation	reflection of real world	*Mother Courage, The Life of Galileo,* etc.	*Brecht on Theatre* 1930–1954
Piscator (1893–1966)	documentary	incarnation of historical figures	functional, architectural expression of social and dramatic relationships	collective elaboration of staging, epic form	didactic, political influence, radical action	incorporation of film segments, images, slogans	*Adventures of the Good Soldier Schweik, Rasputin* documentary theatre: Weiss, Hochhuth, Kipphardt	*Political Theatre* 1929
Artaud (1896–1948)	renewed attack on the text	freed from psychology and literature; embodiment of meaning through breath patterns and physical presence	progression toward the empty space, total spectacle	all-powerful *mise en scène*	cruelty, therapeutic remodeling of life	vision of a unitary culture where there is no distance between form and reality	poor theatre Grotowsky Beck Ionesco	*The Theatre and Its Double* (1938)

5. Performance models

The study of theatre has, over the years, included within its ambit numerous performance practices (inanimate signs such as puppets, in the case of the Prague School, circus, opera), practices which in certain forms of dramaturgy may well be combined. It is not surprising, therefore, that with the abandonment of linguistic and narratological models, research has been concentrated on the development of a specific paradigm: performance.

a) Numerous sociologists have noted that social structures are themselves theatrical in nature. Erving Goffman's studies, for example, which due to the vagaries of critical terminology have been dubbed "dramaturgical analysis," show that we can all be seen as actors involved in situations liable to involve us in theatrical strategies such as disguise or parade. Our daily lives are governed by interactions, and our cultural codes and models (*rituals of interaction*) can also be analyzed in terms of game theory; the rituals of carnival at the basis of our official culture (Bakhtin), Duvignaud's idea of generalized theatricality, and Goffman's notion of the presentation of self in everyday life all indicate that the very basis of our culture is structured around performance models. Theatrical performance itself, or other institutionally marked forms of performance, constitute particular cases, exemplifying in the here and now the functioning of effects within the performance domain. The problem for theatre analysts is thus to establish the means (markers, conventions, limits) whereby performance proper establishes its own distinctive territory, and how it exploits the ritualized functions which can also be seen to regulate our everyday "reality."

b) Analogous presuppositions are at work in the field of biology: Laborit includes performance in a group of behavioral functions (rituals, animal parades) controlled from the right side of the brain; theatrical performance proper demonstrates the mechanisms at work which are masked by the very familiarity of the social/cultural structures of daily life; he sees theatre as a means of liberating us from anxiety-producing inhibitions, as a way of reflecting, through its fictions, the suppressed Imaginary, and as compensation for the prohibitions of capitalist, consumer society.

c) Semiotics takes up these various preoccupations while developing a range of methodical approaches:
• the semiotics of Peirce offers a theory of levels of convention constructed by the culture; this is the point of his trichotomies (e.g., icon/index/symbol), which, he argued, govern our systems of signification.
• the semiotics of Greimas is equally concerned with performance processes (*le faire spectaculaire*) which are made operative through convention in the sequences of discourses (modalities of seeming and being) and in their actantial structure.

d) Theatre semioticians have for their part attempted to relate their definition of performance to the notion of performance discourse made physically manifest in the theatrical event. Three criteria of performance convention are currently the focus of research:

• convention as the basis of theatrical performance to the point of being its fundamental component. The various ritual markers which separate the performance from the real world (bells ringing, lights dimming, curtain) and the reinsertion of the latter into the fictional world (intermissions, pretend near-misses in circus acts) are inextricably linked;

• convention as related to denegation in theatrical performance: a given choice will separate fiction from referential discourse but almost immediately will reconnect the two: the voice of Jouvet reminds us of the actor himself and his immense prestige but then obliterates this in the service of the fictional character;

• convention as a means of drawing attention to the officially authorized nature of performance discourse. It sets the mechanisms in motion, establishes the limits of the contract, and circumscribes—in terms used by Bourdieu—"the I-we sanctioned by the group." The illocutionary value of convention (the condition necessary for illusion and fundamental to the function of denegation) opens up the question of the possible worlds thus created. The discourse of performance is typically made up of a duality: (1) assertion of the convention of the lie: this utterance presupposes a veridictory modality (assertion, reference to knowledge about the truth of the real world) which sanctions a regime (convention) whose impact is denegatory (lie or illusion); (2) pseudo-assertion inscribed within a possible world: a conventional utterance of doing contains an overmodalization of seeming which is (pseudo)justified on the basis of a desire to believe (the spectator accepts the lie as though he were accepting the real world).

e) The influence of historians has induced a certain doubt about the deductive hypothesis of a performance language of which all possible performances would be particular manifestations. The danger here is that one might extrapolate from one field of discourse to others, perceiving as definitely given functions (e.g., deixis, ostension, mimesis, projection) which are culture-specific and situated in a given historical context.

6. Production and reception of performance

Performance theory in its current state seems to have reverted to detailed analysis of the systems of production and reception. Chapter and section headings in the rest of this book provide an overview of procedures in current use, and the summary of these set out below is thus intended to set the parameters of the field as currently defined.

a) Production is concerned with the following:
• the work of the actor, its presuppositions and contractual aspects (I play / I want to listen-see / I comment / I observe)

- the pragmatics of speech acts
- the relationship between fiction and physical performance
- spatialization
- the construction of performance text
- the phenomena of denegation
  b) Reception is concerned with the following:
- visual composition and juxtaposition, linear/tabular perception
- the relation between the readable and the visible
- emotions
- the observer actant (see below)
- enunciation of/by the spectator (re/desemanticizing)
- verbalization by the spectator

   The division between production and reception has to be seen as a pedagogical distinction. A number of recent studies have gone beyond this division
in favor of the concept of the enunciating collective, and the notion of the
observer actant is of central importance to this theoretical formulation. Con-
ceptualized in terms of a cognitive role, the observer represents a specific function, one of the conditions of existence of the performance utterance (*l'énoncé
spectaculaire*). It is indeed the silent presence of the observer—syncretically
integrated into the stage reality (in the case of a play within a play) or auditorium (the theatre spectator has a double presence, both seeing and being seen)
—that enables the performance act or performance behavior to occur. The
watching eye, an indispensable part of the performance, is nevertheless incapa-
ble of any intervention that could change its progression, and the notion of
the observer actant refines considerably the analysis of identification initiated
by Brecht.

7. Pleasure and knowledge

   The theatre is the focus of a range of diverse intellectual practices and is
currently the focus of attempts to elucidate more precisely what constitutes
the pleasure of performance, and, more generally, the nature of the theatrical
experience.
   a) Far from being limited to a semiotic/cognitive experience, the theatrical
event provides a double form of intellectual appeal: primary (pleasure, acceptance of the fiction, feelings, expectations) and secondary (logic, interpretation,
assessment, memory); there is a movement toward trying to connect the theory
of focalization (attention stimulus) with that of emotional response (elementary
and complex emotion).
   b) Psychologists have used the theory of montage with good results: It is
claimed that the spectator, selecting from the available perceptual material,
organizes his/her own montage which runs parallel to that presented on the
stage. Confronted with the continual flow of visual information, the spectator

constructs his/her own "visions" from perceptual elements selected, and this montage (the viewer's "film") makes possible a personal narrative verbalization.

The experience of the performance can thus be described, not in terms of communication, but of active participation: focalization of attention through signalling devices and frameworks of enunciation set up by the stage, inferences based on the rhetorical strategies proposed.

8. Media theory

Analysis in this field has been becoming increasingly specific:
• the study of particular performance practices (theatre, circus, opera)
• improved definition of codes: the narratological dimension has not been abandoned but recontextualized in the total signifying network; the theory of segmentation—derived from film theory and more appropriately associated with cinematic discontinuity and with the mediating function of the screen—has been progressively abandoned by theatre specialists.

Having acquired a more solid intellectual base, theatre studies can now compare its object of analysis with that of other media:
• with mixed forms, particularly the comic strip, which utilizes in analogous ways the interaction of textual and visual elements;
• with the two-dimensional image and its visual components, which share certain optical and meaning-bearing features with the theatre;
• with television, whose structures of enunciation (continuous story presentation, unification of enunciative disjunctions) and communication (transmission and non-representation, contemporaneity of the referent rather than the signifier) can profitably be explored in connection with theatre.

BIBLIOGRAPHY

1. *General references*

Daniel Couty and Alain Rey, 1980, *Le théâtre,* Paris, Bordas.

Oswald Ducrot and Tzvetan Todorov, 1972, *Dictionnaire encyclopédique des sciences du langage,* Paris, Seuil.

Patrice Pavis, 1980, 1987, *Dictionnaire du théâtre,* Paris, Ed. Sociales.

2. *Dramaturgy*

André Antoine, 1903, "Causerie sur la mise en scène," in *Revue de Paris,* April.

Adolphe Appia, 1921, *L'oeuvre d'art vivant,* Geneva, Atar.

Denis Bablet (ed.), 1978–83, *Les voies de la création théâtrale,* vols. 1–11, Paris, CNRS.

Gordon Craig, 1911, *On the Art of the Theatre*, Chicago, Browne's.

Denis Diderot, 1959, *Oeuvres esthétiques*, Paris, Garnier.

Johann Jacob Engel, 1804, *Ideen zu einer Mimik* (1785), in *Schriften*, vols. 7–8, Berlin; 1971, reprint, Frankfurt, Athenaüm.

Gotthold-Ephraim Lessing, 1886–1924, *Sämtliche Schriften*, 23 vols., (ed. K. L. Lachmann, under the direction of F. Muncker) Stuttgart, Berlin, and Leipzig.

Constantin Stanislavski, 1936, *An Actor Prepares* (trans. E. R. Hapgood), New York.

3. Aesthetics

Monique Borie, Martine de Rougemont, Jacques Schérer, 1982, *Esthétique théâtrale*, Paris, CDU-Sedes.

Henry Gouhier, 1968, *L'essence du théâtre*, Paris, Flammarion.

Roman Ingarden, 1958, "The Literary Work of Art," appendix to *The Functions of Language in the Theatre*, Evanston, Northwestern Univ. Press.

Tadeusz Kowzan, 1975, *Littérature et spectacle*, Paris and La Haye, Mouton.

Paul Valéry, 1960, *Eupalinos: L'âme et la danse. Dialogue de l'arbre*, Paris, Gallimard.

André Veinstein, 1955, *La mise en scène théâtrale et sa condition esthétique*, Paris, Flammarion.

4. Performing arts

Denis Bablet, 1981, Filmer le théâtre, in *Cahiers théâtre Louvain*, 46.

Jean Baudrillard, 1972, "Requiem pour les médias," in *Pour une critique de l'économie politique du signe*, Paris, Gallimard.

Walter Benjamin, 1971, "L'oeuvre d'art à l'ère de sa reproductivité technique," in *L'Homme, le langage et la culture*, Paris, Denoël-Gonthier.

Dany Bloch, 1983, *L'art vidéo*, Paris, Limage 2—Alin Avila.

Patrice Flichy, 1980, *Les industries de l'imaginaire*, P. U. Grenoble, I.N.A.

André Helbo, 1986, *Approches de l'opéra*, Paris, Didier Erudition.

Hugues Hotier, 1984, *Signes du cirque*, Bruxelles AISS-IASPA (Tréteaux).

Kodikas/Code, 1984, 7, "Le spectacle au pluriel," Tübingen.

Marshall McLuhan, 1968, *Pour comprendre les media*, Paris, Mame/Seuil.

Edgar Morin, 1958, *Le cinéma ou l'homme imaginaire*, Paris, Minuit.

5. History

Denis Bablet, 1975, *Les révolutions scéniques au XXe siècle*, Paris, Société Internationale d'Art XXe siècle.

Marvin Carlson, 1985, *Theories of the Theatre*, Cornell University Press.

David Cole, 1975, *The Theatrical Event*, Middleton, Conn.

Gilbert Debusscher and Alain Van Crugten (eds.), 1983, *Théâtre de toujours, d'Aristote à Kalisky*, Brussels, Ed. U.L.B.

Paul Delsemme, 1983, *L'oeuvre dramatique, sa structure et sa représentation*, Brussels, Ed. U.L.B.

Maurice Descotes, 1964, *Le public de théâtre et son histoire*, Paris, Presses Universitaires de France.

Guy Dumur (ed.), 1968, *Histoire des spectacles*, Paris, Gallimard (*La Pléiade*).

Erika Fischer-Lichte, 1983, *Semiotik des theatre*, 3 vols., Tübingen, Gunter Narr.

Robert Pignarre, 1967, *Histoire du théâtre*, Paris, Presses Universitaires de France.

Richard Southern, 1964, *The Seven Ages of Theatre*, New York.

Jiřy Veltruský, "La sémiologie du spectacle à la recherche de son passé," in A. Helbo, *Approches de l'opéra*, Paris, Didier Erudition.

6. *Sociology*

Mikhail Bahktin, 1976, "Problema Teksta," *Voprosy literatury*, 10, pp. 122–51.

Pierre Bourdieu, 1979, *La distinction*, Paris, Minuit.

Guy Debord, 1967, *La société du spectacle*, Paris.

Robert Demarcy, 1973, *Eléments d'une sociologie du spectacle*, Paris, UGE.

Marco De Marinis, "Theatrical Comprehension: A Socio-semiotic Approach," in *Theater*, 15, no. 1.

1984, *L'esperienza dello spettatore*, Univ. di Urbino, Nov.–Dec.

Jean Duvignaud, 1965, *Sociologie du théâtre: Essai sur les ombres collectives*, Paris, Presses Universitaires de France.

1965, *L'acteur: Esquisse d'une sociologie du comédien*, Paris, Gallimard.

1970, *Spectacle et société*, Paris, Denoël-Gonthier.

1972, *The Sociology of Art*, London, Harper and Row.

1973, *Fêtes et civilisations*, Paris, Weber.

1977, *Le don du rien*, Paris, Stock.

Jean Duvignaud and Jean-Pierre Faye, 1966, "Débat sur la sociologie du théâtre," in *Cahiers internationaux de sociologie*, pp. 103–112.

Erving Goffman, 1959, *The Presentation of Self in Everyday Life*, New York, Doubleday.

1961, *Encounters*, Indianapolis, Bobbs-Merrill.

1963, *Behavior in Public Places*, The Free Press of Glencoe.

1967, *Interaction Ritual*, New York, Doubleday.

1971, *Relations in Public*, New York, Basic Books.

1974, *Frame Analysis: An Essay on the Organisation of Experience*, New York, Harper and Row.

Lucien Goldmann, 1964, *The Hidden God*, New York.

A.-M. Gourdon, 1982, *Théâtre, public, perception*, Paris, CNRS

G. Gurvitch, 1956, "Sociologie du théâtre," in *Lettres Nouvelles*, 35.

André Helbo, 1983, *Les mots et les gestes,* Lille, Presses de l'Université de Lille.

1987, *Theory of Performing Arts,* Amsterdam and Philadelphia, Benjamins.

Ernest Hess-Lüttich, *Multimedial Communication II,* Tübingen, Gunter Narr Verlag.

Abraham Moles, 1986, "Peut-on construire une sémiologie des actes à propos d'une représentation théâtrale?" in A. Helbo, 1986, *Approches de l'opéra,* Paris, Didier Erudition.

Jean-Pierre Vernant and Pierre Vidal-Naquet, 1972, *Mythe et tragédie en Grèce ancienne,* Paris, Maspero.

M. Wolf, 1979, *Sociologie della vita quotidiana,* Milan, Strumenti Espresso.

7. Economics

C. D. Throsby and G. A. Whriters, 1979, *The Economics of the Performing Arts,* Victoria, Edward Arnold.

8. Anthropology

Eugenio Barba, 1982, "Anthropologie théâtrale," in *Degrés* 29, Brussels.

Jerzy Grotowski, 1968, *Towards a Poor Theatre,* New York.

Franco Ruffini (dir.), 1981, *La scuola degli attori: Rapporti dalla prima sessione dell'I.S.T.A.,* Florence, Usher.

Nicola Savarese, 1985, *Anatomie de l'acteur: Un dictionnaire d'anthropologie théâtrale,* Rome and Carcassone, Zeami- Bouffonneries.

Richard Schechner, 1985, *Between Theatre and Anthropology,* Philadelphia, Univ. of Pennsylvania Press.

Ferdinando Taviani, 1986, "Presenza energica ed espressione amorosa nella Commedia dell'Arte," in *Teatro e Storia* (Dipartimento di Musica e Spettacolo dell'Universita di Bologna), 2.

9. Semiotics

J. L. Austin, 1962, *How to Do Things with Words,* London, Oxford Univ. Press.

Petr Bogatyrev, 1971, "Les signes du théâtre," in *Poétique,* 8, pp. 517–30.

Diez Borque and Luciano Garcio Lorenzo (ed.), 1975. *Semiologia del teatro,* Barcelona, Planeta.

Michel Corvin, 1985, *Molière,* Presses Universitaires de Lyon.

Degrés, 1978, 13, Théâtre et sémiologie, Brussels.

1979, 18, Sémiologie de la musique, Brussels.

1982, 29–32, Sémiologie du spectacle (Actes du colloque AISS-AISPA), Brussels.

Marco De Marinis, 1982, *Semiotica del teatro,* Milan, Bompiani.

Oswald Ducrot, 1972, *Dire et ne pas dire,* Paris, Hermann.

Umberto Eco, 1977, "Semiotics of Performance," in *The Drama Review,* 21, no. 1.

1978, "Pour une reformulation du signe iconique," in *Communications*, 29, Paris, Seuil.

Keir Elam, 1980, *The Semiotics of Theatre and Drama*, London, Methuen.

1984, *Shakespeare's Universe of Discourse: Language Games in the Comedies*, Cambridge, Cambridge Univ. Press.

Etudes littéraires, 1980, 13/3, Théâtre et théâtralité, Montreal.

Algirdas Julien Greimas, 1966, *Sémantique structurale*, Paris, Larousse.

1970, *Du Sens*, Paris, Seuil.

T. E. Hall, 1971, *La dimension cachée*, Paris, Seuil.

1979, *Au-delà de la culture*, Paris, Seuil.

André Helbo, 1975, *Sémiologie de la représentation*, Brussels and Paris, Complexe— Presses Universitaires de France.

1979, *Le champ sémiologique*, Brussels, Complexe.

1983, *Sémiologie des messages sociaux*, Paris, Edilig.

1985, "Approches de la réception: Quelques problèmes," in *VS*, 41, pp. 41– 48.

Jindrich Honzl, "Dynamics in the Sign of the Theater," in Matejka Titunik, pp. 118– 127.

Roman Jakobson, 1963, *Essais de linguistique générale*, Paris, Minuit.

J. Dines Johansen, 1980, "Sémiotique et pragmatique universelle," in *Degrés*, 21, Brussels.

Solomon Marcus, 1975, "Stratégie des personnages dramatiques," in Helbo, 1975, *Sémiologie de la représentation*, Brussels and Paris, Complexe—Presses Universitaires de France.

Ladislaw Matejka and Irwin R. Titunik, 1976, *Semiotics of Art: Prague School Contributions*, Cambridge, MIT Press.

Georges Mounin, 1970, *Introduction à la sémiologie*, Paris, Minuit.

Jan Mukařovský, 1934, *L'art comme fait sémiologique: Actes du huitième congrès de philosophie à Prague*; 1976, trans. in Mateyka and Titunik, pp. 3–10.

1978, *Structure, Sign and Function* (ed. J. Burbank and P. Steiner), New Haven, Yale Univ. Press.

Patrice Pavis, 1976, *Problèmes de sémiologie théâtrale*, Montréal, P.U.Q.

1982, *Voix et images de la scène*, Presses Universitaires de Lille; 1972, trans. Performing Arts Journal, New York.

Michel Pecheux, 1975, *Les vérités de la Palice: linguistique, sémantique, philosophie*, Paris, Maspero.

Charles Sanders Peirce, 1931–58, *Collected Papers*, 8 vols., Cambridge.

Poetics Today, 1981, 2, no. 3, Drama, Theater, Performance, Tel Aviv.

Franco Ruffini, 1978, *Semiotica del testo: l'esempio teatro*, Rome, Bulzoni.

Herta Schmid and Aloysius Van Kesteren, 1984, *Semiotics of Drama and Theatre,* Amsterdam and Philadelphia, Benjamins.

John R. Searle, 1972, *Les actes de langage,* Paris, Hermann.

Alessandro Serpieri, 1977, "Ipotesa teorica di segmentazione del testo teatrale," in *Strumenti critici,* 32–33.

Irena Slawinska, 1978, "La semiologia del teatro in statu nascendi," in *Biblioteca teatrale,* 20.

Etienne Souriau, 1950, *Les deux cent mille situations dramatiques,* Paris, Flammarion.

Substance, 1977, 18–19, Theatre in France, Univ. of Wisconsin—Madison.

Anne Ubersfeld, 1970, *Salacrou,* Paris, Seghers.

1974, *Le Roi et le Bouffon,* Paris, Corti.

1977, *Lire le théâtre,* Paris, Editions Sociales.

1979, *L'objet théâtral,* Paris, CNDP.

1981, "The Space of Phèdre," in *Poetics Today,* 2, no. 3, Tel Aviv.

1982, *L'école du spectateur,* Paris, Editions Sociales.

Jiřy Veltruský, 1976, *Drama as Literature,* Lisse, Peter de Ridder.

Versus, 1978, no. 21, Teatro e semiotica, Milan, Bompiani.

1985, no. 41, Ricezione teatrale, Milan, Bompiani.

Otakar Zich, 1931, *Esthétique de l'art dramatique,* Prague, Melantrich; 1977, reproduced in JAL reprint, Würzburg.

10. *Psychoanalysis*

Degrés, 1980, 21, Communication et sujet, Brussels.

Sigmund Freud, 1969, "Psychopathische personnen auf der Buhne," in *Studienausgabe,* 10, Frankfort.

Octave Mannoni, 1969, "L'Illusion comique ou le théâtre du point de vue de l'imaginaire," in *Clés pour l'imaginaire,* Paris, Seuil.

Christian Metz, 1977, *Le signifiant imaginaire,* Paris, UGE.

Maryvonne Saison, 1981, *Imaginaire imaginable,* Paris, Klincksieck.

Yves Thoret, 1983, "Etude sémiologique de la fonction scénique dans la relation thérapeutique," in *L'évolution psychiatrique,* Toulouse, Privat.

"Place du théâtre dans l'oeuvre de Freud," in *Degrés,* 56.

11. *Life sciences*

Henri Laborit, 1982, "Le geste et la parole: Le théâtre vu dans l'optique de la biologie des comportements," in *Degrés,* 29, Brussels.

Jean Pradier, 1982, "Theatrum scientiae / Scientia theatri: Interrogations et propositions," in *Degrés* 29, Brussels.

II.
Theatre and the media
specificity and interference

1. Theatre within a theory of media

A. *Mediatization of theatre*

Inscribing theatre within a theory of media presupposes—rather hastily—that theatre can be compared with artistic and technological formats such as film, television, radio, or video. This involves comparing theatre with what is usually contrasted to it: (mass) media, technical arts,[1] the techniques of the culture industry. We would do theatre a disservice by measuring it against media grounded in a technological infrastructure that it has done without; we would also endanger its specificity. On the other hand, theatre practice happily moves into other areas, either by using video, television, or sound recording in the performance, or by responding to the demand for television, film, or video recording, reproduction or archival preservation. Exchanges between theatre and the media are so frequent and so diversified that we should take note of the ensuing network of influences and interferences. There is no point in defining theatre as "pure art," or in outlining a theory of theatre that does not take into account media practices that border on and often penetrate contemporary work on stage. But can we go so far as to integrate theatre in a theory of media and so compare it to technical arts and practices? Besides, what are *media*?[2] The notion is not well defined. Media might be defined by a sum of technical characteristics (possibilities, potentialities) according to the technology by which the artistic product is produced, transmitted, and received—infinitely reproducible. The notion of media is thus not linked to content or theme, but to the current apparatus and state of technology. Nonetheless, this technology of technical production and reproduction of the work of art implies a certain aesthetic which is useful only when concretized in a particular individual work, aesthetically or ethically judged. Discussing novelistic technique, Sartre said that every technique points to a metaphysics. We could say the same thing of the technology of media: it makes sense only when linked to aesthetic or metaphysical reflection on the passage from quantity (reproduction) to quality (interpretation). Technically describing the properties of media such as radio or television is not enough; we must appreciate the *visible* dramaturgy as we see it in a given broadcast or as we foresee it for a future production. I would like to invite the reader on this journey, which requires no particular knowledge of computer science.

B. Media in relation to theatre

One could write a chronological history of inventions in the media, showing their connections and technical improvements. It would be possible to situate theatre in relation to these technical stages—before the advent of film and electronic media, and afterwards—in reaction to technological development. This is too difficult a task, so I will show only the opposing tendencies of theatre and media. Theatre tends toward simplification, minimalization, and fundamental reduction to a direct exchange between actor and spectator. Media, on the other hand, tend toward complication and sophistication, thanks to technological development; they are by nature open to maximal multiplication. Inscribed in ideological and cultural practices as well as in technology, and in an active process of information and disinformation, media easily multiply the number of their spectators, becoming accessible to a seemingly ever-larger audience. If theatre relationships are to come about, however, the performances cannot tolerate more than a limited number of spectators—or even performances—because theatre repeated too often deteriorates or at least changes. As a result, theatre is "in essence" (i.e., in its optimal mode of reception) an art of limited range.

C. Quantification and massification

The possibility of an indefinitely repeating and diversifying mass-media production affects the audience's tastes and expectations much more actively than the occasional visit to the theatre. We could thus distinguish between media or arts which have to be sought after and actively constructed—such as theatre or video (insofar as we have to go to the theatre or select a video cassette) —and those media that are *immediate,* ready-made, and almost compulsory, or which are present almost without being summoned (we switch on the television or radio as unthinkingly as an electric light). This active/passive criterion is nonetheless rather tenuous and does not prejudge the spectator's activity in the necessary process of reception and interpretation, whether one is deciphering the performance of a classic or following a Western. Media do not in themselves—by way of their technological possibilities—favor activity or passivity. Rather, it is the way in which they structure their messages and utilize them according to a dramaturgy and a strategy that stimulate the spectator's activity to a greater or lesser extent.

D. Theatre, media, and the spectacular

In what system of the arts, in what classification, in what theory of art or media can we place theatre? Stating that these practices are linked to a theory of performance says little: even if all human activity can be *turned into a performance* (is *spectacularisable*) for a spectator, not everything is *spectacular* in the ordinary sense of the term. We will use the French terms for the various arts:

• *Arts du spectacle (Performing arts)* is the most general and neutral designation; it authorizes the inclusion of any new practice in which an object is submitted to the gaze of a subject (thus including peepshows, striptease, lectures, discussion, etc.). There are other groupings that do not always allow for a differentiation between theatre and media:

• *Arts de représentation (Representational visual arts)*. This term underlines the representational function of theatre and cinema, as well as that of painting and any activity that produces a representation of the world.

• *Arts de la scène (The arts of the stage)* are linked to the live, unmediated use of the stage.

• *Arts mécanisés (Technically reproduced arts)* comprise all techniques of recording and reproduction that produce the same artistic message on every occasion, with the proviso that a reproduced product (such as a symphony or film) loses some of its substance when it is received innumerable times: the experience of vision being in inverse proportion to its repeated presentation and perception.

E. The double game of the media . . . and theatre

At first glance, what differentiates the media from theatre is the double status of their fictionality: a television or radio broadcast sometimes presents itself as real (as in news broadcasts) and sometimes fictional (telling a story). Airwaves are thus used in addressing needs which we normally separate, and spectators must continually work out the status of what they hear or what they see on the screen: Is this fact or fiction? Different media have distinct markers that indicate their fictional status; theatre likewise plays on the two levels of fact and fiction, since its story is continually supported by reality effects and remarks that lend this discourse credibility. Conversely, we could also note that television news has its own story line, its own narrativity, as well as zones of pure fiction and invention.

In order to sketch a theory of media that would grant space to theatre practice, we have to confront a few specific features of several media, comparing them to a minimal[ist] theatre. Establishing a general theory of the media and performing arts depends on the possibility of this confrontation and comparison.

2. Dramaturgy and specificity of the media

The following table invites us to compare media and theatre on the basis of their relationship to the spectator, their conditions of production and repro-duction, their dramaturgy, specificity and fictional status—criteria which have in view the evaluation of technological potential and semiotic use.

Without commenting on every element in the schema, we will return to several key points, such as dramaturgy, specificity, and fictiveness.

A. *The dramaturgy of radio*

• *Character* exists only through the voice, and each must be typical and clearly distinguishable from the others. The characters' voices must be very distinct, chosen according to a system that characterizes the speakers. This casting procedure is a fundamental step in preparing a radio broadcast.

• *Time and space* are suggested by changes in vocal intensity, distancing effects, echo, and reverberation. A sound frame is created by sound or music that opens and closes the sequence; the place of action is immediately situated, then "removed" at the end of the sequence. This framing device, the position of the microphones, the volume control, and the sequence of characteristic sounds provide spatial-temporal orientation for the listener. The possibility of intensifying or reducing the sound, of having an actor speak closer to or farther away from the microphone, lets us clearly indicate a change of frame or movement within the same frame.

A series of "shifters," of musical or acoustic leitmotifs between sequences or spaces allows for the identification of speakers and location in time and space. Often, the editing suggests an erasure of different time frames or an interior monologue. Rhythmic patterns, repetitions, and almost musical varia-tions can produce an effect of physical interiority, setting up exchanges be-tween the visible and the audible. The pleasure of this perception rests on the hallucination of the hearer, who hears everything and sees nothing: the enunciation and transmission of the text give the hearer the impression that the action takes place elsewhere.

More than any other medium, radio is the art of metonymy, of convention, of meaningful abstraction. It is left to the author to provide those indispensable points of reference that will allow the listener to grasp the coherence of the narrative and the organization of the fictional world without any particular effort of memory.

B. *The dramaturgy of television*

Let us leave aside the issue of the live or delayed broadcast of a pre-existing theatre performance: such a procedure is still a form of reporting, and meaning is quoted but also lost (although, in the case of a live broadcast, it keeps some authenticity). Dramaturgy for the TV film (or the play made for TV) rests on a few general principles:

• *The image* must be framed precisely, composed carefully so as to be easily read, given the small dimensions of the screen. There is therefore a stylization, an abstraction of elements in set and costumes, a systematic treatment of space. The miniaturization of the image leads to an increased importance of the sound track.

• *The sound*, by virtue of its quality and proximity, ensures the greatest effect of reality. Language carries well on television, better than in cinema, and often better than on stage, since it can be modulated, transmitted "off-screen," adapted to the situation and the image: the "delocalization" of sound in the image is much less noticeable than on a large screen. Television is often nothing more than visual radio: we listen to it in a way that is both private and distracted, as if to a close and convincing voice whose image is only the confirmation of vocal authenticity.

• *The sets* are usually noticed only in pieces behind the actors, except when the camera provides a close-up or a panorama, so as to emphasize a detail or establish atmosphere. Up to about 1965, the sets for French shows filmed in studios remained close to theatrical stylization; since then, work on location has provided an environment similar to that of film, and realistic effect has been attained at the expense of clarity and stylization.

• *Lighting* is rarely as varied or subtle as in the theatre or cinema; it has to accommodate black-and-white televisions by accentuating contrasts and treating luminous areas carefully.

• *Editing* plays on the effects of heavy punctuation, dramatic breaks, lingering moments. The narrative must be readable, coherent, and quick paced to maintain suspense.

• *Acting.* The camera focuses on the speakers/actors, usually in medium-long shot [*en plan américain*], so as to show their psychological and physiological reactions. Too many close-ups in color risk showing skin imperfections. Like the other elements of film and screen, the actor is nothing more than an element integrated into the director's industrial and signifying apparatus. Hence a certain "disembodiment": the actors exist only in their fragmentation, their metonymy, and their integration into filmic discourse.

• *Plot and theme* are certainly variable, but usually refer to social reality, to journalism, to daily life. This kind of narrative lends itself to serials. Inheritor of the trivial literature of the chapbook and melodrama, TV drama sticks to stories along safe lines, with unhappy heroes, unstable destinies. Television drama is consumed the same way as television news, weather, or commercials. News takes on the appearance of a show on a large scale, with blood, death, or marriages as in soap opera. Conversely, TV fiction maintains a basic realism and the feel of daily life; it lends itself best to a naturalistic repertoire and to an aesthetic of realistic effects.

• *Mise en scène* for television arises out of the preceding elements; it is the vast assembly line on which framing and editing decide on the hierarchy and correlation of all components of the TV film. The more perceptible the coherence, the closer form moves toward identity with content and the more TV dramaturgy proves its specificity, thus moving successfully from *theatron* to *electron*.

C. The dramaturgy of video

We notice in video the same double status of fact and fiction as in radio and TV. The medium is used on the one hand to observe, note, and record facts, and on the other to produce fictions, as in cinema or TV. In the creation of music videos, a narrative is based on image sequences which place the singer or illustrate the lyrics with shots that have a vague thematic connection with the words or musical atmosphere. The dramaturgy of such videos is based on a spatio-temporal anchoring of the song and on the attempt to link the enunciator (singer) and his/her utterance (the song), so as to make the image alternatively a visual commentary on the words and an anticipation of what the following words will say.

D. Specificity of radio

• *Words.* The listener rarely concentrates on listening only to the play. The transistor has multiplied the locations where theatre penetrates. Radio restores an intimate, almost religious quality to the word; it returns us to the Edenesque state of a purely oral literature. Without being completely stuck in one place (as when watching theatre or TV), the radio listener is in something close to a daydream or fantasy. Listening to a radio play, the hearer conducts a sort of interior monologue; his/her body is as though dematerialized as s/he receives the amplified echo of drives and daydreams.

• *The fiction.* The radio play is linked to a fiction, even if this aspect is not always clearly recognized by the audience (cf. the panic caused by an Orson Welles broadcast in 1938). As opposed to reporting, news, and discussions, radio fiction uses voices impersonating characters and creating an imaginary world. It gradually frees itself from journalism, from linear information, and from the dialogic form and realism in voice and action.

• *Studio* production. Unlike the stage, the studio is an immaterial space which supports the fabrication of sounds, the montage of voices, or the synchronization of voice, noise, and music. The listener has the illusion that the aural performance is being manufactured and broadcast at the moment of its reception.

• *Types of radio plays:*

1. live theatre broadcasts: During radio's early years, plays were often broadcast live from theatres in Paris. The set and stage business were described by a commentator. This practice continues with live broadcasts from the Comédie-Française. Neither theatre nor radio, this kind of program is more a documentary than an original work.

2. dramatized reading from the studio

3. radio play with recognizable character voices, dialogue, and conflict, as in naturalist drama

4. epic radio play: dramatizing a character or a voice

5. interior monologue

6. collage of voices, noises, or music

7. electronic simulation of human voices, using synthesizer and musical work on voice and noises

E. Specificity of television

Defining the specificity of television is as difficult as looking for the essence of theatre. Let us begin with the proposition of Patrick Besenval:

> If we look for the real specificity of television, we quickly come to the following definition: "Television is nothing other than the *domestic reception of audio-visual messages* that appear on the screen *at the very moment that they are transmitted.*" That is: something that pertains simultaneously to serials and film, as well as actual perception. In other words, television is first of all *a program,* second *"film in one's own living room,"* and last, the feeling of *immediate contact* with "the world," culminating in the live broadcast. (Besenval 1978:14)

But, once again, the subject is so vast that we will focus more precisely on the issue of television filming theatre, so as to observe the shock of their conflicting specific qualities.

• *The situation of reception.* The television occupies a central place in the home; it is the magnetic center and the umbilical cord connected to a "somewhere else" that is difficult to locate. Voluntary or involuntary interruptions of the broadcast are possible, and TV viewers—wooed by a number of other programs—are fundamentally unstable beings, hence the difficulty of fixing them to their seats and interesting them in a performance that is more nervous than the stage version, which lasts three hours or more. The mise en scène of a performance made for TV must never be boring or lose its narrative power.

• *The mediations between producers and receivers* are infinite, not only technological mediations, but also interference and semiotic transformation of meaning in the different phases of the actors' work, first in the theatre, then in the studio, then in the framing and editing of the film or video, and finally in adaptation and miniaturization for the small screen.

• *The erasure of theatricality.* The TV director of a pre-existing theatre performance or of a TV movie can choose either to erase the most visual and stagy aspects of theatricality by looking for "cinematic effects" and naturalizing the acting style and sets, or else to display this theatricality, underlining it with an abstract set and half-sung diction, as if the camera were reporting from the theatre itself.

• *Principles of the transposition of theatre to television.* In theatre, the spectators themselves sort out the signs of the performance, but in television (as in cinema) a meaningful indication has already been set up through framing, editing, and camera movements. In the transmission of a theatrical mise en scène, this means that the cinematic mise-en-scène has the "last word" on the meaning of the performance. The most compact and complete theatrical object is thus deconstructed and reconstructed in filmic discourse, during filming and editing, and in television discourse (miniaturization, private and deferred reception, and so forth). All this supports the notion of a dramaturgy that is specific to television.

F. Specificity of video

Because of its recency and the diversity in its use, video cannot be reduced to a series of specific features. We would have to specify the definition of the image used in video: 300–450 lines for portable video, 625 for TV. Video can also paradoxically produce the effect of a theatre event: closed circuit video can have an effect of presence and eventfulness; it becomes the theatre of a technical event. Hence the dual relationship to theatre: in theatre, the performance is ephemeral, but the text is permanent; in video, the performance is permanent, but the discourse, meaning, and text are ephemeral.

G. Fictional status of the media

Theatre presents itself as fiction, but this fiction is comprehensible only because perceived reality-effects intervene to authenticate it. Radio and television programming do their best to separate fact from fiction. To do this, they make use of fictional indicators: the anchor's announcement of the program and its content, the credits, the fact that we already know the journalists, their repeated allusions to the deictic situation of non-fictional communication, the assurance that the journalists are trying to get to the truth, and so on. The use of voice, the foregrounding of aesthetic devices signaling fiction or fact enable us to recognize the fictional status of the broadcast. The fact that the listener or viewer rarely makes a mistake here—even if she or he has tuned in at the middle of a program—proves the effectiveness of this discrimination.

3. Interferences between media

We have established that a unified theory of the performing arts, including theatre and the media, is very problematic. It is as difficult to understand the mechanisms of interference and contamination among various media and between theatre and media.

Leaving aside the fundamental question of the economic factors determining media development (see Busson 1983–85; Mattelart 1979; Flichy 1980), we will concentrate on evaluating the interdependence and interaction of the media. We can distinguish two types of influence:

1. *Technological influence* (➡). Development in one medium can affect the others by making available new technical possibilities and thus modifying those media. We begin with the hypothesis that there is a technological and aesthetic struggle among the various media, that each evolves and is contaminated by another. As Alain Busson notes, "the new medium offers broader possibilities for programing and broadcasting than hitherto existing media. The cost of production is much less if one relates it to the potential audience, and the means of purchase are simpler and financially more attractive to the consumer" (Busson 1985, 103). The aesthetic consequences of this rearrangement are our concern here: "the dominated medium is not only obliged to redefine its social and economic role with respect to the new medium that dominates it, but it is likewise required to reposition itself aesthetically" (Busson 1985, 103).

2. *Aesthetic influence* (→). Technological progress has aesthetic consequences for media, either by modifying their meaning or their potential, or by creating new meaning. New possibilities of diffusion influence the aesthetic quality of the product. This influence can take the form either of a direct confrontation (such as "filming theatre") or an indirect modification of its laws and potential (the development of film or radio, for example, which affect theatre writing). We will focus above all on this indirect aesthetic influence, on this mutual contamination of the media. Grasping this interaction is not easy, since it is never tangible and cannot be reduced to technological influence (even if it certainly depends on this influence at the start). We will attempt to retrace this aesthetic interaction of the media in the specific way in which artists use the media in their work. Paradoxically, we see both the contamination of the media or the contamination of theatre by the media *and* a refusal of certain artistic practices to be influenced or to compete, a renewed quest for their own specificity. This leads theatre people such as Brook, Grotowski, and Patte toward a *poor theatre* that does not allow itself to be "impressed" by the all-powerful media.

So as not to obscure too much a media landscape that is already cluttered, I have limited this discussion to radio, cinema, television, and video. Obviously, not all the theoretically possible combinations of these media, including theatre, are equally relevant, but we will examine them systematically, with respect to both technology and aesthetics.

A. THEATRE ➡ RADIO

Theatre "makes its entrance" into radio with the broadcasting, live or delayed, of a performance conceived for the theatre and taking place in a theatre in front of an audience. The first recordings were made in this way, and today we can still listen to live broadcasts of the Comédie-Française on Sunday afternoons, on the program "France-Culture." The absence of the visual dimension is more or less compensated for by a description of the stage at the beginning of each act. The "commentator" provides a rather discreet report of the stage business, especially at key moments. Sometimes, the commentator merely reads the stage directions, which have not always been adhered to by the mise en scène. The listener has trouble hearing the audience reaction, laughter, applause, response, but can still get a rough idea of the relation of real audience to performance; the perceived reactions seem more embarrassing than illuminating.

THEATRE → RADIO

At first, theatre imposed its own dramatic structure on radio plays, particularly reproducing the notion of character, action, plot, attempting to structure "radio drama" as a stage play, lacking "only" the mise en scène. The history of the radio play is a series of moves toward greater freedom, a search for its own minimal specificity. The best radio playwrights know how to submit to the demands of the situation of production and reception, so as to differentiate their work radically from theatre. In a letter to his American publisher (27 August 1957), for example, Beckett refused to allow a theatre performance of his radio play *All That Fall*:

> *All That Fall* is a specifically radio play, or rather radio text, for voices, not bodies. I have already refused to have it "staged" and I cannot think of it in such terms. A straight reading before an audience seems to me barely legitimate, though even on this score I have my doubts. But I am absolutely opposed to any form of adaptation with a view to its conversion into "theatre." It is no more theatre than *Endgame* is radio; to "act" it is to kill it. Even the reduced visual dimension it will receive from the simplest and most static of readings will be destructive of whatever quality it may have, which depends on the whole thing's *coming out of the dark*. (*Modern Drama*, 27, 1 [1985], 38)

RADIO → THEATRE

Radio influences theatre's means of production in the slant of the texts, music, pre-recorded noises "inserted" into the performance. The audience perceives the recording through loudspeakers, just as a radio listener might. The use of portable microphones produces the same effect of delocalizing the sound and of disembodying the performance. This introduction, subtle or not, of a mechanized voice threatens to "denature" theatre, to deprive it of its spontaneous, vulnerable, and unpredictable quality, so that the body is no longer the natural conveyor of the theatre event.

RADIO → THEATRE

Radio dramaturgy exercises a little-known influence on contemporary dramatic production. Dramatic writing today tends toward simplification, ellipsis, epic elements, rapid montage of sequences, collage of diverse materials. Thus radio contributes (just as cinema and television do) to the dematerialization of the stage, to the reduction of the actor to a mere vocal presence, to the banishment of visual signs in favor of the aural dimension of the text. This is the case with Beckett (*Happy Days* or *Not I*) or Handke (*Through the Villages*): in these plays, everything is focused on the projection of the word deprived of the support of visual representation.

B. RADIO ➡ CINEMA

Technological transfer occurs in adding sound to silent film. Even if the technicalities of radio and the film soundtrack are not the same, the result is what counts: the possibility of technically reproducing a fragment of reality, specifically the aural environment, which gives rise to the most powerful reality-effects. Improvements in sound recording techniques (stereo, Dolby, etc.) allow the film audience to experience the illusion of a second reality.

RADIO → CINEMA

The aesthetic and/or ideological influence of radio on film is very difficult to pin down. Consider two apparently contradictory hypotheses: (1) The capacity for documenting reality and informing the radio listener about the external world is surpassed by the documentary film and particularly by television reporting—since cinemas rarely show documentary films any more. Cinema has become the documentary medium par excellence. (2) But, on the other hand, experimental cinema may be tempted to question the imperialism of the image, by reducing the "usual" (rather than "natural") qualities of the medium: the power of the image. "Divesting" the image of its representational function (avoiding changes in the frame or the shot, expanding and multiplying sound effects) creates a cinema—such as the work of Marguerite Duras, for instance—that reverses "normal" perspective and highlights the constitutive properties of sound and the radio voice in relation to the spectator/listener.

CINEMA ➡ RADIO

Technologically speaking, the influence is negligible, due to the different machinery of transmission in each case.

CINEMA → RADIO

Radio cannot match up to film's (or television's) greater capacity for capturing and showing reality; it has to defend itself against its new rival, television, which has cornered the market for family news in the first forty years of its existence. Radio has an inferiority complex because of TV, even to the point of being advertised as "radio in color"; it is quite aware that the consumer prefers soccer on TV and that films take away listeners. Radio does not dare to develop its own specific dramaturgy beyond a pale shadow of theatre or cinema; it is content to announce films shown on TV and to discuss recently released films. It dare not "speak" of soccer or theatre in a different way and tries to compensate for the lack of images with a flood of words and emotions. Such defensive and mimetic attitudes paralyze the search for specific solutions.

C. CINEMA ➡ VIDEO

The format of the video cassette intended for viewing on a TV monitor miniaturizes and individualizes film. This transfer and reduction no longer poses any technical problems, but entail a reduction and decline in the quality of the image.

CINEMA → VIDEO

In the beginning, especially with the use of large TV cameras, video was constrained by the models of TV drama and cinematographic techniques: similar framing, shots, zooms, the same attention paid to narrative coherence. Under the influence of music video, the tendency has been reversed (cf. [10] b, below).

VIDEO ➡ CINEMA

It is now possible to use portable video equipment that greatly simplifies the filmmaker's task, speeds up editing, and thus reduces costs. After aping film for a long time, video has become the dominant medium, imposing its own laws on others, thus affecting new cinematic dramaturgy. The results are not great, especially as regards the quality and definition of the image. Nothing can (yet?) replace good old 35mm Eastmancolor™.

VIDEO → CINEMA

Although video is a new and expanding medium, it has already affected the narrative structure of cinema, which has become less linear and more subject to manipulation, deconstruction, and fantasy, as well as to the fascination of video's capacity for filming brilliant commercial spots. J. J. Beineix, the director of *Diva* and *Betty Blue*, was inspired by the techniques of commercial clips. He also claims that clips have greatly influenced the narrative form and content of contemporary cinema: "By definition, the clip is all or nothing, the best or the worst. One thing is certain; we are moving away from the beaten narrative track . . . we are witnessing an explosion of norms and forms, exactly as in painting years ago, when artists turned to abstraction" (*L'événement du jeudi*, 22–28 November 1984). This kind of representation —in rock videos for example—the visualization of emotion, and of visual tricks, the emphasis on surface impression, all this leads to the dissolution of the narrative, the rejection of causality, of a philosophical, social or psychological background, as if phantasms formed a surface totally detached from reality (cf. [10] below).

D. VIDEO ➡ TELEVISION / VIDEO → TELEVISION

The increasingly frequent use of video cameras for television is justified in terms of simplifying the process of manipulating, storing, and transforming the image.

In aesthetic terms, this leads to overly rigid or imprecise use of the video camera, producing a TV film that is too choppy and badly controlled.

> R. Jacquinet: We often hear that the continuity of fixed video take allows the actors to present themselves much better than in the fragmentation of film shots.
>
> J. C. Averty: Above all, this allows them to enjoy their own way of speaking and to perform at a snail's pace. We get the slow pace of the performance at the Buttes-Chaumont: walking, then speaking, then walking without speaking, then stopping, then speaking. It's terrible. (Quoted by Besenval 1978: 126)

TELEVISION ➡ VIDEO / TELEVISION → VIDEO

Constant research on TV equipment has immediate effects on video equipment and vice versa. The osmosis between these two technologies is almost total, but their aesthetic functions are radically different. They both use the same TV image. The relationship between video and television is both natural (with the same equipment) and conflicting. Jean-Paul Fargier, himself a video artist, describes their interaction in this way:

> Right now, if I think about the video pieces that strike me as the strongest, the specifically strongest, and the most strongly specific, what almost always comes to mind are the tapes and installations that attack television in one way or another that take television as their target, adversary, rival, alter ego, referent, primary material, exemplary model, negative, scrap, in short as other. An other from which video must separate and distinguish itself, but which it cannot not oppose, simply to be what it must be. It seems that video can only give of its best by directly or indirectly, knowingly or not, violently or diplomatically, spontaneously or in a calculated way attacking its links with television. ("Vidéo: un art de moins," Art-Press, no. 47 [1981, April]. Quoted by Dany Bloch, L'Art vidéo, L'image 2 / Alin Avila, 1983)

Video gets from television a sense of the ephemeral and the evanescent together, but with the possibility of *replaying* this ephemerality and thus denying it. Since television has a vast audience, its aesthetic procedures must be comprehensible and more or less transparent. Video, when it is not being used as a simple means of reproducing film or a TV broadcast, addresses an audience of connoisseurs, and experimentation appears to be the rule of the game, hence an abundance of experiments with image, narrative, rhythm, and their relationship to sound. For the moment, video art is in the position of a dominated medium, reduced to experimentation and limited by reason of cost and complexity to a group of aficionados. Even here, socio-economic conditions of production determine artistic specialization and the search for aesthetic specificity: "the unavoidable abandonment of universality leads dominated media to *suggest more specific productions,* better adapted to their hitherto limited targets—the young (film) and the intellectuals (film, theatre) . . ." (Busson 1985, 103).

E. TELEVISION ➡ THEATRE

Television technology does not seem to have had an impact on theatre production, except negatively: the public—captured in the domestic space and by the irresistible sirens of the TV screen—neglects theatre, because of the effort required to choose a play, buy a ticket, go out, and so on. The television spectator becomes one who looks without speaking, the opposite of theatre spectators who "speak" to the stage by attending to it with eyes and ears, modifying it with their attention. They also "speak" to their neighbors in the audience even without saying anything, because they know that while at the theatre they belong to a group, which is *volens nolens* in solidarity, in the same boat, and whose members thus cannot but communicate. Jean Baudrillard has shown that the media

> *are what always prevents response,* making all process of exchange impossible (except in the various forms of response *simulation,* themselves integrated in the transmission process, thus leaving the unilateral nature of the communication intact). . . .
>
> TV, by virtue of its mere presence, is a social control in itself. There is no need to imagine it as a state periscope spying on everyone's private life—the situation as it stands is more efficient than that: it is the *certainty that people are no longer speaking to each other,* that they are definitely isolated in the face of a speech without response. (1981 [1972], 170, 172)

TELEVISION → THEATRE

The qualitative competition of television does not affect theatre; it feels itself superior to television and unhindered by the psychological realism so beloved of TV movies. In this sense, the formation (or rather the *deformation*) of audience taste by television necessarily rebounds on the future audience for theatre, particularly in the demand for realism, verisimilitude, and the desire to be soothed, rather than disturbed, by the performance. On the other hand, we should not forget that an enormous part of theatre production is seen only on television, whether by way of broadcasts such as "Au théâtre ce soir" or by way of cultural series. Television and its "filmic discourse" (that is, its way of filming theatre) have become the normal form of presentation. The repetitive banality of this "filmic discourse" (as in "Au théâtre ce soir," for example) as well as the depressing banality of boulevard plays soliciting the public with the *n*th version of the betrayed husband, means that the potential audience is unprepared for the Théâtre du Soleil or the Théâtre National de Chaillot, even though its members may think they are familiar with theatre.

THEATRE ➡ TELEVISION

Despite its relative technological weakness with respect to television, theatre has nonetheless influenced television by offering itself as such to the inflexible and doubly frontal eye of the camera. This was and still is the era of the live or delayed broadcast of theatre and the now almost defunct era of slow and heavy shows filmed live with TV cameras at the Buttes-Chaumont studio.[3] Once theatre and cinema had entered the realm of television as they were, they could not but lose their original form and power, contaminating and sterilizing television at the same time and preventing it from finding its own language. Theatre's clandestine entry into television has been criticized often, as here, for instance, by J. C. Averty:

> It is a mistake to use fixed video cameras only to make filmed theatre. That is bound to disappear more and more. I am thinking of what we generally call the dramatic art of the Buttes-Chaumont, that is: a play written, specifically or not, for television, filmed in a set created by four cameras, either live or recorded in long half-hour sequences. In my opinion, this is a fundamental mistake. This is not really theatre; it has all its faults and none of its virtues. Nor is it cinema, because it is very heavy. It is certainly not television, since it merely uses television as a means of reproduction. It consists of hemming in the actors with the set and the microphones. It is the idea of cinema, without the analytic finesse of the cinematic camera whose multiplicity of shots allows for an in-depth investigation of the characters' psychology. In the case of live broadcasts, on the other hand, we are stuck with medium shots, close-ups, group shots. Moreover the technique is rudimentary, because we have no choice: television cameras are not flexible, at least in the context of live recording. The actors perform badly because they are very tense. Even though they are performing live, they perform less well than in a theatre, without the aura of theatre, and less well than in a film, where a director can guide them from shot to shot and inspire them with energy. Finally, this is in no sense television, because television is something else entirely: playing with electronics. To reproduce reality, to do the job of an usher in the studio has completely ruined the TV drama that has been produced for the last twenty-five years. (Quoted by Besenval 1978, 124)

THEATRE → TELEVISION

The most disastrous consequence of this eruption of theatre on television has been the failure to adapt theatre dramaturgy to that of television film.

This refusal to adapt has taken antithetical forms: thus in the dramaturgy of Buttes-Chaumont, the unities of place and time were respected under duress for texts that should have been performed in a variety of places and temporalities; on the other hand, filming on location with portable video cameras, television deliberately attempted to avoid being "theatrical" by multiplying places, objects, points of view, and changes in rhythm, thus completely losing the unity of tone and action necessary for drama (and not only *classical* drama). In both cases, what was lacking was a reflection on the means of coherently translating from one form of performance to another.

F. THEATRE ➡ VIDEO

Theatre has no technological influence on video. Only *video performance art* enjoys manipulating machines theatrically, confronting man and machine, *reducing* the most sophisticated electronic technology to the level of the living actor, whose *body* always triumphs over the machine, despite appearances.

THEATRE → VIDEO

Video is obviously inspired by cinema and television (from which it tries to differentiate itself), but not really by theatre, unless in the banal sense of filming characters engaged in action.

On the other hand, theatre seems to have become easy prey for video recording. Theatre people seem no longer able to resist media pressure to film their performances, more or less to adapt them and thus produce a video version. Vitez has filmed his four Molière productions; Brook, the advocate of the immediate and ephemeral, prolonged the career of *Carmen* by recording three different versions for film and television. As La Fontaine might have said: "They would not all die, but all were struck." Indeed, this desire to control everything electronically affects theatre too, which risks losing its identity, only because it hopes to reach millions of spectators and to preserve the performance for future generations and theatre researchers (a breed threatened with extinction). But theatre people are not duped by this video market: they know that this electronic memorialization displaces and reconstructs what was originally a theatre event. As Vitez's poem suggests:

> The pleasure of theatre is linked to the fact. . . .
>   —indestructibly linked—
>   —indissolubly—
> . . . to the fact that it does not last.
>   It is funny to think
>   of the efforts of notation
>   the efforts of archives
>   of videos, in canning plays:
> "We must notate, gather up, store."
> (Copfermann and Vitez 1981, 138)

These theatre people also understand that video cannot destroy theatre, but rather reaffirm that its uniqueness, its ephemeral quality, will emerge strengthened by suggestions from video.

VIDEO ➡ THEATRE

The technological influence of video is hardly perceptible in current theatre practice, except for experimental injections of pre-registered video sequences into the theatre performance. Nonetheless, the living, fragile, unpredictable, and thus incorruptible character of theatre can only emerge reinforced. Video performance is first of all a performance, the artist's concrete activity for an audience, however reduced that audience may be; only afterwards is it a manipulation of video machines.

Theatre is resorting more and more to video recording: for rehearsal, to make the actors aware of their acting style and their image in space; to record a mise en scène in order to remember moves, intonations, rhythm. (This is current practice at the Comédie-Française or the TNP at Chaillot.) (See G below.)

VIDEO → THEATRE

If technological transfer from video to theatre is more or less impossible because of unequal technical development, their mutual aesthetic contamination is remarkable. By using video monitors on stage or in the house, the director inserts visual materials, documentary, film extracts, montage, closed-circuit images of stage or house. The function of this insertion varies considerably: redirecting attention, contradicting the stage and the living actor, treating the stage sculpturally with walls of screens, as Nam-June Paik does, destabilizing the spectators' perception by obliging them constantly to change the status of fictionality and representation. Sometimes the living actor enters into dialogue with his video image or with other characters present only on video. (This technique was used in Ligeon Ligeonnet's version of *Woyzeck.* Josef Svoboda was the first to introduce closed-circuit television into his productions: *Prometheus* by Carl Orff, 1968, and *Intoleranza* by Luigi Nono, 1965.)

We may nonetheless doubt the success of this electronic injection into the living tissue of the performance, as does Evelyne Ertel:

> The conditions of spectator reception in theatre and television are radically opposed to each other. Sometimes the idea is to transform the theatre spectator into a television viewer, in order to play on this very opposition so that the division produces a fissure, from which emotion or consciousness emerges. But this very division is not produced. The theatre spectator can not be divided s/he remains entirely a theatre spectator, in a community of spectators and actors; s/he is not completely alone, or isolated with the family in a small apartment, two feet away from and completely absorbed

by this familiar object that is almost a member of the family. We may multiply the monitors, bring them closer to the audience, but the difficulty remains: the spatio-temporal given of theatre is such that TV monitors can only function as a global sign at the heart of the performance and not as an autonomous medium transmitting its own signals. (*Journal du Théâtre National de Chaillot*, no. 12 [June 1983])

Evelyne Ertel clearly regards the video image in these examples as an intruder in the theatre performance, an interloper that the spectator finally rejects. Conversely, *performance video* plays with the simultaneous utilization of the performer's body and the images s/he produces or manipulates. What comes first is the artist's performance and the *corps-à-corps* that s/he engages in with the medium of video. In the work of Nam-June Paik and Charlotte Moorman, video becomes a partner, making possible an active meditation on the interaction between the human being and the recording machine (cf. Bloch 1983, 24-30):

In T.V. Bra, Nam-June Paik studies the direct links established between the body of the young woman [Charlotte Moorman] and the technical equipment: two small monitors attached to her bra. In *T.V. Cello,* he has a complex apparatus consisting of several monitors piled on top of one another. . . . According to Nam-June Paik, Charlotte is in control since she generates images that she can direct while playing her cello. . . . Charlotte is not within the video apparatus; the apparatus is within her. (Bloch 1983, 116)

G. THEATRE ➡ CINEMA

No influence, since theatre lacks the technological infrastructure necessary for the cinema.

THEATRE → CINEMA

Theatre's dramaturgical influence on early cinema was enormous during the last years of the last century: the weak development of cinematic technique and the habits of stage writing affected the very "theatrical"—i.e., frontal, static, and redundant acting style in the first films by Mélies, that "creator of the cinematic spectacle" and, through Mélies, of a cinema that is still under the influence of theatre performance (acting, segmentation of the action, frontal rather than disorienting camera angles, recourse to playwrights for scripts).

In reaction to this embarrassing filiation, cinema quickly found its own specificity, set against a rather partial and limited image of theatre: it insisted on multiplying shots, perspectives, and locations so as to bind the viewer to the editing rhythm, to play counterpoint on the sound and image, on the movements of objects and the camera. Only recently have we abandoned those vast cosmogonies in which theatre and cinema were opposed according to criteria that were "specific" and metaphysical rather than historical and material. We no longer try to define them once and for all but we are interested in the exchange of procedures that characterizes their incestuous relationship and in the relativity of notions of "theatricality" or "filmicity" (as the neologism might go). Eric Rohmer remarked jokingly: "The worst insult used to be calling a film 'theatrical.' Today, the worst is that it is 'cinematic'." (*Cahiers Renaud/ Barrault,* no. 96, 1977, 11).

CINEMA ➡ THEATRE

The technological impact of cinema on theatre becomes obvious as soon as one tries to film theatre. There are certainly innumerable ways of capturing theatre on celluloid or videotape, but we will examine two major cases: (1) *Filming* theatrical performances that existed prior to and independent of requirements for shooting. (2) Instead of the pre-existing performance, *filming* something specifically prepared for the camera, but with some of the properties of a theatre event.

1. FILMING A PERFORMANCE

We could legitimately claim that, once we bring cameras into the auditorium, however discreetly, the acting is disturbed and changed; therefore we cannot film theatre without destroying it. The argument cannot be dismissed, but we can allow for a minimal degree of disturbance while a performance is being filmed live.

(a) This is the case with *1789* by the Théâtre du Soleil, which was filmed over twelve performances, and which has the advantage of showing the audience, the wings, the performance in the making, and not a hypothetical, typical, or perfect performance. Mnouchkine's film captures the theatrical relationship, shows the space, multiplies the points of view on an already fragmentary scenography, restores the simultaneity of the narratives. (See, for example "Taking the Bastille" in *1789.*)

(b) This is quite different in the case of *Le Bal,* filmed by Ettore Scola and based on the performance of the Campagnol company, "coordinated" by Jean-Claude Penchenat. Here we have an adaptation for the cinema—not a film of an actual performance—with more or less the same actors and made in Cinecittà studios. The actors' performances, inspired by the original mise-en-scène, but tailored to the new space, are directed at the camera and edited as in a normal film. In this sense, the film belongs in the second category; prior to the shooting, it did not exist—at least not in this form and place —as a live performance directed at an audience in a theatre.

(c) *Carmen,* filmed by Peter Brook and based on his opera at the Bouffes du Nord, is close to the second case. The essential difference is that Brook directs both the opera and the film, and that he shot the film at the Bouffes du Nord, transformed into a closed studio without an audience. This is not the only difference. The stage set involved a sand-covered arena bounded by the orchestra pit in back, the back wall, the side walls and the audience very close to the singers. The shots of the film point to several sub-locations and focus on the singer or the two singers at the center of the drama, underlining the psychological details of their behavior.

2. FILMING FRAGMENTS OF THEATRE

In this case, theatre no longer exists prior to being captured on film (as in *1789*), nor is it adapted to the technical demands of filming. The film rearranges the dramatic text, makes an extremely partial choice of fragments. In *Falstaff* by Orson Welles, the only remaining theatrical element is Shakespeare's text, which has been cut, edited, and rearranged to make it say almost anything Welles required. The theatrical dimension is concentrated in certain scenes, as when Falstaff and Hal parody the conversation between the king and his son in the manner of psychodrama. For the rest, the filmic discourse owes absolutely nothing to any theatre performance of Shakespeare. The rapid editing, based on the contrasts of faces and places and on a segmentation of the text, gives the film its dynamic montage.

CINEMA → THEATRE

Since the twenties, cinema has been used on stage to illustrate the action or provide the spectator with documentation (Piscator, Brecht). Its function has been to disturb traditional perception, to provide background or ironic comment on the stage action. Today, directors such as Richard Demarcy (in *Disparitions* or *Parcours*) and Henri Gruvman (in *Gru-Gru*) play with this disturbance of theatrical perception, making the actor react to an animated image.

The dramaturgical influence of cinema on theatre language has been much more profound and lasting. The introduction of epic elements or the montage of the plot in Brecht, the manipulation of time or space have become tried and tested techniques in dramatic writing. As in the cinema, mise en scène can frame an actor or a group, focus on or de-emphasize a point on stage, effect a close-up or a "traveling shot" on an actor. Eisenstein, man of the theatre as well as of the cinema, described mise-en-scène in theatre as a process of montage:

> Mise-en-scène in which characters move from foreground to background and back again offers the equivalent of montage. We could call this latent montage. (From Theatre to Cinema, *Film Form* 15)

Vitez adds:

> Finally, there is another more subtle area in which theatre has been infected by cinema. . . . From the end of the Thirties and under the influence of

Central European and especially Russian directors, theatre decided to be as full of signs as an egg. . . .We [Patrice Chereau and I] imitated the cinema, investing the same amount of work in each play as one might in a film, or in a work not destined to be ephemeral. The real difference between theatre and cinema is that theatre is made to be destroyed by the rising tide, whereas cinema is made to be preserved and reproduced. (Vitez 1980, 64–65)

H. TELEVISION ➡ RADIO

No technological influence.

TELEVISION → RADIO

Radio necessarily occupies an inferior position with respect to television, since the latter can for the most part perform the tasks assigned to radio (reporting, news, broadcasting shows, etc.) with the added presence of the image that authenticates the message in the eyes of the audience. As a result, radio feels obliged to compete with television, multiplying its news and broadcasting sources, sticking to real events to inform the audience immediately, by continually repeating the same news (France-Inter in the morning, National Public Radio), by allowing for listeners' questions, and so forth. The "realistic" character of the TV image appears to impose itself in the style of radio dramaturgy: radio plays stick too often to verist notions of character and story, with real places and conventional chronology.

RADIO ➡ TELEVISION

Radio research has not yet been fully utilized for the TV apparatus, which is still a rather rudimentary music box.

RADIO → TELEVISION

Television programs reproduce the same major categories as radio—news, fiction , variety, commercials—cut up into timed and relatively immovable segments. As for TV drama, the producers seem unable or unwilling to experiment as much as some radio playwrights. The reasons for this are many: TV drama looks in vain for its own way; it remains within the narrative domain of theatre or cinema. Television addresses—or, driven by the ratings, claims to address —a larger audience than radio, which it dares not displease by too much formal experimentation.

I. TELEVISION ➡ CINEMA

For reasons of economy or efficiency, video cameras are sometimes used for filming.

	theatre	radio	cinema	television	video
1. relationship between production and reception	relatively stable and based on human body	body reduced to voice and ear; impoverishment but also enlargement	photographed body gives a reality effect	immediate broadcast but no immediate feedback; phatic communication to keep viewer on one channel; extremely mediated relation to advanced technology	significant mediatization, but can be reinserted into live performance
1.1. voice	delivered and received "naturally"	body reduced to voice	reality effect of voice, but delocalized sound	voice has limited effect	limited effect
1.2. audience	present during production	live but remote	maximum mediation	variable mediation; possible live broadcast	extreme mediation
2.1. signifier	varied and live	limited and mediated	signifier of signifier	possible confusion between signifier and referent	signifier subject to infinite modification
2.2. mode of representation	stylization despite appearances	metonymic representation	representational enlargement	representational reduction	extreme reduction of representation; loss of information
3. conditions of production	simplified, tends to use elaborate technology	mass medium; stable technology, diversified institution	advanced technology closely linked to commercial institutions	mass medium par excellence; complex production apparatus; weighty institution	needs advanced technology but still accessible to individual use
3.1 reproduction	live and non-technical	technical but live if desired	technical, detached from productive instances, tied to institution	technical, linked to institution, live or delayed broadcast	technical support for TV; privatization of technological sophistication
3.2. distribution and reception	live, in unique time and place; necessarily active construction of meaning	ubiquitous distribution of listeners; inattentive reception possible; radio as background	in diverse locations; absolutely distinct in time and relatively in space	in private interiors; choice determined by available programs; TV set has significant place in daily life	linked to TV (recordings), live, in theatre or installation

4. dramaturgy	extreme variety in historical forms	re-uses theatrical dramaturgy with some specific research (voice, sound frame, etc.)	problematic search for "cinematic language" based too rigidly on image	little specific research for TV dramaturgy, audio-visual adaptation for TV use	identity crisis in relation to TV image; experiments without clear theorization, especially for fiction
4.1. specificity	sought after through history, currently in doubt	technological specificity but hybrid thematics and usage	problematic search for "cinematic language" based exclusively on image	hardly any; often adapts theatre dramaturgy to screen production	takes up research abandoned by TV; simple techniques; enables experiment with montage and rhythm of image
4.2. framing	fixed by stage/house relation and semiotic framing of events	sound framing	framing fundamental to image-making before and after narrative montage	as in cinema, with additional constraint of small screen	as in TV, with even more impoverished image
4.3. norms and codes	historically known and categorized	limited number of norms, as regards radio play as opposed to music	specific and non-specific norms	norms not yet well known	norms of music video not well known; norms rejected in video art; no distance for definition
4.4. repertoire	dramatic texts according to author and period; different mises-en-scène of same text possible; repertoire of exemplary mises-en-scène	not well known, often no trace of script of a radio play. Product is complete; can be re-broadcast in entirety only	published scripts pale shadow of film; possible (teaching or specialist) repertoire of classics	INA archives closed to public; vast, but unreliable memory bank	difficult to establish repertoire because of unclassified diversity
5. fictional status	presents itself as fiction, despite reality effects	coexistence of "pure" fact and "pure" fiction, with mutual contamination	distinction between documentary and fiction film	as in radio	information (control with closed circuit or fiction (music video / MTV)
5.1. indices of fictional status	no	yes	yes	yes	yes

TELEVISION → CINEMA

According to the experts, the influence of television on cinema is enormous and devastating. Alain Busson describes the transfer in terms of a transfer of the economically weakest consumers:

> An examination of customer structures shows that the economically weakest social groups have most changed their habits. Empty cinemas in the suburbs are connected with a more general refusal of collective consumption and a return to individual domestic activities, of which television is the fullest symbol. (Busson 1985, 103)

When we remember that 68.8 percent of the French watch television every day, 49.6 percent go to the cinema at least once a year, and only 10.3 percent go to the theatre (Busson 1985, 105), we can see that television dominates the other media, economically and aesthetically ravaging the theatre. Even the once dominant cinema is modified by this power relation. As the Malécot Report (January 1977) notes: "It is because the French have never seen so many films [as they are seeing now] that cinema is in such bad shape" (quoted by Busson 1985, 104).

We have come to the point where films are made with the financial support of television, with a view to future use on the small screen. The result for filmmaking is a tendency to use television-specific thematics, cutting, editing, and acting technique. This distortion is further aggravated when films made in this way are used for television: the image loses definition, the miniaturization makes it difficult to decipher the image. Cinema and television are thus both the worse for it.

CINEMA ➡ TELEVISION

Television has become the principal channel for showing films, with some channels (Canal+ or HBO) specializing in this kind of program.

CINEMA → TELEVISION

Despite the current tendency to produce films which will be distributed on video cassette and on television, TV drama is still made like miniature film: with the same cutting, the same excessive use of exterior shots and location changes, the same kind of shot and narrative rhythm:

> This "nostalgia for the cinema" [which J. C. Averty detects in his colleagues (1975, 128)] flatters the dominant public taste and limits what can pass for the technological specificity of television (video in the studio with tricks,

insertions, reshaping of the image) to an experimental game without a future.

J. RADIO → VIDEO → RADIO

This last case is the most surprising. It deserves special attention from the mass-media industry. The music video serves two masters: the record industry (radio) and the video market. The music video is in no way a referential illustration of the song or the music; it does not interpret or imitate anything.

Detached in this way from any textual reference (as theatre was "once upon a time"), from any interpretation (such as mise-en-scène), and from any classic cinematic narrative (such as television), the music video tries to match the rhythm of music (particularly rock) with a visual rhythm. Rock, which loves to play "big bad wolf," adapts perfectly to surprise shots and fantastic scenes. Given that a rock song generally does not tell a story, it does not tie down the visual accompaniment of the video. The video must not bore the spectator with a fixed decor, but must rather offer a series of shocking visual ideas, of marvelous events activated by friendly tricks, to make the singers and musicians little imps that are simultaneously the producers of the music and its first listener/dancers, engaged in the marvelous fiction of the video. As a product for immediate consumption and disposal, the music video can at least be praised for forcing us to reconsider the relations among the media and leading to a new practice of visual representation.

In this overview of technological and aesthetic interference between theatre and the media, we have shown, even if in a rather mechanical way, that theatre cannot be "protected" from any media and that the "work of art in the era of technical reproduction" (Benjamin 1936) cannot escape socio-economic-technological domination, which determines its aesthetic dimension. Technological and aesthetic contamination is inevitable, whether as effective interaction of media techniques or as the frantic desire to maintain the specificity or poverty of theatre (Grotowski). The time has passed for artistic protectionism, and the time has arrived for experiments with different possibilities. The most marked influence of the media has been to found all aesthetic reflection on the notion of technological progress and mass diffusion; this reflection can thus be materially linked to production, diffusion, and reception. Reflections of this kind on these practices of performance and visual representation cannot allow themselves to be overawed by the technical complexity of the media or the socio-economic phenomena of the culture industry but should rather examine, from the perspective of an aesthetic of form, the processes of semiotic transformation from one form to another, the emergence of meaning in these contaminations, and the dynamism of practices of performance and representation in the media of our time.[4]

NOTES

1. Translator's note: Following Pavis's allusion to Benjamin here (and throughout this chapter), I translate *arts mécanisés* as *"technical"* rather than "mechanical arts," to highlight, as does Benjamin's *"technishe* Reproduktion" and Pavis's argument, if not his adherence to the French (mis)translation.

2. Translator's note: In order to maintain Pavis's implied distinction between the singular nouns *médium* and *média* (unavailable in English), I have used the English plural wherever possible.

3. Translator's note: This is the French TV studio where the first TV plays were broadcast.

4. Author's note: Grateful thanks to Mary and Hector McLean for their help with the first draft of this article.

BIBLIOGRAPHY

Jean-Françoise Barbier-Bouvet, 1977, *De la scène au petit écran,* Paris, Ministry of Culture and Communication.

Jean Baudrillard, 1972, "Requiem pour les médias," in *Pour une critique de l'économie politique du signe,* Paris, Gallimard; 1981, *For a Critique of the Political Economy of the Sign* (trans. Charles Levin), New York, Telos.

Walter Benjamin, 1970 (1936), "Das Kunstwerk im Zeitalter seiner technischen Reproduzierbarkeit," in *Gesammelte Schriften,* I.2; "The Work of Art in the Age of Mechanical Reproduction [*sic*]," in *Illuminations* (trans. Harry Zohn), London, Fontana.

Patrick Besenval, 1978, *La télévision,* Paris, Larousse.

Dany Block, 1983, *L'art vidéo,* Paris, L'image 2—Alin Avila.

Alain Busson, 1983, *La place du théâtre dans le champ culturel,* Paris, Université de Paris, 1.

1985, "L'innovation et structuration du champ culturel," in *Théâtre/public,* 64/65.

E. Copfermann and A. Vitez, 1981, *De Chaillot à Chaillot,* Paris, Hachette.

Degrés, 1986, 48, *La Captation,* Brussels.

Les Dossiers du petit écran, CNDP, Paris.

Anne-Marie Duguet, 1981, *Vidéo: La mémoire au poing,* Paris, Hachette.

Hanns Eisler (and T. W. Adorno), 1947, *Music for the Film,* New York, Oxford Univ. Press.

H. M. Enzensberger, 1970, "Baukasten zu einer Theorie der Medien," in *Kursbuch,* 20; 1974; "Constituents of a Theory of the Media," in *The Consciousness Industry,* New York, Seabury Press.

Martin Esslin, 1985, "Drama and the Media in Britain," in *Modern Drama,* 28, 1.

Patrice Flichy, 1980, *Les Industries de l'imaginaire,* P. U. Grenoble, I.N.A.

Max Horkheimer, and T. W. Adorno, 1977 (1947), "The Culture Industry: Enlightenment as Mass Deception," in *Dialectic of Enlightenment,* New York, Continuum.

France Huser, 1975, "La vidéo et le temps," in *Revue d'Esthétique,* 4.

Marshall McLuhan, 1964, *Understanding Media,* New York, Signet.

Alain and Michèle Mattelart, 1979, *De l'usage des médias en temps de crise,* Paris, A. Moreau.

Modern Drama, 1985, 28, 1, Special Issue on Drama and the Media.

Edgar Morin, 1958, *Le cinéma ou l'homme imaginaire,* Paris, Minuit.

Jean-Marie Piemme, 1975, *La propagande inavouée,* Paris, U.G.E., 10/18.

    1984, *Le souffleur inquiet,* in *Alternatives théâtrales* (Brussels, Atelier des Arts), 20–21.

Serge Serror, 1970, *Petit écran, grand public,* Paris, I.N.A., La Documentation Française.

Antoine Vitez, 1980, "Antoine Vitez, le signifiant et l'histoire," in *Ça Cinéma,* 17.

Raymond Williams, 1974, *Television: Technology and Cultural Form,* London, Fontana.

III.
Four approaches

I. Historical survey of theatrical forms

At the very basis of the phenomenon of theatre as it is found in a wide variety of cultures is the assumption of a particular spatial configuration suggested by the word *theatre* itself—a place where one sees. Many theorists and historians have emphasized the centrality of this configuration. Richard Southern's *The Seven Ages of Theatre* undertakes to "peel off" the various "accretions" theatre has taken on over the centuries and to discover its "essence." At the core he finds two separate pieces, the Player and the Audience. "Take these apart and you have nothing left" (Southern 1961, 21). Eric Bentley's "minimal definition" of theatre makes a similar point: "A impersonates B while C looks on" (Bentley 1964, 150). Other approaches, such as David Cole's anthropological analysis, bring us to this same dialectic by a different route. For Cole, theatre occurs in a mystic place where two worlds confront one another—the uncanny, dangerous, and fascinating space of the archetypical *illud tempus* inhabited by our representative shaman/actor while we watch from the duller but safer world of everyday reality. It is not these separate spaces for player and audience that make theatre, but their confrontation: "*as against* the Actor, we take on the collective character of the Audience" (Cole 1975, 71). For this confrontation to occur, of course, both actor and audience must be physically present.

Theatre as a cultural system is thus based on a given spatial relationship different from those involved in other spatial systems. Every culture has its own systems for the arrangement of space within a dwelling, for example, but the dwelling has no wide-spread relationship of spaces corresponding to the basic code of theatre; neither does a commercial structure, despite the given dialectic of buyer and seller. The church or temple has perhaps the closest systematic architectural relationship to the theatre, since it represents a meeting point of the secular celebrant and the sacred celebrated, yet the sacred may be only spiritually or symbolically present, not spatially, as a player must be. Certain religious structures, such as the traditional Quaker meeting house, are thus able to avoid the setting aside of "sacred" space within their confines. Certain modern experimental performances seek to extend the same freedom to the theatre. Among the "axioms" for "environmental theatre," for example,

Richard Schechner lists "actor and audiences employ the same space" (Schechner 1968, 43), but this tends to be literally rather than psychically true. Those who have been in audiences sharing the same physical space with actors in performance will have felt the tenacity of Cole's observation—the actor almost always remains an uncanny, disturbing "other," inhabiting a world with its own rules and which the audience, however physically close, cannot truly penetrate. A history of spatial signification in the theatre will thus be in large part a history of how different cultures have altered the location, size, shape, and exact relationship of acting and audience spaces according to changing ideas about the function of theatre and its relationship to other cultural systems.

A theatre was one of the architectural objects that defined a Greek city, an essential element in its repertoire of architectural objects according to Pausanius and others, though its size and the method of its construction normally placed it outside the city center. The heart of this theatre was the orchestra, surrounded on three sides by an amphitheatre so that the performance space was thrust forward into the audience space. It might be helpful at this point to consider the possible variations of actor-audience space, ranging from entirely separate (as in film and television) to fully integrated, as in Schechner's environmental theatre, where each performer may create her own "pocket" of performance space. The most integrated form with clearly defined audience-actor space is what is sometimes called the arena form, with performance space entirely surrounded by audience. This is a natural arrangement in an otherwise undifferentiated area and is often found in theatrical performance outside physical structures. The thrust stage projects the performance space into the audience space; scenery may be behind an actor in such an arrangement, but the audience perceives the actors as spatially embedded in the audience world more than in that represented by the scenery. The confrontational model, which we will examine more closely in its historical context, clearly moves the actor from the audience space to within the space of the theatricalized world. (See Figure 1.)

The Greek theatre, which probably began as an arena stage with audience surrounding the orchestra, retained the integrated thrust arrangement even when the development of the skene house as a dressing and scenic area had made a full arena arrangement impossible. Moreover, this theatre sought not only to integrate performance and audience but to integrate the audience itself. The architectural codes which would evolve in later periods to mark social

separate (film)   confrontational (Italianate)   thrust   arena   environmental

Figure 1

differentiations in the public were not to be found in the Greek auditorium, with its sweeping curves of socially equal benches.

The development of the skene house at the beginning of the classic period provided another element in the repertoire of theatrical spaces to be variously encoded in subsequent periods. The basic function of this element was to provide an "offstage" area for actors to don and change costumes and masks, and which could provide rapid and easy entrances and exits for the acting area. These practical considerations remained the same for the great variety of tiring houses and backstage areas in later periods, but from the beginning this space was given additional signifying functions as well. In its first known appearance (in Aeschylus' *Orestia*), the skene represented the palace at Thebes and the Temple of Diana. Its main door became a display area for scenic tableaux; its roof represented city walls, palace roofs, even the abode of the gods. So there developed a standard spatial feature of the thrust stage that would be shared, in time, by the confrontational (Italianate) stage. Behind the acting area there is commonly another area, with support spaces for the actors, the wall between these areas becoming a space for the display of scenic elements signifying the fictive world of the dramatic action.

Perhaps as early as the Greek theatre and certainly later, theatre structures offered a parallel "retiring space" for the audience, the lobbies and foyers. There are interesting connotative parallels in these two types of support areas (Figure 2). Each serves as a sort of transitional space between the outside world, where actors and audience mingle in different relationships, and the special world of the stage and auditorium. Both actors and spectators normally use these intermediate spaces to prepare themselves for their different "roles" in the central confrontational space. Actors get into costume and makeup and prepare themselves physically and psychologically for their contact with the audience. The spectators make more modest but similar adjustments in their support spaces. In a modern theatre they may check their coats, chat with others preparing to share the same experience, read programs and perhaps posted reviews, and generally remove themselves, as these spaces encourage them to do, from their extra-theatre concerns. At intermissions, both actors and spectators retire to their separate support spaces, where both may relax briefly with their fellows, away from the tensions and obligations of the stage/ auditorium confrontation.

The theatre structure was not a part of the architectural repertoire of the late medieval city, though a great variety of other spaces, created for other

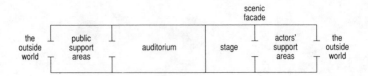

Figure 2

purposes, were utilized for theatre, each contributing its own connotations to this experience. The liturgical dramas, staged in cathedrals and monasteries, drew upon the spatial and decorative codes of those buildings, utilizing specific shrines and chapels with appropriate symbolic overtones as well as standard features such as the high altar, the crypt, the baptismal font, and the architectural alignment of the cathedral as a whole with the East (Jerusalem and Eden) to West (death and resurrection) world axis.

In the great processional dramas the city itself became the space of performance, a visual and spatial equivalent of the mixing of Biblical and contemporary references in the paintings of the period and in the texts of the medieval dramas themselves. Thus the Viennese Passion of the fifteenth century that began in the markeplace doubtless assumed the secular and social connotations of that area, but when the actor portraying Christ subsequently bore his cross through the winding streets of the city to the distant cemetery where the crucifixion was to be represented, the city itself took on the connotations of the universal city, Jerusalem (Königson 1975, 95).

Reduced to the simplest of spatial elements, a populist theatre continued to thrive in secular form during the Renaissance. A raised platform was set up in a public square or at a fairground to set apart and make visible the performance area, the rear of this platform normally curtained off to form a simple backstage area, the front serving as a rudimentary scenic façade (sometimes nothing more than a curtain with slots for entrances). The actors on the platform enjoyed the sort of integration with the audience offered by the thrust-stage arrangement.

A very different sort of theatrical space was developed in the private theatres of the Renaissance princes, involving a totally different set of spatial and decorative codes. The first thing to be noted about this so-called Italianate stage is the implications of its location. The classic theatre was an independent structure, open to the populace at large and located in a site accessible to them. The medieval theatre, lacking a permanent structure, was offered in public areas such as the cathedrals or public marketplaces. The princely theatres of the Renaissance followed neither model. Normally not independent structures, they were built into princely residences and were thus an architectural part of them, like a kitchen, chapel, or audience chamber. As such, they were of course not readily accessible to outsiders, but could be attended only by invitation from the master of the palace. Wagner's complaint that the Renaissance princes appropriated the arts for their private entertainment is nowhere more evident than in the theatre, where the physical space of the art was literally a part of the princely home.

Equally radical changes took place within the theatre space itself. The integrated actor/audience space of the classic and medieval theatre was here replaced by a confrontational model; the proscenium arch appeared as a "frame" (and a barrier) between the world of the audience and that of the actor, with the curtain to further reinforce the separation. Perhaps the single most important spatial feature of this theatre was the enormous symbolic influence of perspective in it. Instead of the façade backgrounds of earlier stages, the Italian-ate began employing a one-point perspective which could be perfectly enjoyed only from a single position in the auditorium, that of the sponsoring prince. Audience members along the sides of the auditorium had to imagine the effect from that point of view, to enjoy the performance, as it were, through the prince's eyes. His position now rivaled or even surpassed the stage as a focus of attention (Murray 1977, 282). Those unaware of this double focus are often surprised to find that the auditoriums of Renaissance and baroque theatres were as a rule better illuminated than the stages themselves. The auditorium, as an area of display, was decorated at least as richly as the stage. The actors, removed from the intimacy of a thrust stage, lost the physical dimensionality such staging offered, a loss correspondingly offset by the prince, who was usually seated on a dais in the center of the auditorium, to be observed in his full dimensionality (Figure 3).

Of course the public theatres of the Renaissance developed very different spatial configurations. As commercial ventures, they priced different parts of their auditoriums differently, so that none could be said to have offered demo-cratic seating. On the other hand, a commercial operation had no incentive to emphasize a particular part of the auditorium at the expense of all others as the princely theatres did. Thus, perspective scenery remained essentially a court phenomenon during the Renaissance, while public theatres in England, France, Spain, and elsewhere utilized neutral or multiple backgrounds.

Renaissance public theatres, architectural entities outside the princely pal-aces, had to find their proper place in the new urban systems, and this varied according to the place that theatre as an activity was assigned within the cul-ture. The first public theatres (*corrales*) of Spain were founded as charitable institutions, and they remained generally respected elements in the society, often with close ties to the state religion. The *corrales* of Madrid's Cofradía de la Pasion were located in the Calle del Sol and the Calle del Príncipe in the very heart of the city. Seville's Coliseo shared a wall with the residence of the Marquis of Ayamonte, who furnished water from his private fountain

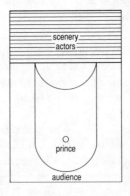

Figure 3

for the establishment, and who was granted a private entrance from his home directly into a theatre box (Rennert 1909, 53).

In England, on the contrary, the social marginality of the theatre was echoed in the physical marginality of its structures, located in the "liberties"— contiguous to the city but not a part of it, and in the case of the south bank (the favored location), separated by the formidable barrier of the Thames. The neighbors in such locations were other culturally marginal establishments such as bear-baiting arenas and bordellos. When at least certain English theatres during the Restoration were accorded an official place in the social system, their position in the urban text at once reflected this change, with the companies holding the royal patents erecting houses in the center of London. During the following century the theatre was widely accepted in Europe as a cultural monument, and by the late eighteenth century city planners were regularly using theatre buildings as nodes for the convergence of the great boulevards that crisscrossed their new cities. Thus Baron Haussmann in Paris had huge new theatres built at the Opéra and the Châtelet to provide just such an urban focus.

The interior spaces of European theatres underwent various changes between the Renaissance and the nineteenth century, but the auditorium remained rigidly codified in terms of social classes (and sometimes in other terms as well —Spanish theatres, for example, provided sexually segregated seating). The raised dais for the princely patron in the center of the auditorium was generally replaced by the elaborately decorated royal or ducal box located at the back and center of the auditorium. Other boxes, naturally of lesser status, extended to the right and left of this around to the stage, normally in three or four tiers. The possession of a box at the Opéra became a widely accepted sign of membership in the privileged classes. Indeed New York's Metropolitan Opera was originally built not to satisfy a passion for this art but because the new wealth represented by the Vanderbilts, the Astors, and the Morgans was unable to obtain boxes at the old Academy of Music, where all the "aristocratic" space was already filled by older families. Rather than settle for symbolically inferior spaces, the new society felt compelled to build its own theatre (Eaton 1968, 1–2).

While the aristocracy filled the boxes of European seventeenth- and eighteenth-century theatres, with appropriate subdivisions according to rank, the area surrounded by the boxes, the pit (*parterre*) was traditionally the space for merchants, clerks, and professional men, while the gallery (*paradis*) above the boxes provided space for footmen, grooms, and the lower orders of society. Each class was assigned not only its own seating space, but usually its own support space as well, so that the patrons of each area entered by their own door, ascended by their own stairs, and during intermissions gathered in their own lobby or salon—each of these of course treated spatially and decoratively as befitted the class being served.

The French Revolution, a period of high official awareness of the signifying power of objects and spaces, completely remodeled the Théâtre de la Nation in Paris in 1794 to replace all boxes and balconies with a single democratic sweep of seats. This reform lasted only two years, until the Thermidorian reaction, when the social spatial divisions were restored, including, under Napoleon, even a restoration of the royal (now the imperial) box. Not until Wagner built his revolutionary theatre at Bayreuth did Europe see another major attempt at a democratic auditorium, this time a lasting one, with continual influence on subsequent design. Wagner's often-mentioned reform of dimming the auditorium lights during performance is usually tied to his desire to concentrate focus on the stage, but this change had its social message as well. The auditorium was no longer to be treated, as it had been since the Renaissance, as a space for the display of aristocratic power and pomp.

The confrontational style of staging favored by the Renaissance court theatres remained predominant in most Western theatres until early in the twentieth century (and still remains the traditional arrangement of a Western theatre). Changes in theatre forms and practice during the eighteenth and nineteenth centuries generally tended to reinforce this pattern. Early in the 1600s some aristocratic audience members invaded the sides of the Italianate stage, restoring for more than a century something of the actor/audience spatial relationship of the thrust theatres, but by the mid-1800s they had disappeared. The English forestage, another encouragement to this relationship, gradually disappeared too. In the latter part of the eighteenth century the baroque idea of the actor standing at the front of the stage presenting conventionally understood signs to the audience began to be replaced by another idea of acting, drawing more on the signs of everyday life and relating the actor more to his fellows (as in Diderot's beloved *tableaux*) than to the dominant princely eye in the auditorium (Fischer-Lichte 1983, 2:131–33).

The concern of romantics such as Hugo for visual spectacle and historical detail, along with the subsequent realist emphasis on physical environment, carried this reinterpretation of the space behind the proscenium arch further still. From antiquity through the baroque, actors were displayed in front of scenery, whether that scenery was a neutral façade or a highly elaborate perspective. In the nineteenth century, actors were thought of as living *within* the scenic space, which was no longer displayed for the public but, as it were, accidentally observed by an audience of voyeurs through the transparent "fourth wall." Wagner's darkened auditorium was an important contribution toward the reinforcement of this separation of worlds (Figure 4).

Twentieth-century experimentation with theatrical form has largely been directed against this totally divided theatrical space. This experimentation has been extremely varied. It has included the conscious revival of earlier spatial arrangements, the conscious creation of new ones, both permanent and temporary, the development of spaces whose use can be varied, and the utilization of non-theatrical space which may suggest hitherto unexplored actor/audience relationships or bring external social or cultural connotations into the theatre experience.

During most of the periods briefly surveyed here, the spatial codes of the

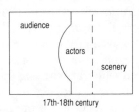
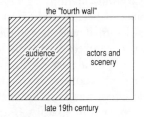

Figure 4

theatre were fairly limited and generally acknowledged; but today in theatre, as in much of modern culture, an enormous variety of codes are utilized, and theatrical competence now requires the knowledge of not just one of them but many. There remain certain general structural principles, however, to help viewers find their bearings. The general urban spatial codes for theatre still operate with remarkable consistency in most major Western cities. Here one finds three basic types of theatre, each in its own area, with its own type of offering in a fairly standardized space. First there are the generally well-subsidized national theatres, the twentieth-century palaces of culture, found in sites befitting their role as national monuments, in landscaped parks or as central elements in modern building complexes. These have generous interior spaces, often including eating facilities. They may also contain a smaller theatre or two for experimental work, though their own fare tends to be traditional classics or major premières.

The second type is the standard commercial theatre, so closely identified with a certain urban area and a certain type of play that one may speak of a boulevard theatre or boulevard drama, a West End theatre or play, or a Broadway theatre, play, or musical. Spatially these are not free-standing monuments like the national houses, but façade theatres, part of the commercial rows which characterize their districts. They tend to cluster in a fairly limited area, with hotels and restaurants nearby, and their interior spaces are usually largely devoted to seating, often rather cramped at that, to maximize profits in an expensive location. Lobbies and other support spaces are correspondingly small. Their stages are almost invariably in Italian proscenium style, while the national theatres, many of them of more recent construction, are more varied. The third type of theatre, the "off-Broadway" or "fringe" theatre, may be found scattered throughout the city, sometimes singly but often in small groups, especially in the artistic quarters where recent performance experimentation has encouraged the collaboration of theatre with other arts. These theatres have often been converted from other spaces and tend to be small, intimate, and correspondingly the most flexible in actor/audience spatial relationships.

The theatre audience today is thus generally much better informed about the spatial codes operating there than the plurality of possibilities would suggest. Almost any large theatre is a fairly stable structure, and previous acquaintance with this theatre or another of the same general type will normally provide any necessary information. Certain theatres—both large (like the Theatre am Lehninerplatz in Berlin) and small (like the Performing Garage in New York City)—are designed with a completely neutral interior, the so-called "black box" that is organized differently spatially for each production, but that very flexibility becomes a part of the pattern of expectation for the audiences of these theatres. For those with an interest in contemporary theatre, the plurality of available codes has become itself a part of the experience of theatre. We select the proper anticipatory frame just as we select the proper wardrobe, and just as we wear suits, dresses, and jewelry to one theatre and jeans, slacks, and sneakers to another, so we bring to each an expectation of the spatial and performance codes our culture has led us to expect from that type of performance situation.

BIBLIOGRAPHY

Eric Bentley, 1964, *Life of the Drama*, New York.

David Cole, 1975, *The Theatrical Event*, Middleton, Conn.

Quaintance Eaton, 1968, *The Miracle of the Met*, New York.

Erika Fischer-Lichte, 1983, "Vom 'künstlichen' zum 'natürlichen' Zeichen: Theatre des Barock und der Aufklärun," in vol. 2 of *Semiotik des Theaters*, Tübingen.

Elie Königson, 1975, *L'espace théâtral mediéval*, Paris.

Timothy Murray, 1977, "Richelieu's Theatre: The Mirror of a Prince," in *Renaissance Drama*, NS 8.

Hugo Rennert, 1909, *The Spanish Stage in the Time of Lope de Vega*, New York.

Richard Schectner, 1968, "6 Axioms for Environmental Theatre," in *Drama Review*, 12, no. 3.

Richard Southern, 1961, *The Seven Ages of Theatre*, New York.

II. Sociology

1. *Premise*

Within the limits of the social sciences, it is the sociological perspective that has been that most extensively applied to the study of the theatrical event in its numerous aspects. This is not surprising when one considers the social characteristics of the theatre and the evidence that the theatre is a phenomenon deeply rooted in the fabric of a collective existence. Nevertheless, it would be difficult to maintain that there is at present or that there has ever been a sociology (or an anthropology) of the theatre, that is, a true and proper discipline worthy of the name.[1]

In the first place, the extensive sociological material related to the theatre rarely presents the minimum theoretical and methodological homogeneity required. Besides, worse yet, the results of the various uses of sociology in the theatre field have always caused disappointment. Usually they end up being superficial statistical polls of the audience or abstract studies, sometimes even metaphysically oriented, on the relationship between theatre and society, both understood as static and monolithic entities.

To my knowledge, the first work explicitly devoted to this new approach appeared in 1956. It was by Georges Gurvitch, the great French sociologist, who, in his effort "to enumerate the different parts and branches that it could explore" (Gurvitch 1956, 202), said, "the sociology of the theatre is only at its very beginnings." Ten years later, Jean Duvignaud started his ponderous and now classic volume *Sociologie du théâtre* with far more critical and pessimistic considerations: "In spite of being under-developed to date, the sociology of the theatre has already gained a bad reputation because it has left its doors open to many confusions and misunderstandings. The very intensity of the relationship between social life and theatre is responsible for the superficialities and the exaggerations which are often brought about. In this way, we usually feel satisfied simply reflecting the general social conditions in the dramatic creation while establishing a mechanical connection between cause and effect and between the appearance of collective life and dramatic experimentation. [. . .] Without doubt, the sociology of the theatre suffers from an extreme mediocrity since it is pleased with the parallels that it has established between a static society and a dead theatre, that is, two abstractions" (Duvignaud 1965a, 37).

During a conversation with Jean-Pierre Faye which appeared in *Cahiers Internationaux de Sociologie,* Duvignaud confirmed his opinion a year after the publication of his book. On this occasion, the French sociologist explicitly questioned the perspective of idealistic historicism that, according to him, occupies a large part of sociological theatre research: "The sociology of the arts, and more precisely the sociology of the theatre, seems to lead only to *impasses.* This is due mainly to three causes: in the past one speculated about an "essence" of the theatre, or one was satisfied with evoking a continuous evolution that, for instance, would transform the contemporary theatre into a successor of the Greek theatre. Moreover, one would start from such a stiff and cadaverous image of social life that it was impossible to establish any relationships different from mechanical dependency on this cold and inert 'milieu'" (Duvignaud and Faye 1966, 103).

2. Theatrum mundi

So, how do we go about studying the complex correlations "that are established between the diverse forms of the collective experience at its various levels and the multiple aspects of the theatre?" (ibid.). How do we avoid the traps of simple-minded and mechanical sociologism while aiming at escaping, however, from the opposite but equally serious risk of "pure aesthetics," idealism, and formalism which claim the total autonomy of the work of art from the society and history?

The theoretical "gesture" that in the 1960s allowed the sociology of the theatre to overcome at least partially this double obstacle of sociologism and idealism consists of trying to think in a new, more fluid and dynamic way about the two categories of "society" and "theatre" in order to facilitate further assessment of the "deep and surprising affinity" (in Gurvitch's terms) that exists between them. On one hand, indeed, the most advanced social theory and the "new history" have revealed in a very convincing fashion that a given society never represents a monolithic and immobile entity, but rather that it consists of a dynamic whole of levels (structural and suprastructural: economic, social, political, cultural, aesthetic, etc.) whose historical functioning is not necessarily parallel or convergent and whose steps for transformation (or "duration") are not always the same. This explains the well-known phenomena of remnants and of contradictions between one level and another, and so forth. It is a matter of "transversal" stratification which obviously overlaps the canonic "vertical" stratification organized in classes, sub-classes, particular groupings, and so forth. Scholars such as Gurvitch and Ralph Linton have detailed the components, the typologies, and the diachronic functioning of this stratification. On the other hand, the progressive dilatation of the category "theatre" (a dilatation, it is important to remember, that is almost imposed by contemporary theatrical experimentation) has agreed to focus on the "dramatic" elements of which the life of social groups and of individuals is full, and to realize that the phenomena of performance, representation, and the mask (in the broadest sense of these terms) are not limited exclusively to the theatrical space.[2]

DRAMATIC CEREMONY AND SOCIAL CEREMONY

Duvignaud has certainly been the scholar to pursue this matching between social phenomena and theatrical phenomena with the greatest determination and the greatest *esprit de finesse* in the *macrosociological* plane (see especially 1965a, also Duvignaud 1970, 1971, 1973, 1977). In order to reveal the theatrical dimension of social life, Duvignaud applies, following Gurvitch's suggestion, the Durkheimian notion of "ceremony," while proposing to study the similarities and differences between *dramatic ceremonies* which take place in actual theatres and *social ceremonies*—those spontaneous dramatizations with which the history of groups and of nations is disseminated. Naturally, one of the principal goals of his approach is to show how difficult it often is to separate one from the other in a clear way. Besides, it is important to note that when he talks about social ceremonies he does not refer only to those great forms of "spontaneous" theatricalizations of *rites* and *public celebrations* performed in both so-called primitive societies and those considered civilized or historical: "In different degrees," writes Duvignaud (1965a, 4–6), "a political gathering, a mass, a family, or a neighbourhood party are also dramatic acts," as are a "court session, a competition jury, the inauguration of a monument. . . ". In this respect, "they are ceremonies in which the people involved interpret a role according to a scenario that they are not able to modify since nobody can escape from the social roles that he or she must assume" (ibid.).

In fact, in this way, the Duvignaudian perspective gets transferred from the macrosociological plane to the microsociological one, meeting Goffman's and other theorists' areas, as I will soon discuss. However, still from the level of the large-scale phenomena, one wonders what the meaning of this diffuse theatricalization is and what the functions of ceremonies in social life are. Duvignaud's answer is the following: "One could say that society applies to the theatre every time that it needs to assert its existence or perform a decisive act that might put it into question" (ibid.).

According to Duvignaud, social groups (like individuals) must represent themselves to each other in order to continue (or in some instances to start) to exist as such and principally, to be periodically put into question and to be transformed. This is a thesis supported by the incontestable historical circumstance that the "rate" of collective theatricality of societies, or of an entire civilization, increases enormously during crises or passages from one period to the next, from one socio-economic structure and from one political system to another. The social "effervescence" seems to produce theatricalization, or, more precisely, it seems to have an inherent need for representation and masking in order to manifest itself and to produce its effects. It so happens that in revolutionary periods—that is, in those historical moments in which the collective dynamism and the ability of a society to put itself into question reach their maximum degree—the diffuse theatricalization might even arrive to replace the actual theatre. In these cases, it is the social existence itself that becomes theatre, performance, and continuous "feast" as such (Duvignaud 1971, 59).[3]

EVERYDAY LIFE AS REPRESENTATION

When Duvignaud began dealing with the ceremonies of social life and their relationships with the theatre in the 1960s, the famous American sociologist Erving Goffman had already spent some time on the study of the theatrical elements implied in even the smallest rituals of everyday life, especially in interpersonal relationships. The hypotheses briefly summarized here are the bases of his work on the subject:

> 1) "The ordinary social relationship is by nature organized as a scene, with changes of actions theatrically swollen, counteractions, and final lines." (Goffman 1959, 83)
> 2) "I am suggesting that often what talkers undertake to do is not to provide information to a recipient but to present dramas to an audience. Indeed, it seems that we spend most of our time not engaged in giving information but in giving shows." (Goffman 1974, 508)

Although we are not always aware of our "public behaviour" (as Goffman calls another of his well-known findings),[4] or at least not willing to admit it, our personal interactions—both public and private, and even the most banal —are always in some way related to the fiction of the *"mise-en-scène."* It is not that all of us deliberately tend to lie or to fake (some people might do so incidentally, but this is a different subject altogether). It is rather our constant need to represent our self, our role, our social "persona" in front of others or, more simply, our need to give an image of ourselves that responds to the way in which we wish to be seen by others. To this effect, we—social actors—in a more or less conscious way bring into play a repertory of abilities and techniques similar to those of theatre actors: appropriate mimicry, tones of voice, gestures, pauses, and so forth. And for a piece of incontrovertible evidence, one need look no further than the role playing that is interwoven in the fabric of our daily behavior, according to Goffman and others, and to think of the embarrassment almost to the point of schizophrenia that we experience when we are in the combined presence of individuals to whom we usually exhibit very different images of ourselves, such as parents, friends, employers, and colleagues. What gets us in trouble in these cases is the conflict between our diverse masks or, more precisely, the impossibility of showing them all at the same time.

In reading Goffman superficially, there is a serious risk of believing that he makes no distinction between theatre and everyday life. This would be a distortion. He does not equate theatre with everyday life or propose that we are all inevitably liars and dissimulators. Goffman has tried to demonstrate something quite different through his analysis—that "performance is not confined to the realm of fiction but constitutes an essential device of everyday life as well" (Wolf 1979, 90).

Therefore, it is not a matter of identifying or confusing two distinct kinds of communicatory situations—theatrical performances and everyday performances—but to realize, as Goffman explains in the famous last page of *The Presentation,* that in both situations the actors must apply the same repertory of "real techniques"[5] in order to succeed: "A character staged in the theatre is not in some ways real, nor does it have the same kind of real consequences as does the thoroughly contrived character performed by a confidence man: but the *successful* staging of either of these types of false figures involves use of *real* techniques—the same techniques by which everyday persons sustain their real social situations" (Goffman 1959, 291).

During the 1960s and 1970s Goffman's dramatic perspective moved toward a non-substantialistic direction, without falling into hurried and abstract temptations for holistic systematizations. Even more clearly, theatre for him constitutes only a model, a paradigm, i.e., a method of analysis.[6]

THEATRE AS A BEHAVIOR MODEL

Independent of the fact that social and individual behaviors can be recognized or analyzed as theatrical, there exists (or, better, one can also postulate) a different kind of link between theatre and real life. Briefly, this consists of the fact that "the theatre provides usable paradigms for conduct" (Burns 1972, 34). It is a phenomenon that surpasses the explicitly and intentionally didactic level in dramatic texts and in performances (a non-specific level, however, since it can be present in every kind of artistic production). In European history we can observe that the theatre—understood mainly as representation and performance—after being born from the re-elaboration of cultural codes of its time, often ends up influencing and even modifying those codes, thus operating as a "secondary modeling system," in the vocabulary of Lotman's school of Russian semiologists. More specifically, the actor's way of moving, gesticulating, and talking—his or her "style" on stage and off—is considered more or less deliberately as a model in certain social milieux. The history of the European actor, from the eighteenth century on, is full of examples of this sort, going beyond infatuation and fashion to point out a broader and deeper phenomenon, i.e., the possibility for the theatre to function as a "device for codifying human behavior [. . .] in the reality of life and costume" (Lotman 1973, 277f.).[7]

3. Sociology of the dramatic production

Up to this point we have dealt with a very heterodox sociology of the theatre, so to speak, because within its limits theatre illuminates certain aspects of the society and its functions; it is nonetheless obvious that at least part of this light will in turn reflect upon theatre itself. Now we must wonder, from a more orthodox point of view, how and whether society can, in turn, shed light on the theatre to help us study and understand it better. For the sake of clarity, I will divide the rest of this chapter into two parts, to discuss in the first place the sociology of production in its various aspects and levels, and in the second place the sociology of reception.

Among the different branches of the future sociology of the theatre that Gurvitch lists in his "program" (1956) there are three that could be usefully gathered under the label of the sociology of theatrical production:

1) "the study of groups of actors as a company, and of acting as a profession in general";

2) "the study of the functional relationship between the *content* (and style) of texts and their social context—with particular reference to global social structures and classes";

3) "the study of the social functions of the theatre in different types of global social structures" (Gurvitch ibid., 203–204).

SOCIOLOGY OF ACTORS AND COMPANIES

Gurvitch's list of questions for study on this subject is still so precise and complete today that it does not seem to have been compiled more than thirty years ago: "The size and cohesion of different companies, their organization, the professional and extra-professional relationships among their members, and the social origin of the latter; the integration of the companies in the profession; the structuring of the actor's profession into groups; the relationships of professional groups of actors with other professional groupings (writers, costume designers, directors, technicians, etc.), with their unions, and finally, with their social classes and the inherent hierarchies of social strata" (ibid., 203).

However, despite the numerous available works on this broad research field, we must admit that the response to Gurvitch's questions about the life of professional actors and companies in Europe in the last few centuries, for instance, is still insufficient. Generally, one goes from overly abstract studies (Duvignaud's brilliant sociology of the actor [1965b] is not an exception of this approach) to empirical surveys that deal mainly with our times, and usually limit themselves to the collection of a certain amount of quantitative data. In the first case, facts are considered from too great a distance, and in the second case they are watched too closely to seize the phenomenon of the actor and the theatrical profession in its specific historical complexity or to define with precision the place of the theatre in the cultural topography of modern Europe. It is important to remember that the biggest difficulty in this respect is our tendency to read or analyze the theatrical phenomena of the past (including the condition of the professional actor in the last few centuries) under the deforming light of the reality of our present time, which leads us to project on these phenomena the image of what they have become only later on.[8] For instance, we risk understanding very little about theatrical professionalism in the sixteenth and seventeenth centuries and its relationship to "amateur" theatre if we insist on considering it in the socio-cultural terms that it assumed only later on, after the institutionalization of the theatre in the eighteenth century. In this way, one forgets that before this time the professional actor was considered, with few exceptions, as someone who practiced an almost shameful trade, closer to the world of the charlatans and acrobats of the fairs than to that of "art and culture," to which the non-professional theatre of aristocrats and academicians belonged. To deal with this issue, it is necessary to refer to the enlightening proposals of Ferdinando Taviani, particularly to the fundamental book he wrote on the commedia dell'arte in collaboration with Mirella Schino (Taviani-Schino 1982).[9] Among his particularly interesting notions is that of *microsociety*—a term by which he attempts to define the hybrid socio-cultural status of the theatre companies who traveled in Europe between the sixteenth and eighteenth centuries. These companies were always foreigners with respect to the environments in which they were periodically hosted. However, while being the carriers of an irreducible anthropological "difference," they were consistently eager to integrate themselves with their hosts, and forever willing to hide or at least to reduce their difference through their eager adhesion to the ruling values.[10]

SOCIOLOGY OF THE DRAMATIC CONTENTS

What Gurvitch (1956, 203) calls "the sociology of knowledge applied to the theatrical production" is probably the theatrical/sociological area that is most dealt with. It mainly consists of the analysis of the relationships "between the kind of global society (for instance, the kind characterized by feudalism, absolute illuminism, economic liberalism, organized capitalism, communism, etc.) and the contents of the theatrical production" (ibid.). We shall limit ourselves to well-known examples.

• Using such an approach, one can easily see in Greek tragedy of the fifth century B.C. the uncertain and risky transition from the culture and law of an archaic society to that of a democratic *polis* (think, for instance, of Aeschylus' *Oresteia*); hence one can consider this transition the material and mental conflictual context of a peak of Western dramaturgy, i.e., as its "social and psychological conditions" (Vernant and Vidal-Naquet 1972).

• In many of Shakespeare's plays, it is possible to decipher the vivid echo of the fall of the old feudal order with its hierarchies and values, what Stone (1965) called "the crisis of the aristocracy" (*Richard III, Macbeth, Hamlet,* and *King Lear*, for example).

• One can—and could in the past—throw new light on Corneille's and Racine's masterpieces (*Le Cid, Bérénice, Phèdre*) by reading the conflicts of passion against duty and of self against society in the context of the monarchic absolutism of seventeenth-century France and the different reactions that it aroused in the social milieux and classes to which the dramatists were linked (cf. Goldmann 1955).[11]

• Finally, in the eighteenth century, one can easily relate the new dramaturgies of Diderot, Lessing, Goldoni, and Beaumarchais to the ascent of a new social class, the bourgeoisie, and to the spread of its world view.

Naturally, it is also possible and useful to establish tighter and more detailed connections between certain pieces and determined social institutions or determining social facts. For instance, just looking into the ancient theatre, Vernant and Vidal-Naquet (1972, 88–120) have related Sophocles' *Oedipus Rex* to the ritual procedure of the *pharmakos* (scapegoat) and to ostracism. (This Athenian political institution was born with the tragedy in the fifth century, and likewise disappeared with the tragedy.) In general, Aristophanes' comedies and the works of the three great Greek tragedians have been analyzed many times to decipher and understand the reactions and events of their times— such as the Peloponnesian War, the fights between oligarchs and democrats, the controversy about Socrates and the sophists, and the crisis of Pericles' golden age—to the point of arriving, in certain cases, at a precise clarification of the most trivial historical circumstances lying in the background of some dramas (cfr. for example, Thomson 1946; Ehrenberg 1951; Goossens 1962; Di Benedetto 1972).

Beyond the irrefutable usefulness and the important results that this kind of approach can sometimes yield, it also presents an evident limitation and risk. The limitation is that of using the theatrical event, text, and performance only as documentation (i.e., only as the source of information about the social and political context). The risk has been in fact very serious and diffuse until recently, and consists of a preference for reduction (usually called "sociologism") or for considering the play as a mere *reflection* of a given social reality and to explain it only by the particular historic conditions that have produced it. In so doing, one forgets about the aesthetic and intellectual autonomy of the work and its ability to re-elaborate in an original way the data of its point of departure, without paying attention to the numerous mediations that intervene between culture, social context, and the work itself. For this reason, one can confirm that the semantic values of an aesthetic event (in our case of a theatrical text or a performance) go far beyond the historic circumstances inherent in both its origin and the creator's intentions. The multiple and endlessly renewed meaning of each artistic event is primarily linked to its connection with those who receive it; more exactly, it depends on the communication that such an event is able to establish, each time, with different receivers. Besides this, in the case of the dramatic text, it is necessary to take into consideration the possibilities of a re-interpretation by another writer or by the director. (In this sense, think of the Brechtian concepts of *Bearbeitung* and *Umfunktionierung*.)

THE SOCIAL FUNCTIONS OF THE THEATRE

The considerations presented above in reference to the sociology of dramatic content are also valid for any kind of research on the social functions of the theatre (or of the actor): functions of support and propaganda in favor of the political system in power and of celebration of its values; subversion, transgression, and protest; evasion and entertainment, social and cultural animation, and so forth. It is obviously impossible to enumerate these functions exhaustively, especially when referring to the present, now that cultural and ideological fragmentation have produced an almost unstoppable multiplication of the concepts of art and in particular of the theatre. In any case, if one carefully avoids the risks of a simple-minded sociologism, the functional analysis of theatrical events can prove to be valuable when done with rigorous research on the historical environments of the production and reception of these events. Two examples from Gurvitch's program (1956) are of particular interest here:

(1) It is probably correct to assert, as Gurvitch does (ibid.: 204) that "the famous 'mysteries' of the Middle Ages serve the function of confirming the faith and of supporting the priority of the Church above all other hierarchic chains in competition within the feudal society"; but surely this is not enough. We still understand almost nothing about the social, cultural, and artistic specificity of this theatrical phenomenon (a very diverse phenomenon, besides) if we forget to pose the question of its material dimensions, its spatial and temporal typologies, its location in the city, the contiguity with the marketplace and the fair (besides the church and the liturgy), its interchanges with what Bakhtin has called the "comic popular culture," the urban and rural composition of its audience, the structure and the functioning of the corporations to which the organization of the mysteries was entrusted (see Rey-Flaud 1973; Konigson 1975, ed. 1980; Kinderman 1980).

(2) It is not incorrect to say that "the theatre under the liberalist regime of competitive capitalism has the function of entertaining the ruling classes" (Gurvitch, 1956). However, in order to understand seriously anything about last century's theatre, one must introduce some decisive distinctions within the category of "entertainment" between the function of the boulevard theatre (*pochade,* vaudeville, *grand guignol,* etc.), that of the dramatic theatre of the great actor, and that of the opera, with their respective audiences.[12]

SOCIOLOGY OF THE DRAMATIC AND SCENIC FORMS

It is evident that it is not only the content of theatre pieces but also their *form* and *style* that can undergo sociological analysis of the type indicated in the previous pages. When I speak of forms and styles, I am obviously thinking of both dramatic-literary and scenic concerns. Therefore, I am referring to both the various 'genres' of texts and performances and to different types of signs and expressive means that can be used by theatrical representation, as well as the possible connections among all of these.

I will consider here only one of these sign systems, no doubt one of the most important of them all: this is the *scenic space* or *lieu théâtral.* With the exception of Duvignaud's schematizations, often having little concern with historical data, there are no available global studies pursued from a sociological point of view that reveal the various scenic typologies that existed in the European theatre, from the *mansiones* of medieval performances to the Italian stage of the sixteenth and seventeenth centuries and modern playhouses, up to the revolutions of the twentieth century. Nevertheless, there are some interesting analyses done in this light, such as Rey-Flaud's and Konigson's on the medieval scenic space, quoted above. Also, there is excellent work by the sociologist of art Pierre Francastel on the Renaissance "figurative space" and especially on the social and intellectual conditions in fifteenth century Italy that promoted the spatial system of representation of linear perspective (a new "visual order" corresponding to the new socio-political order represented by the great commercial bourgeoisie and by the 'Signorie') and that led (at the beginning of the sixteenth century) to its passage from painting and architecture into theatrical scenography (see Francastel 1951, 1965, 1967, 1986).

4. Sociology of reception: from the audience to the spectator

As I said at the beginning of this chapter, a highly developed branch of the sociology of the theatre has been (and still is) the one that deals with empirical surveys of the audience. They are mostly studies using the techniques of sociography (i.e., various types of interviews and written tests) to gather quantitative data on the socio-cultural composition of the theatre audience and also to elaborate statistics relative to their tastes and preferences for performances. I have also reminded the reader of the long-standing opposition to this kind of research, even within sociology itself. Gurvitch, for instance, blames these investigations for the adoption of "overly mechanical techniques which do not allow for the recognition of the diversity of audiences, their different degrees of cohesion, the importance of their possible transformation into proper groupings" (1956, 202). Ten years after Gurvitch, Duvignaud (1965a, 42–43) blamed statistical analyses for considering only "the numbers of spectators in a theatre hall, with no interest in the reasons that attract them to the theatre," without trying to address "the inclinations that should help define the real tendencies that characterize the general configuration of an audience, their *expectations.*"

This question of different perspectives gives us a fair idea of the "abyss" in the 1950s and 1960s, between the "theoretical sociology" and the "sociology of the passive observation of the facts," as expressed again by Gurvitch (206). However, during the 1970s the situation started to change in this respect. In fact, the consistently closer encounter between the theatre and the human sciences began to produce studies on the theatre audience that were more theoretically grounded than ever before. There already exist a good number of multidisciplinary research projects on theatre reception in which the traditional sociographic methods are integrated with and enriched by the instruments of semiology and psychology. The most interesting among these studies adopt (although not exclusively), the theoretical and epistemological framework of semiotics. They attempt to translate the reflections produced today in semiology on the functioning of signification in the theatre, and on the relationship between the performance and the audience, into scientific operational terms, thus attempting to surpass the simplicity of descriptions and the rigidity of formulations drawn from traditional surveys on theatre "consumers" (see, for instance, Coppieters 1981; Schoenmakers 1982; Tan 1982; De Marinis-Altieri 1985).

In my opinion, there are two principal theoretical differences that counter-distinguish these recent investigations (even if they end up very different from each other):

a) The passage from the notion of *public*—a homogeneous and therefore abstract sociological entity—to that of *spectator*, an anthropological notion far more complex and precise, determined not only by socio-economic factors but by psychological, cultural, and even biological and other factors as well.

b) The concept of *theatrical relationship*, i.e., the rapport between the performance and the spectator as a rapport of communication or, more precisely, as a meaningful interaction in which cognitive, intellectual, and affective values are not imposed in a unilateral manner by one pole (the performance, the actor) on the other pole (the spectators) but are somehow produced *together* by both. Naturally, the term "together" refers to a broad spectrum of possibilities, ranging from harmonious cooperation (in those rare but historically documented cases of a great cohesion between stage and auditorium) to a negotiation that might sometimes become very conflictive. According to this pragmatic view of the theatrical relationship, the role of the spectator always appears decisive, since she or he is the only effective realizer of the semantic and communicative potentials of the representation.

The impossibility and the uselessness of an approach that isolates only one of the two poles of the theatrical relationship has forced the most recent studies to rethink the sociology of the audience in the more adequate terms of an analysis (which I propose to call "socio-semiotics") of the entire *theatrical circuit*, which involves the production-reception of the performance and of the numerous processes and sub-processes that it implies (see, for instance, Pavis 1983). Within this circuit it is still possible to distinguish at least two principal components (the term 'circuit' itself indicates the possibility of a continuous movement back and forth in both directions, from the performance to the spectator and vice versa):

I) *The productive strategies of the "authors" of the performance* (writer, director, set designer, actors, the other "practitioners": they compose what Helbo [1983, 1987] calls "the collective of theatrical enunciation"): at the same time it is a matter of strategies of signification and of communication-manipulation which lead not only to *faire-savoir* (causing to know) (and therefore to carry information, meanings, messages) but also, and especially, to *faire-croire* (causing to believe) and *faire-faire* (causing to act), in Greimas and Courtes' terms (1979), that is, to modify the intellectual and affective universe of the spectators and sometimes even to push them directly to action (as in the revolutionary political theatre of this century: agit-prop, Brecht's epic theatre, etc.).[13]

II) *The reception strategies of the spectator,* within which one must distinguish at least the following:

(a) A certain number of *processes* and *sub-processes* that comprise the receptive act at the theatre: perception, interpretation, emotion, evaluation, memory (cf. Schoenmakers 1982; Tan 1982; De Marinis 1984; Deldime 1986, 1988);

(b) *the result* or *results* of the receptive act, i.e., the understanding that the spectator "constructs" out of a given performance, an understanding which in turn is composed of at least semantic, aesthetic, and emotional aspects. It is important to clarify at this point that these aspects must be conceived of as intimately linked to one another although independent in their functioning. A subject might indeed experience a very positive and intense impression about a performance that s/he has not quite understood from a rational point of view and to which s/he is therefore unable to assign a precise meaning (see Holm 1972; Tan 1982);

(c) a certain limited number of *presuppositions* of the receptive act which function as determinants of the reception processes while influencing their development and results.

As for the presuppositions, it can be useful to structure them in a *theatrical system of receptive preconditions* in which the traditional sociological factors (social class, education level, profession, etc.) leave room mainly for the cognitive and non-cognitive psychological parameters. These parameters should particularly refer to:

i) *general knowledge* of the spectator, theatrical or extra-theatrical;

ii) *particular knowledge* of the spectator, in reference primarily to the dramatic text employed in the production and to all other prior information on it that the spectator can infer from the communicative context: typology and organization of the theatrical space, etc., and the so-called "para-texts": posters, house programs, reviews, etc.;[14]

iii) *goals, interests, motivations,* and *expectations* of the spectator in reference to the theatre in general and to the specific performance in particular (see De Marinis 1984 on distinction between general and specific motivations and expectations);

iv) *material conditions of the reception,* which refers primarily to the physical position of the spectator in relationship to the performance and to the other spectators. In this sense, it becomes almost automatic to think of contemporary examples (which have already become classical) in terms of non-traditional organization of the theatrical space and the relationship between the performance and the audience, as in *Orlando Furioso* by Luca Ronconi, the Théâtre du Soleil's *1789* directed by Ariane Mnouchkine, or *Ka Mountain and Guardenia Terrace* by Robert Wilson. But beyond these "extreme" examples, one fact must be clarified: even in theatre *all'italiana* (and therefore in the usual frontal and monofocused relationship between stage and auditorium), the spectator's material conditions (seated or standing, close to or far from the actors) are always decisive as to the modality and the results of reception, since they with other factors determine the very conditions and limits of visibility: *what* and *how* the spectator sees. In the historical European theatres, for instance, the usual distance between the seats and the stage prevented the majority of the spectators from seeing all the mimico-facial details in the actors' performance. The spectator's material conditions of reception can also include *the spectator's relationship to other spectators,* although this is obviously a very complex and specific question primarily involving the communitary aspect of the theatre audience and the collective functioning of the spectator's reception. These two elements have perhaps been overemphasized in the past by a literature that has chiefly treated them with a spiritual, even mystical optics. However, for the last few years one has been able to speak of serious attempts to study the issue of the constitution of a theatre audience as a "collective actant" (see Poppe 1979; de Kuyper 1979; Ceriani 1988).

With the type of theatrical reception model described briefly here,[15] we are beyond the mechanical connections being made by some current surveys which focus on social class and the corresponding type of understanding achieved by a given spectator (see, for instance, Jaumain 1983; and Gourdon 1982, 130–31).

To conclude, I would like to suggest the need to leave room for the notion of *theatrical competence* right next to that of the theatrical system of receptive preconditions discussed above. This theatrical competence must be understood as the sum of everything that the spectator has at his or her disposal under the conditions of understanding a theatrical representation (attitude, ability, knowledge, motivations, etc.). Therefore, theatrical competence is not only *knowing* (i.e., the sum of knowledge and codes) but also and primarily *knowing how,* which is indeed the whole of the abilities, attitudes and other factors that allow the spectator to execute the diverse receptive operations.

The experimental socio-semiotic approach to the spectator's reception in the theatre is still at its very beginnings, and many theoretical and technical obstacles stand in the way of its development. Think, for instance, of the problems presented by the somewhat crucial passage from an *indirect* reconstruction of the event and of the receptive processes that it implies through the results (and therefore only to the extent to which these results can be inferred from the answers given by the people interviewed, their questionnaires, and other types of verbal or audiovisual texts) to a *direct* research on these same processes by the mechanical recording, for instance, of the behavioral (external) and psychophysical aspects of reception while the performance unfolds. However, in spite of tremendous difficulties, there have already been a certain number of pioneering attempts in this direction: from the bizarre machine invented by N. C. Meier in the 1950s to measure the degree of spectator interest and appreciation (cf. Goodlad 1971) to the recent use of video to document the external reactions of the audience (Schoenmakers 1982; Tan 1982) and particularly to record the "trajectory" described by the spectators' attention (Thorn

1986), to the current experiments by Schälzky, who studies the neurophysiological variations that take place during the reception of a performance event with the aid of the psychogalvanic response test and the electrocardiographic and electroencephalographic tracings (see, for instance, Schälzky 1980).

NOTES

1. In an interesting essay, Meldolesi (1986) maintains that the pretension of giving life to a socio-theatrical discipline, from the 1950s on, has always been based on an "illusion"—that of "being able to produce a true and proper integrated culture out of the theatrico-sociological experience" (111), thus systematizing Gurvitch's and Goffman's "disorganic acquisitions." According to Meldolesi, the failure of every attempt in this direction (Duvignaud, the American theoreticians after Goffman, Schechner) would confirm the "impossibility of constituting a unitary theatrico-sociological culture" and would prove that actually the theatrical sociologies are two, one sociological and the other theatrical. These could interact and collaborate but never fuse, given their intrinsic "discontinuity" (130).

2. For more on the topic of theatrico-sociological relationships, see the chapter "Theatre and Everyday Life" in De Marinis (1988).

3. On theatre-feast-revolt-revolution connections, see also Duvignaud (1973) with socio-anthropological optics. For historical research on the subject in reference to Europe, see Bercé (1976), Ozouf (1976), Vovelle (1976) and Le Roy Ladurie (1979). In an essay written in 1976 (now in De Marinis 1983) and devoted in large part to traversing the stages of Duvignaud's theatricological elaboration, I came to distinguish between a "first" and a "second" Duvignaud (which would start more or less with *Spectacle et société* [1970]) on the basis of a progressive dilatation in his work of the category of the "theatre" and of the emergence at one level of the notion of "feast" as a sort of anti-theatre (70–71). On that occasion, I pointed out, although briefly, how these theorizations of the second phase, far more important to my eyes, sometimes ended up short in the documentation and accuracy of the historico-ethnological information, while they appeared strongly indebted to the most radical experiments of theatre of the 1960s (happening, environmental theatre, street theatre, etc.) and to the polemics against the so-called "society of the spectacle" provoked by the French Situationalists (especially Guy Debord). Now Meldolesi returns to this division of Duvignaud's theatrico-sociological itinerary into two moments, expressing himself in very negative terms about the second one, and seeing in two ambitious books—*Spectacle et société* and *Le Théâtre, et après*—which, in his opinion, missed the point, the confirmation of the "impossibility of culturally systematizing the relationships between the theatre and sociology" (114). Regarding these and other works by Duvignaud, he also discusses "an only apparent radicalism" that actually hides "a closed system of references, arbitrarily presented as the only possible one": from this derives an "expository extremism" in which, due to "the lack of original links between one enunciation and the next," "the ideas tend to become slogans while the connecting thread shows itself to be impregnated with commonplaces, and overly emphasized in order to maintain the level of the ideas" (ibid.).

4. Cf. Goffman (1963). But other references are extended to almost all the titles of Goffman's bibliography; from 1961 (particularly, the chapter on "Distance from the role") to 1967, 1971, 1974, and the last one, 1981.

5. On this point, see the chapter "Anthropology" in De Marinis (1988).

6. From this point of view, Goffman's (1974) comparison of "theatrical perform-ance" and "face to face interactions" on the basis of *frame analysis* appears interesting.

7. The example studied by Lotman (1973) is that of the Russian aristocracy in the first half of the nineteenth century, who in particular circumstances and mainly in their literary autodescriptions (letters, memories, etc.) used to model their behavior on the basis of codes of the stage and of the paintings of their times, both inspired, naturally, by ethic and aesthetic ideals of solemnity and heroism.

8. On the subject, see also the chapter "History and Historiography" in De Marinis (1988).

9. But cf. also Taviani (1978, 1979). Mariti (1978) is also very useful on the relation-ship between professional comedians and *dilettanti* in the Italian society of the seven-teenth century.

10. One should not forget that, as Meldolesi (1984, 104) remembers when comment-ing upon Taviani's notion of the microsociety of the actors, the world of professional actors in the seventeenth and eighteenth centuries represented many internal differences quite evident from the socio-economic and cultural point of view. It actually constituted a pyramid with the great actors, cultivated and academicians (like Isabella Andreini) on the top, and the jesters and marketplace acrobats at the bottom.

11. In his fascinating and classic study, Lucien Goldmann (1955) realizes the "*inser-tion*" of Racine's theatre and Pascal's *Pensées* "in the currents of the thinking and the affectivity that are closest to them; this means, primarily, within what we will call *Jansenist thought and spirituality*, and then in the whole of the economic and social life of the group or, to be more precise, of the social class connected with this mentality and spirituality, what corresponds, in the specific case of our study, to the economic, social, and political situation of the aristocracy [*noblesse de robe*]" (110). The latter, in fact, had hidden behind Jansenism, often abandoning the world to live in solitude, as a reaction against the absolute monarchy and its affirmation throughout the seventeeenth century.

12. In this sense, it is interesting to note the study done by the director and theorist Richard Demarcy on the reasons for the popular success in France, during the 1950s and 1960s, of two genres apparently far removed from each other: the musical theatre (the *musical* and the "operetta") on one hand, and the theatre of the classics on the other. The author finds the explanation in the fact that these two types of theatrical performances satisfy two fundamental aspirations of the audience (or, at least, of the French audience of this given period): evasion and entertainment, and the complimen-tary value of cultural elevation as a form of social promotion (Demarcy 1973, 21–22).

13. It is clear that these productive strategies must be explicated and reconstructed from the work, thus, in our case, from the *performance text*, and only as long as they are inscribed in it. Consequently, they are independent from the empirical authors' extratextual intentions (either implicit or explicit). In other words, these strategies refer to the *intentio operis* and not to the *intentio auctoris* (to see the difference between the two, see Eco 1986).

14. On "para-texts" in the field of the mass media, cf. Casetti, Lumbelli, and Wolf (1980–81). In reference to the literary field, see Genette (1987).

15. For further information, see De Marinis (1984, 1986).

BIBLIOGRAPHY

M. Bakhtin, 1965, *L'œuvre de François Rabelais et la culture populaire au moyen âge et sous la Renaissance,* Paris, Gallimard.

Yves-Marie Bercé, 1976, *Fête et révolte,* Paris, Hachette.

Elisabeth Burns, 1972, *Theatricality. A Study of Convention in the Theatre and in Social Life,* London, Longman.

F. Casetti, L. Lumbelli, and M. Wolf, 1980/81, "Indagine su alcune regole di genere televisivo," *Ricerche sulla comunicazione,* 2–3.

Giulia Ceriani, 1988, "'Oversights': Notes on Theatrical Montage," in *New Theatre Quarterly,* 4, 15.

Frank Coppieters, 1981, "Performance and perception," in *Poetics Today,* 2, 3.

Roger Deldime, 1986, "La rémanence théâtrale" (paper presented at the First Congress of Sociology of Theatre, Rome), 27–29 June.

Roger Deldime and Jeanne Pigeon, 1988, *La mémoire du jeune spectateur,* Brussels, De Boeck Université.

Eric De Kuyper, 1979, *Pour une sémiotique spectaculaire,* thèse de troisième cycle, Université de la Sorbonne, Paris (unpublished).

Richard Demarcy, 1973, *Eléments d'une sociologie du spectacle,* Paris, UGE.

Marco De Marinis, 1982, *Semiotica del teatro,* Milan, Bompiani.

   1983, *Al limite del teatro,* Florence, Usher.

   1984, "L'esperienza dello spettatore: Fondamenti per una semiotica della ricezione teatrale," *Documenti di lavoro,* 138-139, Centro di Semiotica e di Linguistica, Urbino.

   1986, "Processi cognitivi nella comprensione dello spettacolo: Teoria dei frames e competenza teatrale," (paper presented at the International Congress *Gedächtnis und Repräsentation von Wissen,* Stuttgart, 17–20 November); 1989, in *Versus,* special issue on the reader.

   1988, *Capire il teatro: Lineamenti di una nuova teatrologia,* Florence, Usher.

M. De Marinis and L. Altieri, 1985, "Il lavora dello spettatore nella produzione dell'evento teatrale," *Sociologia del lavoro,* 25.

Vincenzo Di Benedetto, 1972, *Euripide: teatro e società,* Turin, Einaudi.

Jean Duvignaud, 1965a, *Sociologie du théâtre: Essai sur les ombres collectives,* Paris, Presses Universitaires de France.

   1965b, *L'acteur: Esquisse d'une sociologie du comédien,* Paris, Gallimard.

   1970, *Spectacle et société,* Paris, Denoël-Gonthier.

   1971, *Le théâtre, et après,* Paris, Casterman.

   1973, *Fêtes et civilisations,* Paris, Weber.

   1977, *Le don du rien,* Paris, Stock.

J. Duvignaud and J. P. Faye, 1966, "Débat sur la sociologie du théâtre," *Cahiers Internationaux de Sociologie.*

Umberto Eco, 1986, "Appunti sulla semiotica della ricezione," *Carte semiotiche,* 2.

V. Ehrenberg, 1951², *The People of Aristophanes,* Oxford.

Pierre Francastel, 1951, *Peinture et société,* Lyon, Audin.

1965, *La réalité figurative*, Paris, Gonthier.

1967, *La figure et le lieu: L'ordre visuel au Quattrocento*, Paris, Gallimard.

1987, *Guardare il teatro*, Bologna, Il Mulino.

Gerard Genette, 1987, *Seuils: Le paratexte*, Paris, Seuil.

Erving Goffman, 1959, *The Presentation of Self in Everyday Life*, Garden City and New York, Doubleday.

1961, *Encounters*, Indianapolis, Bobbs Merrill.

1963, *Behavior in Public Places*, London and New York, The Free Press of Glencoe.

1971, *Relations in Public*, New York, Basic Books.

1974, *Frame Analysis: An Essay on the Organization of Experience*, New York, Harper and Row.

1981, *Forms of Talk*, Philadelphia, Univ. of Pennsylvania Press.

Lucien Goldmann, 1955, *Le dieu caché*, Paris, Gallimard.

J. S. R. Goodlad, 1971, *A Sociology of Popular Drama*, London, Heinemann.

R. Goossens, 1962, *Euripide et Athènes*, Brussels.

Anne-Marie Gourdon, 1982, *Théâtre, public, perception*, Paris, CNRS.

A. J. Greimas and J. Courtés, 1979, *Sémiotique: Dictionnaire raisonné de la théorie du langage*, Paris, Hachette; 1980, Engl. trans., *Semiotics and Language: An Analytical Dictionary*, Bloomington, Indiana Univ. Press.

Georges Gurvitch, 1956, "Sociologie du théâtre," *Les Lettres nouvelles*, 35.

André Helbo, 1983, *Les mots et les gestes*, Lille, Presses Universitaires de Lille.

1987, *Theory of Performing Arts*, Amsterdam and Philadelphia, Benjamins.

Ingvar Holm, 1972, "Il pubblico di *Ferai*,: in *Biblioteca teatrale*, 5.

Michel Jaumain, 1983, "Théâtre et public: Approches méthodologiques de l'audience théâtrale," in *Cahiers théâtre Louvain*, 49.

Heinz Kindermann, 1980, *Das Theaterpublikum des Mittelalters*, Salzburg, O. Müller.

Elie Konigson, 1975, *L'espace théâtral médiéval*, Paris, CNRS.

Elie Konigson, ed., 1980, *Les voies da la création théâtrale*, Paris, CNRS, vol. VIII.

Jurij M. Lotman, 1973, "Le scena e la pittura come dispositivi codificatori del comportamento culturale nella Russia del primo Ottocento"; 1975, in *Tipologia della cultura*, Milan, Bompiani.

Luciano Mariti, 1978, *Commedia ridicolosa: Storia e testi*, Rome, Bulzoni.

Claudio Meldolesi, 1984, "La microsocietà degli attori: Una storia di tre secoli e più," in *Inchiesta*, 14, 63/64.

1986, "Ai confini del teatro e della sociologia," in *Teatro e storia*, 1, 1.

Mona Ozouf, 1976, *Le fête révolutionnaire (1789–1799)*, Paris, Gallimard.

Patrice Pavis, 1983, Production et réception au théâtre," in *Revue des sciences humaines*, 60, 189, 1985[2], reprinted in *Voix et images de la scène*, Lille, Presses de l'Université de Lille.

Emile Poppe, 1979, *Analyse sémiotique de l'espace spectaculaire*, thèse de troisième cycle, Université de la Sorbonne, Paris (unpublished).

H. Rey-Flaud, 1973, *Le cercle magique: essai sur le théâtre en rond à la fin du moyen âge*, Paris, Gallimard.

H. Schälzky, 1980, *Empirisch-quantitative Methoden in der Theaterwissenschaft*, Munich.

Henri Schoenmakers, 1982, "The Tacit Majority in the Theatre," in E. W. B. Hess-Lüttich, ed., *Multimedial Communication*, II: *Theatre Semiotics*, Tübingen, Gunter Narr.

Lawrence Stone, 1965, *The Crisis of Aristocracy (1558–1641)*, Oxford.

Ed Tan, 1982, "Cognitive Processes in Reception," in E. W. B. Hess- Lüttich, ed. (cited at Schoenmakers, 1982).

Ferdinando Taviani, 1978, "Ideologia teatrale e teatro materiale: Sugli attori," *Quaderni di teatro*, 2.

1979, "L'acritica, gli attori," *Quaderni di teatro*, 5.

F. Taviani and M. Schino, 1982, *Il segreto della Commedia dell'Arte*, Florence: Usher.

George Thomson, 1946[2], *Aeschylus and Athens*, London.

Benjamin Thorn, 1986, "What They Looked At: Two Studies of Audience Attention and Perception," Italian Department, Sydney University (unpublished).

J.-P. Vernant, and P. Vidal-Naquet, 1972, *Mythe et tragédie en Grèce ancienne*, Paris, Maspero.

Michel Vovelle, 1976, *Les métamorphoses de la fête en Provence de 1750 à 1820*, Paris, Aubier-Flammarion.

Mauro Wolf, 1979, *Sociologie della vita quotidiana*, Milan, Strumenti Espresso.

III. Theatre anthropology

Preface

"Theatre anthropology" is an expression used to cover very different fields of research. In this essay we shall deal only with theatre anthropology as a science. This preface is therefore to be read from a "negative" point of view, i.e., as a list of the things (necessarily simplified) with which we do *not* intend to deal.

The most widely known field of theatre anthropology is the one that we shall call *phenomenological,* in which one tries to identify the anthropological aspects pertaining to theatre, and the theatrical aspects pertaining to anthropology. "Theatre" and "anthropology" remain in this field clearly separate: the attention is focused on their points of contact. Its fundamental notion is that of the *ritual,* inasmuch as it represents a performance which has its own code, which is externalized into a public spectacle, and which is socially rooted. The notion of *festa* ("feast"), which has had a wide, although erratic, diffusion in the theatre field, derives from that of the ritual, even though it essentially differentiates itself by the origins of its codes and by its particular milieu and social rooting.

There is then another field of research that we shall define as *ontological.* Here we explore the vocation and even the anthropological *essence* of theatre. Rather than speaking of a specific field here, one ought to speak of a distinctive mark which characterizes all theatrical thinking, especially in the twentieth century, one which emerges unprompted every time economic, political, and market forces become more pressing. The underlying assumption is a sort of utopia in negative, in which theatre, if exempt from those forces, would rediscover its anthropological "heart": thus a community of actors not dependent on (or in opposition to) their "professionality," their "doing theatre" independent of (or in opposition to) their duty to produce a show, a community of spectators not restricted by (or in spite of) their being a paying audience, the community of actors/spectators freed from the contingencies of the law of supply and demand within a market. Within the competence of this field we shall also add the opposition didactics/pedagogy seen respectively as training practice connected to the devising of a show and to "doing theatre." Within this field we can also include those attempts (theoretical or practical) aimed at breaking down the actor/audience division, at pursuing "involvement" and meaning, at destabilizing the traditional theatre space, searching for an "original" spectator or for an "original" means of expression through theatre: all these instances share a craving for a more intense and genuine communion between actors and spectators during a performance.

There is finally a field that we shall define as practical. If we compare a typically "ontological" instance, that of Copeau for example, to a typically "practical" one, we shall discover that they are the specular opposite. Copeau

starts off from the theatre, from an eminent position in the theatre. He acknowl-
edges (by rejecting them) all those economic and market forces which we mentioned earlier: his utopia—a kind of negation of "theatre"—sees the actors
organized "in a community" experimenting with elementary forms of spectacle
outside the commercial circuits. This is obviously a wholesale assumption that
cannot take into consideration potential problematic elements. In the practical
field many events have developed in reverse: starting off from forms of relationship which are not necessarily theatrical ones, drawing on the "community"
for theoretical and practical strength, and making its way, in certain instances,
to the "theatre-theatre." A similar pattern of events can be witnessed in many
groups of the "third theatre," i.e., in that theatre which by definition is neither
"institutionalized" nor avant-garde theatre, and whose official appearance
dates back to the Belgrade International Workshop organized by Eugenio
Barba in 1976. We cannot here give the history of this theatre or consider
it in detail. In any case, the notion of group and that of group culture are
acquisitions without which it is now very difficult to study any theatre, either
past or present. Although the "third theatre"—as alive as ever in today's
reality—no longer enjoys that critical attention it received during the 1970s
and early 1980s, it remains a fruitful experience for the aesthetic and ethical
standards it established.

Each of these areas of theatre anthropology has its own bibliography and
its own protagonists, and is of vital importance for an adequate comprehension
of theatre: none of them, however, has addressed with clarity or with any
order of priorities the problems of "how to do theatre." The questions have
certainly been numerous and very important: Why, for whom, in which forms,
where, in which conditions should one "do theatre"? All of these explore,
in a way, the direction and meaning of theatre but not the (possible) science
of theatre.

In this essay we shall deal with the *scientific aspect* of theatre anthropology.
In so doing we shall operate a drastic selection, setting forth, as organically
as we can (and integrating with other authors' contributions), the ideas that
Eugenio Barba has formulated in various writings over the years. My choice
is neither accidental nor arbitrary. Eugenio Barba, director and founder of
the Odin Teatret, has for many years been concentrating his research on
identifying and formulating a science of theatre and above all science of acting,
to which Barba himself gave the name "theatre anthropology." The main
source of this paper is an articulate bulk of material which was discussed
and debated at the five public sessions of ISTA (International School of Theatre
Anthropology) (Bonn, 1980; Volterra, 1981; Paris and Blois, 1985; Holstebro,
1986; Salento, 1987), sessions which in themselves turned out to be great
experimental laboratories.

Barba's research, just like any other, owes much to other studies which
have explored parallel fields of research without necessarily sharing the same
objectives. We shall here mention Richard Schechner and above all Jerzy
Grotowski, who paved the way for theatre anthropology as a science. Apart

from its aesthetic and practical importance, Grotowski's notion of "negative way" represents the methodological pivot for any scientific study on the actor.

"Rigorous" science and "pragmatic" science

Theatre anthropology as a science deals with human behavior in a performance situation. Before we go any further we ought to define the term "science" as we intend to use it in this context. This is to avoid being accused, on the one hand, of scientism by those who (quite rightly) argue that there are aspects of the actor's work that cannot be formalized, and, on the other, of superficiality by those who regard only the "mechanical" aspects of an actor's work (i.e., physiology, biochemistry, etc.) as fit subjects for scientific scrutiny.

In a period of scientific rigor, the term "science" is antagonistic to both the purely intellectual exercise of philosophy, and the empiricism of certain methods which, although based on facts, fail to accommodate (and simply do not use) *scientific explanation*. While philosophy's permanent statement is that from *a* one deduces *b,* and that of pragmatic empiricism is that to *a* one can associate *b,* "rigorous" science states "from *a* necessarily follows *b*" as a law of cause and effect. Scientific explanation consists in identifying the cause (or the causes) and understanding its (their) functioning. In the light of this definition, theatre anthropology is not a science. It becomes science in the light of what we called earlier "pragmatic empiricism." It was Jerzy Grotowski who drew attention to the pragmatic character of the laws of theatre anthropology. We can argue that if "scientific science" (in the most rigorous sense of the term) declares its validity by showing *why* b *follows* a, pragmatic law declares its validity by showing *that and how* b *follows* a. Pragmatic law states "what to do" and "how" to obtain a specific result; it does not explain why this result occurs. If we look at the notion of "law" we can identify two aspects of pragmatic science which mark its difference from "rigorous" science.

The first aspect concerns the rapport between law and facts. "Rigorous" science piles up facts until they enable one to formulate and verify a law; from then on, the facts are no longer necessary: they are forseen, implied, and therefore embraced by the law. Pragmatic science operates in a different way. The accumulation of facts is never neutralized by a law, and in any case the period of phenomenon-gathering is much longer for pragmatic science than it is for "rigorous" science.

The second aspect concerns the notions of truth and generality. A scientific law does not have degrees of truth. Unless contradicted by fresh evidence, it remains true. We can argue that the "evolution" of a scientific law is a sequence of formulations which are all true within different boundaries. The truth of the law consists in explaining why b *necessarily follows* a; the different truths in the "evolution" of the law concern the different boundaries of *a* and *b.* A pragmatic law evolves in a completely different way: we can describe it as an evolution by successive approximations. Pragmatic law does not enunci-

ate the *cause* of a given rapport, but only its *existence* and its *modalities*.
As the facts accumulate and vary, it keeps updating its formulation without
nullifying the previous "approximations." In scientific law the facts are organized vertically; in pragmatic law they are lined up horizontally. New facts
and further investigation might lead, in scientific law, to proving a formulation
false and to establishing a new, *true* one. In pragmatic law, new facts and
further investigation can lead only to a more accurate approximation.

Pre-expressivity and presence

Now that we have clarified our use of the term "science" we can move
on to consider the key notion of theatre anthropology: the notion of pre-
expressivity. It is generally assumed that in the situation of performance outside
the demands of daily life, the actor's only task is that of expressing (feelings,
passions, concepts). Theatre anthropology has however identified another level
which is also outside daily life, but which cannot be described as expressivity.
It is the pre-expressive level whereby the actor expresses nothing but his presence. This level, then, although it belongs to the situation of performance outside daily life, precedes (logically, if not chronologically) the ultimate task (and
outcome) of expressivity. For the time being, we shall leave to the word "presence" all its ambiguity and therefore all the richness of meaning that common
usage has attributed to it. The actor's presence strikes us every time we watch
a form of theatre with conventions unfamiliar to us and whose meaning we
find difficult to understand. On the other hand the actor's presence escapes
us when it is *hidden* by conventions we all know and by meanings we can
all understand. Our ability to comprehend overshadows, almost to its total
disappearance, the seduction of presence. But the fact that this presence (and
the pre-expressive level in which it is situated) escapes our attention does not
mean that it does not exist, or that it is not an integral part of that same
process of comprehension that is obscuring our view of it. It is worth pointing
out now that the presence has nothing to do with the elements of charm that
the actor might have in his/her daily life, and which s/he will retain (magnified)
in performance; nor has it anything to do with the seduction of being in the
audience's eye. The presence we are talking about is a scientific datum: something which is pragmatically verifiable and independent of the contingencies
that compel the spectator's attention, regardless of the actor's sex-appeal and
the mere fact of being the center of attention on stage. From this point of
view we can say that the pre-expressive level is the level at which the actor
builds his/her own "intrinsic stage."

The pragmatic laws of presence

After more than twenty years of research on Oriental theatre—a theatre
in which unfamiliar conventions and difficulty of comprehension tend to lay
bare the pre-expressive level—three "laws" (or lines of action) related to the

Balinese theatre of *Topeng* (ISTA, 1980). *Photo © Nicola Savarese*

Demonstration by the Japanese teacher Azuma and her Indian counterpart, Saniukta Panighrai (ISTA, 1980). *Photos © Nicola Savarese*

actor's presence have been formulated. It is worth remembering that these are pragmatic laws (or lines of action): they do not explain *why*, but declare *that* and *in which conditions* this presence is verified. The three laws are (1) alteration of balance, (2) the dynamics of oppositions, and (3) the use of "coherent incoherence." In daily life, balance is regulated by the principle of minimal effort: one tends to widen as far as possible the area of support, to keep the center of one's body well within this area, and to "reduce" one's height by allowing the spine to bend, surrendering to the law of gravity. In non-everyday behavior, on the contrary, we can observe the tendency toward unstable, precarious balance, in opposition to the principle of minimal effort. The actors of the above "unfamiliar" theatres show us different means of achieving this precarious or "de luxe" balance, as Eugenio Barba calls it. In Balinese theatre, the actor makes the median of his body slant and lifts his shoulders while raising his toes. In so doing he increases his height, narrows the base of support and pushes his centre of gravity to the limit of his base of support. The Kathakali actor who stands on the outer edge of his feet, a ballerina on point, and a European mime *en déséquilibre* achieve in different ways the same result. The fact that all these different ways are codified in their respective forms of theatre does not imply that they are the only possible ways: on the contrary, despite the fact that they are codified, their variety shows that the same law (the same principle) can be realized in very different, personal and original ways by each actor.

The second law is the "dynamics of oppositions." In daily life these dynamics are manifested only in situations which require an exceptional use of energy: for example, pulling back one's arm to deliver a stronger punch, or crouching down in order to jump higher. In non-everyday behavior this technique is applied even in small actions that do not require a great deal of energy. A typical rule of Peking Opera style is to begin an action in the direction opposite to its intended one, and all the forms of Balinese theatre are built around a series of oppositions between *kras* (hard, strong) and *manis* (soft, tender). According to the law of oppositions, a static position is the result of opposite forces, just as movement is characterized by abrupt acceleration and deceleration, by sudden changes of direction, and so on.

Finally the law of "coherent incoherence" shows that "incoherent" actions (i.e., actions regarded as illogical in everyday life)—which effect an alteration of balance and a dynamic of oppositions—must be used "coherently" (i.e., logically according to the "illogical" non-everyday behavior). We shall return to this crucial point later in this chapter.

Artificiality and artifice

So what is the actor's presence and how can it be defined? Let us here resort to physics. The law of the alteration of balance may be interpreted (not explained) as an *opposition to the force of gravity*. In daily life balance is regulated by favoring the force of gravity: we respond to the downward pull by expanding our base of support, verticalizing the median of our body, and decreasing our height. In stage behavior, on the contrary, balance is regulated by opposing the force of gravity, using resistance, so that the balance becomes unstable, precarious.

The law of the dynamics of oppositions may be interpreted as an *opposition to force of inertia.* In daily life we obtain a static equilibrium by applying a null force, not by applying a number of non-null forces which will give a null resultant; the motion tends to maintain its velocity and trajectory, starting off with an impulse in the same direction of the motion. On the whole, one favors inertia. In stage behavior, on the contrary, one tends to oppose inertia in a number of ways: by rendering the static positions dynamic by means of opposite forces, by adding impulses opposite to the direction of the principal motion, and by changing the velocity and trajectory of the movement.

The law of "coherent incoherence" can be interpreted as the law of *the conservation of energy.* Let us take the following example. If a stone is subjected to certain forces (such as gravity, inertia, and others) the overall resultant will determine a certain trajectory. It will be one and one only, definite. It makes no sense, as regards the stone, to ask oneself whether this trajectory is coherent: it is what it has to be; therefore, by principle, it is coherent. This is because the stone cannot deliberately alter the forces to which it is subjected; it is compelled to conserve them. The same happens with a "passive" human body (i.e., the body in daily life). But in stage behavior, the body is in opposition to the forces to which it is subjected. The law of "coherent incoherence" says that these dynamic "artificial" conditions must be maintained, so that the behavior (=trajectory) can be coherent despite the incoherence of any forces taken separately. Eugenio Barba talks about a "new colonization of the body," of "new culture." The important point is that the "anomalous" forces of the actor presence must become a "norm," an "anomalous norm." What conclusion can we draw from this parallel with physics? First of all, we can say that the actor's presence is a condition of "artificiality." Secondly we can say that this artificiality is related to a surplus of energy. Thirdly, that this surplus must be controlled and must not degenerate into an indiscriminate waste. This conclusion may appear so banal that recourse to physics would seem unnecessary. It is obvious that the laws of alteration of balance and oppositions determine a condition of artificiality of the body, but the ways through which the two pragmatic laws manifest themselves (especially in Oriental theatre) might indicate that this artificiality is only the adjustment to some strange convention. In actual fact, underneath the many varied forms through which the actor is present, there is a common principle which defines (and qualifies) the resulting artificiality of the body. This common principle is a surplus of energy. The artificiality of the presence, in whichever way it is realized, entails an energetic surplus if compared to the sphere of daily life: we can say that the presence, its force of seduction, is precisely this surplus of energy. The actor's presence is uneconomical: it costs more, it is a condition of luxury. This "de luxe" quality, however, must not degenerate into ostentation or waste. There is a certain economy in the uneconomical stage behavior; there is a coherence in the incoherence, naturalness in the artificial opposition to the everyday principle of minimal effort.

Artificiality, however, must not be *artifice*. Economical waste, coherent incoherence, natural artificiality are all still metaphors, small logical paradoxes whose truth reveals itself only when we witness the actor's presence in action, when the seduction it exerts on us as spectators is neither boneless pleasantness nor mere provocation. These paradoxes exist; they are the "norm" for the exceptional situation that performance is.

Apart from the test *de visu*, the notion of surplus energy can be analyzed by looking at the difference between amplification and distortion of organic tensions. We shall do this by looking at actors of the past, belonging to that familiar "unfamiliar" reality called "Commedia dell'Arte."

Amplification and distortion

F. Taviani has attempted to reconstruct the acting style of the commedia dell'arte actors of the second half of the sixteenth century through an analysis of the illustrations in the *Recueil Fossard*, which date back to the period 1575–89 ("Un vivo contrasto": Seminario su attrici e attori nella Commedia dell'Arte, in *Teatro e Storia*, 1, 1986). These illustrations are the work of different hands, and they present the most popular commedia dell'arte characters: Harlequin, the Old Man, the Lovers. Each of these characters is captured in different "expressions." Let us examine Taviani's analysis of Harlequin. Despite the fact that the character is represented in different attitudes and drawn by different artists, one can notice in every illustration a kind of standard position, presenting an elongation of the neck, a lowering of the shoulders and tension of the spine, which forms an arch that goes from the head to the tip of the toes when standing, from the head to the waist when sitting or kneeling.

A similar phenomenon—that is, the recurrence of a standard position—is to be noticed in all the "expressions" of Tristano Martinelli as Harlequin in the illustrations in the booklet *Compositions de Rhétorique* addressed by Martinelli to the French royal family in 1601. This time the standard position is completely different from the one described before. The position is here based on a raising of the shoulders resulting in a hollowing of the neck and elongation of the torso which is accentuated by a belt worn very low.

What can be deduced from these illustrations? First of all, the existence of "artificial" positions which are independent from "expression." Second, the variety of these positions; and third, their "energetic" character: they require more effort than is required for the "relaxed" position of daily life.

But there is another, more important aspect—*crucial* we should say at this stage of our analysis. If we compare the Harlequin of the *Recueil Fossard* (certainly based on real actors seen in performance during the first flourishing of *commedia*) to the Harlequin of Callot's *Balli di Sfessania* (more widely known, but fictional), what strikes us at first sight is an identical artificiality in the disposition of the body. After a thorough examination, however, we perceive that Callot's "imaginary" Harlequin distorts the organic tensions like a contortionist trying to show the "impossibility" of his positions, their almost nonhuman quality; the artificiality of Callot's Harlequin demonstrates itself as an artifice. In contrast to this, the Harlequin in the *Recueil Fossard* and that of Tristano Martinelli amplify the organic tensions: their artificiality is "natural."

We can say that if in daily life man is "erect," the Harlequin of the *Recueil Fossard* continuously and energetically forcing himself to be erect (just like an aging Don Giovanni, if you will excuse the irreverent parallel), unfolds his "presence" by holding back his breath and his belly, thrusting his chest forward, and therefore tightening his spine.

Obviously the "artificial" position of both Harlequins requires energy: the surplus energy of the Fossard Harlequin, though, is not employed to *distort* the tensions of daily life, but to *expand* upon them, to amplify them, retaining their natural functioning. The opposite happens for Callot's Harlequin.

While the body of the contortionist or the acrobat strikes us with the unnatural quality of its artificiality, the body of an actor having "presence" seduces us with the natural quality of its artificiality. Barba's "new colonization of the body" is incoherent coherence, the natural functioning of the actor's "dilated body": a body which opposes everyday laws without contradicting them. The "de luxe" condition of the "presence" is not "against nature," but a condition of "another nature": literally, "second nature."

Presence, expressivity, acting

Now that we have talked about the characteristics of the actor's presence, let us go back to Taviani's study to enquire into its "function."

Taviani proposes a curious experiment: erase all signs of physical expressivity in the illustrations of the *Recueil Fossard* by "beheading" Harlequin and the Old Man in particular, and the result is amazing. Once you have eliminated the white hair and the wrinkly skin of their faces, every sign of physical decadence disappears from their bodies. Those same bodies which—"exceedingly" bent and topped with white hair—looked like the caricature of old age, now appear, without these conditioning suggestions, vigorous, athletic bodies. The bent position now shows the opposite of feebleness or lack of energy: it shows, in fact, a stooping achieved through a surplus of energy. The exceedingly long steps are not the senile wavering of a loss of balance, but the powerful amplification of a "search" for unbalance. The same is true for Harlequin: if we forget his motley as well as his face, we see statuesque postures, energetic but not grotesque.

What conclusion can we draw from this experiment, which is obviously the result of laborious documentary and historiographic research? That the performance style—and, in this particular case, the comic strength (*vis comica*)

—of the commedia dell'arte actors was based neither on caricature nor on generic grotesque but on the *dialectic between an energetic pre-expressive presence and an expressive comic gesturing*. The *vis comica* of *commedia* actors (we are here referring in particular to characters of servants and the Old Man) derived precisely from the grafting of a comic "expressivity" onto a vigorous presence, completely independent of the repertoire of gestures and positions related to expressivity. What is revealed here is the great scientific relevance of the pre-expressive level. The presence is not only the actor's "scenic nature," something that precedes expressivity and is independent of it. It is above all the dialectic complement of expressivity, the other pole with which expressivity interacts, giving shape to the acting. The practical and methodological implications of this important result have not yet been fully explored. Acting is not expressivity alone, but the result of a dialectic between expressivity and presence, between the expressive and the pre-expressive level.

Similarly, from the spectators' point of view, reception is not only comprehension or seduction, or some mixture of both (depending on options of theory or taste). Once again it is the result of a dialectic between the seduction (of the presence) and the comprehension (of expressivity). It is not a case of privileging the expressive or the pre-expressive level: ultimately there is no acting without expressivity, just as there is no acting without presence. From the spectators' point of view, there is no reception without comprehension, just as there is no reception without seduction. The seduction is not part of the reception: it is an essential and integral condition for it in exactly the same way that comprehension is. The accompanying figure is a synopsis of the argument developed so far.

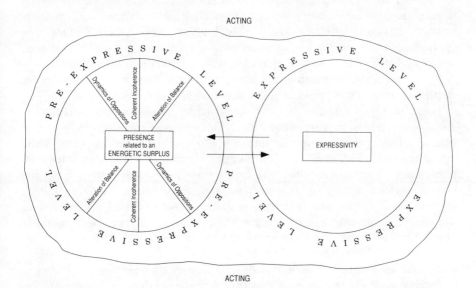

Second nature and training

Let us go back to the actor's presence. We defined it as "natural artificiality" or artificial nature. We mentioned that non-everyday behavior opposes the conditions of nature but does not contradict them. It is, in Taviani's proposed terminology, the "stage" equivalent of that "first nature" which, in daily life, is one's psycho-physical character. A "second nature," then, is not an occasional, accidental behavior. Let us go back to examine the example of the "Don Giovanni" who unfolds his presence. What makes him so un-seductive is the fact that he shows no acquired *nature*, only an extemporary *posture*.

Just as in daily life the *action* springs from the dialectics between one's actions and one's *personal nature*, in the same way in the non-everyday sphere the *stage action* (i.e., acting) springs from the dialectics between "expressivity" and "presence." But the "presence" must be "second nature"; it must have constant characteristics just as first nature has.

The presence as second nature (and the stress here falls, almost paradoxically, on "nature")—if it irreparably condemns the stupid illusion of being able to produce, as an impromptu manufacture, one's own stage presence—shows that the pragmatic laws that determine stage presence are literally *lines of actions*. The actor wants to "re-colonize" his/her own body, not alienate it by command. In actual fact, alienation by command is precisely a condition against nature: even if the pragmatic laws are closely followed, the result cannot but be an *inorganic distortion*, a waste (even if it seems economical) of one's energy.

The pragmatic laws, in all the possible ways they can be put into practice, show themselves to be the analytic equivalent of a continuous activity which is independent of expressivity and is *a fortiori* independent of the performances in which the actor might be engaged. Thus, lines of action: *lines* (i.e., something continuous, uninterrupted, without a programmed ending) and *action* (i.e., something concrete, something that materially engages one's activity).

This (macro) line of action of the actor, this continuous practice independent of performance, has a name: it is called "training."

There have been a number of misunderstandings about training, mainly because of the undeserved indentification with only the exterior aspects of that practice of self-pedagogy and self-identity adopted in the recent years by the "third theatre." The athleticism of this type of training, its spectacularity, its (sometimes) effective "usability" as performance, and, last but not least, the lack of performances that show a high aesthetic standard, all these factors (each of which deserves to be dealt with in much greater detail) have generated a widespread attitude which we shall summarize as follows: (a) training is purely physical activity related to a "theatre of the body" and a "rejection of the word"; (b) training is of no benefit for performance, and the evidence is that the actors of the "institutionalized" theatres do not train.

Leaving aside the truthfulness that these statements may have (or may have had) in specific circumstances, we can say that, in general, these statements are both false, and that they spring from want of recognition and evaluation of the pre-expressive level. First: training is *also* (but not only) a physical activity, and in any case its physical component does not entail the athleticism which characterized, on the whole, the training of the "third theatre." As a corollary, training has nothing to do with the "poetics of the theatre of the body" and the "rejection of the word," unless we want to indicate with this poetics the importance of the body in the whole of the actor's work. Second: training is independent of performance, but not useless to it. On the contrary, the performance, any type of performance, is established in the dialectic rapport between expressivity and a presence which is unachievable (as *second nature*) without continuous training. As a corollary again, one should understand that all actors, including those of the "institutionalized" theatres, must train. The problem, if anything, will then be to identify the methods, without regard to those adopted by the "third theatre" under the specific name of training. We cannot dwell on this extremely important point, but let us ask ourselves this: When the actors of the "institutionalized" theatre, who take as their starting point the psychology of the character they are about to perform, practice in *a continuous way* to transform their bodies, what are these actors doing if not training themselves? From this point of view, the relationship of the "third theatre" to the "tradition" is not different from that of the "institutionalized" theatre: it is only more explicitly marked by a systematic point of departure from the physical aspect.

It might seem at this stage that training, as we have been describing it so far, should go beyond the pragmatic laws of presence, and in fact, nullify them. In other words, if the relevance of pragmatic laws is their proposed role as continuous activity (lines of action) aiming at the acquisition of a "second nature," what seems to disappear is the specificity of these same laws: the alteration of balance and dynamics of oppositions. And all the more so inasmuch as the activity that realizes them need not be exclusively physical.

But one should observe, first, that the relationship between pragmatic laws and presence is not necessarily a bi-univocal one. If the application of certain laws determines presence, that does not mean that presence can be obtained *only* through *these* laws. Second: one has to bear in mind that pragmatic laws express only the *minimal* (and therefore *essential*) core of presence: a core that points out that the minimal conditions of artificiality consist in opposing gravity and inertia. Third, and finally: it is argued that pragmatic laws are lines (of action) not only for their *temporal continuity* but also (and perhaps above all) for their *intrinsic cohesion:* a kind of "spine," a deep line that directs much more diversified activities (including the non-physical ones) toward the acquisition and use of that surplus of energy which characterizes the presence.

Physical and non-physical

We now come to a point of extreme importance, but before dealing with it, it is worth recapitulating the main argument.

The pre-expressive level is that in which the actor's presence is situated. Step by step in our analysis we reached the definition of "second nature": *second* because it is different from everyday nature; *nature*, however, because it does not contradict a natural functioning. The artificiality of the *second nature* consists in a surplus expenditure of energy, deriving from the opposition to the principle of minimal effort. Its naturalness consists in not allowing this surplus of energy to degenerate into waste, in expanding natural tensions without distorting them. The acquisition of presence, in order to become "second nature," requires a continuous activity independent of performance. Although *also* physical, training is *not only* physical, and it may or may not be athletic.

What emerges from the argument so far is an element which was present from the start but that only now stands out with clarity. This element is the *non-physical* or, if you like, the *mental*. Training reveals that presence, although physical, does not have exclusively physical roots: there must be a non-physical, mental equivalent of the pre-expressive level.

We can say that the physical side is the most *exposed* part of the pre-expressive level: "exposed" because "most visible" and therefore more immediately susceptible to attack; and "exposed" because it is at the same time a "weakness" of the pre-expressive level inasmuch as it distracts us from perceiving less obvious points. It is only when we have penetrated the pre-expressive level through its *more* obvious physical side that we are able to discover the *less* obvious non-physical one. On the latter lie the present frontiers of theatre anthropology. We need to understand that the physical and the mental are only the two ends of a *single bridge*, and to grasp how these two sides are linked up: the structure and the functioning of the bridge. The shores of the mental and the physical—and the bridge that links them—are the terms with which Eugenio Barba tackles this still unexplored field in his study "The Dilated Body" (1985). We shall here limit ourselves to giving some directions and asking some questions.

At first the mental side seems to emerge by simple transposition of the notions related to the physical side. There is a "minimal physical effort" which occurs (essentially) by favoring gravity and inertia; by transposition there is a "minimal mental effort," which occurs by favoring mental gravity and inertia. If on the physical side one can resist the principle of minimal effort, the same can be done on the mental side.

First question: How can this opposition to minimal effort occur at a pre-expressive level? And, more radically, is it right to speak of a pre-expressivity of the mental activity? And if so, in what terms?

There are pragmatic lines of actions to contrast the "minimal physical effort", and here the transposition to the mental side becomes difficult. What would be the mental equivalents of the laws of alteration of balance and the dynamics of oppositions?

The body, we can say, is naturally in a realm of constraint; the mind is naturally in a "realm of freedom." Let loose, the body succumbs to all its constrictions; so too does the mind succumb to all its freedom. Probably then the "bridge" between mental and physical must be sought not by considering the *superficial opposition* between freedom and constraint, but by considering the *profound identity* of their subjection.

Both the body and the mind can be *subjected,* and this is the pertinent datum of minimal effort: the norm of everyday life. The body's minimal effort, however, realizes itself in the *subjection to limits* (gravity and inertia are only the most basic of these limits), whereas the subjection of the mind realizes itself in the *subjection to total freedom.* If the body's opposition to minimal effort is obtained by *freeing oneself from limits,* one would think that the mind's opposition to minimal effort would be obtained by *limiting one's freedom.*

Is this only a metaphor? Or does the logical chiasm "freeing oneself from the limits" / "limiting one's freedom" indicate that we will have to look for an analogous anti-symmetry even for the pragmatic lines of action. As regards mental pre-expressivity, Eugenio Barba speaks of a "creative pre-condition." If the prerogative of physical pre-expressivity is the "dilated body," the prerogative of "creative pre-condition" is (on the other side of the "bridge") the "dilated mind." In the creative condition (the mental equivalent of physical expressivity) the essential factor is *orientation;* in the creative pre-condition, *dis-orientation.* In the creative condition *meaning* is essential; in the creative pre-condition *precision* is essential.

Dis-orienting oneself means denying the orientation of the creative condition without either falling into that "freedom without limits" of everyday life or simply replacing it with another, different orientation: it is "a negation which has not yet discovered the new entity which it affirms," according to Eugenio Barba. It is, on the other hand, a renunciation of meaning without either falling into the chaos of "the mind in freedom" or simply substituting another, different meaning: it is, rather, a condition which allows meaning to emerge without (pre)determining it.

As regards orientation and precision, how do they relate to that limitation of freedom which we have postulated as the essential condition to oppose the principle of minimal effort? These are all stimulating questions which have not yet been given answers. It is important, however, to have pointed out the vital relationship between the physical and the mental in the actor's work. In the light of this acquisition one can look back with a different awareness at the traditional dichotomy between the physical and the mental (psychological) which has divided the ideological (more than the practical) options in the actor's work. The physical and the mental are not *two different paths,* but only *two different starting points* which necessarily have to meet. Ultimately, it is irrelevant whether the actor starts from the physical or the mental since there is no dilated body without a dilated mind, and vice versa.

Presence reveals itself even more clearly as a second nature, which—just like one's first nature—is intrinsically psycho-physical, mental and physical.

Actor and director, actor and spectator

The identification of a mental equivalent to the physical side puts the actor-director and actor-spectator relationships in an entirely new light.

The shores of the physical and the mental are no longer linked by the bridge which is the actor, but by a bridge which links the actor's physical performance with the mental activity of the director and the spectator.

From the perspective of production: How does the actor's physical performance relate to the performance that the director has imagined? How does the one reflect or influence the other? From a spectator's point of view: How does the actor's physical performance relate to the performance in the spectator's mind?

Here is disclosed, from the point of view of research, a whole field which overcomes the dynamics of performer/spectator and encoding/decoding or even fascination/seduction, and which forms the scientific bases for exploring the deeper rapport of consonance that every spectator has at least once experienced and which a lack of research has so far relegated to the level of the unrepeatable and unpredictable *personal experience*.

Perhaps it is not accidental that, almost like a transcultural and meta-historical topos, literature should often present one's encounter with the performance as associated with a deep, almost mystical shock in which one re-lives the meaning of one's own life. And this happens also to spectators who (like Wilhelm Meister) are by no means strangers to theatre.

Literature is art, and it may consider mysterious what it would not talk about (or does not consider interesting) in terms other than those of intimate, secret experience. But the science of theatre cannot do so. If the performance-spectator consonance occurs, it is necessary to look for its pragmatic laws, to try to discover *what* to do and *how* to do it in order to bring such consonance about, even if we do not yet know *why* it occurs.

BIBLIOGRAPHY

Eugenio Barba, 1981, *La corsa dei contrari. Antropologia teatrale*, Milan, Feltrinelli.

1982, "L'Archipel du théâtre," in *Bouffonneries*, Carcassonne.

1982, "Anthropologie théâtrale," in *Bouffonneries*, 4, Carcassonne.

1982, "Intercultural Performance," in *The Drama Review*, 26, 2, New York.

1985, "The Dilated Body," in *New Theatre Quarterly*, 4.

1985, *The Dilated Body, followed by The Gospel according to Oxyrhincus*, Rome, Zeami.

1985, *Aldilà delle isole galeggianti,* Milan, Ubulibri.

Eugenio Barba and Nicola Savarese, 1985, *Anatomie de l'acteur. Un dictionnaire d'anthropologie théâtrale,* Caeilhac-Roma, Bouffonneries-Zeami; 1988 (Spanish version), *Anatomia del actor,* Mexico City, Gaceta.

Jerzy Grotowski, 1970, *Per un teatro povero,* Rome, Bulzoni.

1982, "Techniche originarie dell'attore" (lecture given at Instituto del Teatro e dello Spettacole dell'Università di Roma).

Franco Ruffini (dir.), 1981, *La scuola degli attori. Rapporti dalla prima sessione dell'ISTA,* Florence, Usher.

1984, "La trasmissione dell'esperienza in teatro," in *Quaderni di Teatro,* 23.

1988, "L'attore e il dramma. Saggio teorico di antropologia," in *Teatro e Storia,* 5.

forthcoming, "La danse du théâtre," in *Bouffonneries.*

Nicola Savarese (dir.), 1983, *Anatomia del teatro. Un dizionario di antropologia theatrale,* Florence, Usher.

Richard Schechner, 1983, *Performative Circumstances from the Avant Garde to Ramlila,* Calcutta, Seagull Books.

1985, *Between Theatre and Anthropology,* Philadelphia, Univ. of Pennsylvania Press.

Sipario, 1980, 404, *Jerzy Grotowski e il Teatr Laboratorium,* special issue.

Ferdinando Taviani, 1986, "Un vivo contrasto" (Seménario su attrici e attori della Commedia dell'arte), in *Teatro e Storia,* 1.

IV. Semiotics

1. Introduction

Theatre semiotics is a part of general semiotics and will necessarily draw from this broader conceptual basis in any study of drama and theater production. The subsequent aim of this chapter is to introduce a few basic semiotic concepts: *text, sign, discourse, semiosis, structure, reference and referent, code,* and so forth.

But none of these concepts is so overarching as to guarantee both a sufficiently precise and universally applicable analysis. In order to ensure this *theoretic precision* and *analytic relevance,* each respective concept must be considered in direct relation to the scientific theory establishing it and to the domain in which it will be applied.

Semiotics, as applied here, should be taken in its broadest sense, as the general framework within which we shall establish the basic characteristics of certain concepts. It is not our intention to let the definition and exposition of these concepts follow one specific semiotic tradition; on the contrary, we seek a mediation between two different and equally important tendencies: continental structuralism headed by Saussure in company with Russian formalism on the one hand and Peirce's semiotic conception on the other. We deem this mediation necessary since both traditions have their strengths and weaknesses: the strength of Peirce's semiotics lying in its generality and its dynamic conception, the strength of its transatlantic counterparts in a high degree of textual intimacy so far as linguistic texts are concerned.

These few concepts are presented with this as a background in order to show more clearly their relation to *theatre semiotics* and their relevance for its *object*—the theatrical or spectacular event.

2. Text and sign

The *concept of the text* is the point of departure for this presentation because, at first glance, it seems to be the most concrete and because the other concepts can be understood only relative to it. Yet a definition of the concept of text proves difficult for several reasons. In the first place, a more precise definition depends on which semiotic theory one presupposes, and, secondly, a consistent definition of "text" is hindered by everyday language usage. Indeed, "text" is used in reference to a confusing array of phenomena: written or spoken linguistic communications, pictures, road signs, carnivals, towns, costumes, and so forth. It is used in drama as well, both about the linguistic text and the theatrical rendition of this text (cf. Peirce's definition of the sign below).

The relationship between the concepts *text* and *sign* presents another difficulty. The semiotic tradition deriving from and related to linguistics typically distinguishes between these two concepts. Hjelmslev, for example, equates the concept *text* to a *linguistic process,* the *syntagmatic,* which is in opposition to the *paradigmatic* or a *linguistic system.* Hjelmslev views the *text* as a *manifestation* of an underlying system; it may exist as a concrete manifestation, and it is this possibility which interests us here. A given (linguistic) system need not, however, be realized in a process, a text; it can exist as mere possibility and is thus said to be virtual. For Hjelmslev it is essential that a text always manifest a system (Hjelmslev 1966, 16).

In a classic structuralist sign theory such as Hjelmslev's, the difference between text and sign is *not* that the text belongs to the syntagmatic and the sign to the paradigmatic. For, strictly speaking, *the sign itself is a unit of the process or of the manifestation,* which is constituted by the solidarity between the elements from the most important paradigms in linguistic analysis: the planes of expression and of content. Consequently it is only below the sign level—among the elements representing the "building blocks" of the sign at these two respective planes (for example, the expression plane's *phonemes* and the content plane's *sememes*)—that elements are realized which (in theory) are purely paradigmatic, which *differentiate* meaning but which in themselves do not *bear* meaning. The sign, on the other hand, is defined functionally. It is the smallest meaning-bearing unit generated by the combination of elements of content and expression. This means that the concept of the linguistic sign covers not only whole words but also endings, prefixes, suffixes, and so forth. Words can be composed of several signs, and the sign need not be independently manifested. One of Hjelmslev's examples of a sign is the Latin inflexional *-ibus,* which can not be analyzed into further signs. It can, however, be resolved into smaller units on each of the two planes: into the four phonemes /i/, /b/, /u/, and /s/ on the plane of expression and, on the content plane, into the sememes "dative/ablative" and "plural."

The functional definition of the sign as the smallest meaning-bearing unit realized through the combination of elements of expression and content means that *sign* and *text* can in concrete instances coincide perfectly. If, for example, we find the linguistic expression "poison" on a bottle, we can speak simultaneously of a *sign* and of a *text.* This is not strange, since the same expression can be analyzed at several different levels. An example of this is the Latin /i/, where the same expression can be analyzed as phoneme, syllable, sign, and sentence (the latter in the present imperative, second-person singular of the verb "*ire*"). Normally, however, one would see a text as the product of a combination of signs and hence as a phenomenon analyzable into an inventory of elements, of signs and their combination rules (for example, syntactic and semantic rules).

The relevance of this point of view is demonstrated in the fact that even if a very large number of signs exist in a given language and even if new signs appear continuously, the number of signs remains finite and, more important, only a very limited number of signs are necessary for the production and comprehension of a modern text. This is evidenced by the fact that 80.5%

of actual discourse uses the same basic vocabulary of 1000 words (see, for example, Kondratov 1966, 106–19). This means that even at the level of the sign, where the inventory is very large (compared, for example, to the repertory of about 20 phonemes common in many languages), there is, on the one hand, good cause for distinguishing between signs (the lexical and morphological entities) and, on the other, their combination into texts (longer or shorter processes), whose number is practically infinite. For even though it would be possible to calculate mathematically the number of texts possible in a given language at a given time, the resulting figure would be akin to the number of particles in the Milky Way. Roman Jakobson explains the reason for this difference between sign and text as follows:

> In the combination of distinctive features into phonemes, the freedom of the individual speaker is nil; the code has already established all the possibilities which may be utilized in the given language. Freedom to combine phonemes into words is circumscribed, it is limited to the marginal situation of word-coining. In forming sentences out of words the speaker is less constrained. And, finally, in the combination of sentences into utterances, the action of compulsory syntactical rules ceases, and the freedom of any individual speaker to create novel contexts increases substantially, although again the numerous stereotyped utterances are not to be overlooked. (1963: 47–48)

Although Jakobson emphasizes the ever-increasing degree of freedom we are given in combining units, from sign elements to texts, this need not imply that texts are not subjected to various types of codes. In the first place, the codes to which signs are subject are not suspended when the latter are combined into longer linguistic chains (texts); secondly, the texts will be governed by other codes as well—by discursive types and genre conventions, for example.

In pragmatics, the other great semiotic tradition which stems from Peirce, there is no operational distinction between *sign* and *text*. It is very characteristic of Peirce to apply the term "sign" to phenomena which could just as well be called texts. This is confirmed in the following definition of the *sign concept:*

> Signs in general, a class which includes pictures, symptoms, words, sentences, books, libraries, signals, orders of command, microscopes, legislative representatives, musical concertos, performances of these. . . . (MS 634, 1909, ISP 18)[1]

This very open-ended definition of sign does not, however, mean that Peirce makes no distinction between signs of different complexity: it means simply that it is not a linguistic distinction between the sign elements, signs, and texts, but that used by logicians between term, propositional function (Peirce's *Rhema*), proposition, argument, and discourse:

> Discourse consists of arguments, composed of propositions, and they of general terms, relative and non-relative, of singular names, and of some-

thing that may be called copulas, or relative pronouns, etc. according to the family of speech that one compares the discourse to. (MS 939, 1905, ISP 27)

Common to both traditions is the conception of the textual process (the text or the discourse) as being composed of classes of elements which are analyzed through a consistent division or segmentation of the process. The difference in these two processes of analysis and these two systems of classification is a function of the objective of the analysis. This latter point is essential for the establishment of the minimal elements of analysis. For the logician, the entities entering into the proposition (i.e., the terms and propositional functions) will be the smallest elements of analysis. Within linguistics the nearest equivalent to a propositional function would be the smallest meaning-bearing unit, the sign. Linguistics, on the other hand, carries the analysis further, thus registering inventories of the smallest meaning-differentiating units, which are not meaning-bearing as such.

Neither of these traditions is very precise when it comes to specifying the distinction between the sign and the text, since a single element can be both (for example, the word "poison," the iconic sign depicting a skull and crossbones, and the Latin /i/). The difference between *sign* and *text* is not primarily one between signifying elements which manifest the two categories (even though a text most often consists of several signs). Instead of examining the difference between *sign* and *text* on the basis of the elements which constitute them, we suggest a distinction based on their different functions: the *sign* then becomes the smallest meaning-bearing manifestation in a given semiotic (a language, iconic system, etc.) capable of entering into a virtually unlimited number of syntagmas formed in compliance with the combination rules of a given semiotic. The sign is thus conceived as a *virtual entity* invested with a definite *meaning potential* (otherwise we could not discern an unusual or incorrect usage of the sign), but which—in principle—cannot be exhausted by the contexts in which it has appeared at any given moment. This is not of course to imply that the sign lacks a definite stability, for, if this were true, all communication would be impossible. On the contrary, this means that this stability is relative, in the sense that a gliding or displacement of the sign's meaning can and often does occur. This is an essential idea in Viggo Brøndal's semantics, where the word is posited as the linguistic sign.

The *text,* in contrast to the sign, can be conceived of as a concrete manifestation—Brøndal would say an occasional usage—of a syntagma in a communicative context, as an *utterance.* Contextualization, as the characteristic trait of the concept *text,* can be illustrated by the bottle bearing the sign "poison" because here the linguistic sign *together with the bottle* is best understood as a *text* containing the *utterance* "This bottle contains poison."

Some of the characteristics attributed to the concept of *text* in our *common-sense understanding* have already been demonstrated. We in fact generally regard the text as something which can be localized in time and space, produced in a given place at a given time. In the same way, we think of the text as a phenomenon received and perceived at certain moments which can be localized within a spatio-temporal system. From the fact that a text is perceivable it follows that it has or has had material character and, from the fact that it is localized, that it can be described, given qualities which, according to its spatio-temporal situation, make it distinguishable from other phenomena (one can presumably find thousands of bottles marked "poison," that is, thousands of identical texts but which enter into different situations of communication).

3. Text, object, context

What we have said until now concerning the concept *text* has distinguished it from the concept *sign* by emphasizing its occasional material character. But these determinations are not wholly sufficient for differentiating between a *text* and a material *object*. It must be emphasized that *in either sense a text always possesses a material substratum and thereby an objective character.* The difference, moreover, between the object and the text depends on the point of view and the description to which a given phenomenon is subjected. The text, however, as contrary to the object, is characterized by its reference to something outside itself: *aliquid stat pro aliquo* thus becomes the sign's fundamental definition, which also characterizes the text. When a given object, for example an alpine landscape, is designated as a text, this designation is a legitimate usage if it is supposed that the landscape serves some referential function, for example, as a sign of God's might and omnipotence. In the discussion, on the other hand, between two typographers about the formal and material characteristics of the typeface for an editorial, the referential function is suspended. Hence, the text is viewed as an object characterized by a number of material qualities. These examples should demonstrate that the difference between the object and the text depends more upon the context in which a given phenomenon is placed rather than a number of previously attributed qualities (placing them in one of the two categories). This potential duality, as text and object, characteristic of all phenomena is essential for the theatrical production because it is precisely this which provokes a perpetual shifting in the spectator's point of view (see below).

Although the above has clearly shown that any phenomenon can be understood as a potential text even if not produced with a communicative intent based in a conventional semiotic system (i.e., a sign system), let us commence by concentrating on the type of text with these two characteristics: *to be produced based on a conventional semiotic system and with a communicative intent.* A book or a play, for example, meets both conditions; however, before offering a more detailed description of our *common-sense* understanding of such a text, one difficulty must be pointed out, that of the *upper* limit of the individual text, of how a given text can be delimited in relation to other, surrounding texts.

A moment's reflection suffices to show that the answer immediately presenting itself, that of the text as a materially delimited unit, is insufficient, however,
indispensable it may be as a helping tool. For example, an anthology is a collection of texts written by different authors at different moments, usually published separately in various publications. So even though they are presently
bound in a single volume, it can very well be doubted that they constitute
one text. The problem is not resolved through simply referring the texts to
their respective authors because this same problem can again be met at the
level of individual authorships. If we limit ourselves for instance to Shakespeare, we meet this problem of upper delimitation in a collective production.
For example, it is supposed that *Pericles* is the work of two authors, though
Shakespeare scholars stand divided as to the other's identity. We may ask,
however, whether this dual, collective production make *Pericles* two different
texts. Furthermore, *Henry VI* comprises three parts intended to be staged independently. Are we then to treat these parts as three independent texts or as
one? Even more interesting is the question of whether Shakespeare's royal tragedies and, in particular, the two tetralogies (*Henry VI* to *Richard III,* and
Richard II to *Richard V*) constitute eight texts, two texts, or one text. And
what about Shakespeare's contribution to *Sir Thomas More?* The incomplete,
fragmentarily transmitted texts requiring reformulation and restructuring in
association with concrete productions present delimitation problems, too.
Which version of Büchner's *Woyzeck* is more authentic and which is more
effective on stage? And which of these two considerations is more appropriate
in a given dramatic model?

It is no doubt possible to give reasonable answers to the above questions;
however, the mere fact that such questions are relevant makes it clear that
every definition of a linguistic process as a delimitable, independent text must
be well founded. It is therefore interesting to note that in each of the two
great semiotic traditions (for example, among scholars so different as Hjelmslev
and Peirce), we find a text concept radically differing from our everyday understanding. This understanding yields a generalized concept of the text so that,
instead of being applied primarily to definite delimited units, it is applied
to all the textual processes produced in conformity with a given semiotic
system.

The linguist Louis Hjelmslev defines text as a (semiotic) process and, as
concerns natural language, considers it one, continuously expanding text. Even
though this definition runs against the grain of common, everyday understanding, it accords particularly well with the linguistic objective, as it must necessarily transcend the individual text and any limited body of texts. It must
be able to account for all utterances in a given natural language in order to
trace the generative principles which allow us an unlimited production of linguistic meaning.

The logician and philosopher Peirce arrives at the same conclusion by
combining the sign concept with the idea of a continuously expanding argument:

There is a science of semiotic whose results no more afford room for differences of opinion than do those of mathematics, and one of its theorems increases the aptness of that simile. It is that if any signs are connected, no matter how, the resulting system constitutes one sign; so that, most connections resulting from successive pairings, a sign frequently interprets a second in so far as this is "married" to a third. Thus, the conclusion of a syllogism is the interpretation of either premise as married to the other, and of this sort are all the principal translation processes of thought. In the light of the above theorem, we see that *the entire thought-life of any one person is a sign;* and a considerable part of its interpretation will result from marriages with the thought of other persons. So *the thought-life of a social group is a sign; and the entire body of all thought is a sign,* supposing all thought to be more or less connected. (MS 1476, ca. 1904: 38)

Hjelmslev and Peirce's conception of the text as an expanding syntagma is counter-intuitive but possesses obvious advantages compared with our common-sense understanding (even if we cannot dispose of the latter in our practical analysis). Their conception makes it evident that in establishing a particular corpus of texts as the research object we impose limits on an ongoing production of meaning. It is imperative that the foundations of this operation be made explicit. Hjelmslev and Peirce's inclusive conception of the text demonstrates moreover that the limits evinced in the choice a given text or a corpus of texts are, so to speak, semi-permeable because the production, transmission, and interpretation of a passage (e.g., a single text in the ordinary sense) in the formation of meaning, conceived as a historic process, always occur on the basis of a greater textual corpus not necessarily mentioned in the individual text, its transmission, or in its interpretation. Both the production and the transmission of the individual text occur in a dialogical context: a dialectic movement between question and answer (according to the German hermeneutic philosopher Hans-Georg Gadamer), or as a simultaneity of reading and writing.

If the frequently misused concept of *intertextuality* is to be used in connection with the generalized and dynamic(al) conception of the text, then our notion of intertextuality must include at least three elements: (1) If Hjelmslev and Peirce's conception of the generalized text is incorporated, then the individual text's dual affiliation in the broader context is emphasized. On the one hand, there is a *formal* relationship between different individual texts by virtue of their common linguistic codes and the logical rules of inference which are used. (2) On the other hand, Peirce's discussion of thought-life as an argumentative process also stresses the text's *referential character* (Hjelmslev's "content" or "substance") because the thought-process, or the text, refers to a universe. This universe can be understood socio-materially, fictively, physically, ideally, etc., without any of these dimensions being given a privileged status beforehand. Such a juxtaposition of "forms of representation or intuition"

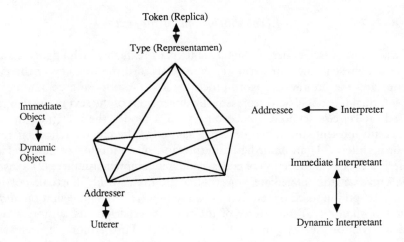

also constitutes an essential part of Brøndal's semantics. (3) From this follows the importance of immediately emphasizing that the interdependence of the text with other texts is not solely a question of a code-community but also of a total or partial community with respect to the universe, thereby relating it to a certain *intersubjectivity* (which has been discussed particularly in hermeneutics and psychoanalysis, and which in linguistics and semiotics is often articulated in the concept of discourse).

As theater spectators, directors and actors, or critics and scholars, our interest naturally lies only in the finished text, the dramatic text as a completed linguistic process or the performance as a limited theatrical event. However, it is only in the interplay between the common-sense notion of the text and the generalized concept of the text (as described, for example, by Hjelmslev and Peirce) that the semiotic analysis of the text can be fruitfully effected, since the isolated text can be understood only as a meaning-bearing unit on the basis of the general production of meaning.

The problem of the delimitation of the individual text and of its interpretation are obviously closely related. In fact they presuppose each other, in the sense that every interpretation constitutes a new text in which elements from the interpreted text are registered. Hence each interpretation is a *contextualization* of the object text. This means that it is through the interpretation of the text's meaning potential that the textual boundaries are drawn. Our common-sense understanding of the text renders it a limited material entity, and it is not until the moment that its sign character—its reference to something else—comes into play that it is differentiated from objects in general; its boundaries are therefore indeterminate until an explication of its meaning has occurred. Thus it would be impossible to determine if a text is a fragment or a relatively completed whole without taking both its structure and content into consideration.

4. *The dimensions of the text*

If we limit ourselves here to linguistic texts or texts in which linguistic structures are present and, furthermore, if we disregard the monkey at the type-
writer and the fire-ravaged word-processor and presuppose a communicative
intent, then it is possible to represent the dimensions of the text in the diagram,
based on Peirce's semiotics. According to this model, the text (i.e., the text
materially present, the token or type) has four different references: it refers
to or manifests (1) an immediate interpretant, or a plurality of interpretants,
that is, a code or a collection of codes lending it comprehensibility; (2) a discursive universe (the immediate object), that is, the "world" (factual, possible,
or fictive) presupposed or referred to by the text (cf. the sign definition *aliquid
stat pro aliquo*); (3) the utterer of the text, its sender or its author; and (4)
the receiver of the text, its reader or audience. Furthermore, it seems that
each of the five instances connected to the production of meaning, the semiosis,
can be divided into internal and external aspects.

The theatrical performance in this connection evidences a number of complicated problems with respect to the dramatic text conceived as a linguistic process. The question is in fact how many of the elements and events of the performance's spatio-temporal process can be interpreted as a coded expression and
which ones are contingent (i.e., incidental in relation to performance considered
as textual process). In other words, how much of what is *visible* is also *legible*
(that is, subject to interpretation as meaning-bearing)? This problem seems
in fact to become even more significant in the analysis of performance than
in literary analysis, which is of course due to the fact that, during the performance, the linguistic text is encased in a *concrete situational context*. Thus the
task becomes not only one of interpreting a series of linguistic utterances based
on linguistic competence, but also of a delimited, focalized, and stylized *physical scenic space*.

The interpretation of the actual phenomenon as a text presupposes its being
conceived as a meaning-bearing object. This means, among other things, that
its expressive elements are differentiated from their background in such a way
that they become identifiable and mutually combinable so that the ensuing coded
expression can be related to a content. This we define simply as its translation
into another text which refers to the same universe as that of the original
(the text's reference to an *interpretant*). The interpretant is a concept from
Peirce's semiotic generally defined as an interpretation or translation of one
sign (or text) into another; for example, the French lexeme *homme* may have
the English lexeme *man* for its interpretant and vice versa. The essential in
Peirce's concept, however, is the distinction between various types of interpretants, one of the most important of which being the difference between
the *immediate interpretant, dynamical interpretant,* and *final interpretant*.

The *immediate interpretant* is defined differently in different places in

Peirce's work, but the following definition will be retained here: "My immediate interpretant is implied in the fact that each Sign must have its peculiar interpretability before it gets any interpreter" (Peirce 1977, 111). The sign or text's *interpretability* thus exists, according to this definition, as a *possibility* which is realized in the *dynamical interpretant,* that is, the objective *content of the concretely realized interpretation:* "The dynamical interpretant is the actual effect produced upon a given interpreter on a given occasion at a given stage of his consideration of the sign" (MS 339 [d], 346). The *final interpretant* is the interpretant that will result from an exhaustive and unlimited study of the sign, and it will be accepted as a true interpretation of the sign (or text) by an unlimited community of investigators.

The *immediate interpretant* can then be understood as that domain of possibilities existing for an interpretation of a given text. This domain is limited for the respective linguistic texts by the meaning potential of the signs entering into the text, their combination in the concrete textual process, the genre of the respective discourse as well as the presuppositions concerning the non-explicit qualities of the discursive universe to which the text refers. All of these determinations can be considered *codes* of the given text.

5. Discourse: process and subjectivity

The conception of discourse that we meet in the linguist and language philosopher Viggo Brøndal can contribute to a presentation of the concept of discourse in its relevance for theater semiotics. He places the discourse on an autonomous plane between the concrete linguistic process (here called the text) and the virtual repertoire of sign and the elementary linguistic unit which, following Saussure, he links to language "as system" (Fr. *la langue*). Concerning discourse in this position, he says:

> "Discourse, in this sense, is a rhythmical totality, an order in time (hence irreversible) where each element (phonic or semantic) has its place and plays the role determined by this place. Through this positional value, words transcend the limbo of the dictionary, enlivening themselves, acquiring a precise meaning and, at the same time, a real and personal character. (Brøndal 1943, 55)

In his concept of discourse, Brøndal maintains that the condition for the realization of the virtual elements in a meaningful text is that one admits *an independent level for the irreversible logic governing the textual process.* This reflection was not particularly well received in classic linguistic structuralism. This is for the most part due to the fact that one adhered to a concept of the sentence modeled after Aristotelian logic; the textual process was already determined by the limits of the sentence, and the ideal structure of the textual process was hence determined through structures reducible to logical rules of inference. There is another reason an independent level of discourse was denied: a level of this nature—verifiable both at the level of the virtual form and the concrete textual manifestation—did not fit into the binary logic of classical structuralism.

The necessity of working with an independent discursive level becomes evident when one can no longer take the limit of the sentence or the sentence's ideal primitive form as an immediate given and when one can no longer accept as a given the identity of the basic unit in the different media of manifestation. It is in fact not given that the same type of sign relation exists in verbal, visual, or multi-dimensional medias. Whether one works with film, theatre, or literature, the limits of a relevant processual unit will be dependent on the medium and its concrete forms of manifestation, and likewise upon the establishment of elementary or fundamental units.

Considering the particular nature of the theatrical event, an independent reflection on the processual logic and its irreversible nature will be especially important in respect to a segmentation of the textual process. In the *narrative* genres, there will always be a narrator who creates a distance between the reader and the events spoken of, even in diary fiction. The reader is never contemporaneous with the events, no matter how absolutely enraptured by the reading. The *theatre,* on the other hand, is from start to finish a here-and-now phenomenon. The happenings on stage and the experiences among the spectators are simultaneous; the physical existence of actor and spectators in a simultaneous now is the heart of the theatrical event. This means that, unlike the spectator, the reader enjoys a certain freedom in controlling the experiential process; one has similar liberty with a novel, a picture, or a video recording, where one can stop, disrupt the action, skip parts, or begin at the end. The theatrical experience is irreversible as it rolls on. Neither can it be repeated in quite the same form, as is possible with a film or video recording; nor can it be replaced by an actor who relates what shall or what has happened on the stage. The theatrical event is at all times a present, concrete activity bound to the specific situation. And this means that the processual logic which dictates the concrete development of these events possesses exactly that mediary position which Brøndal assigns it between the concrete manifestation and the virtual meaning elements which enter into the process.

Every segmentation of this process will have to depend on the situation. The criteria for any given segmentation will be explicated in relation to this situation of presence. The literary reception in the reading also clearly depends on the context. But it is possible to abstract from this and still complete a significant part of the analysis. But such an abstraction is not possible in the analysis of the theatrical event. It would be to reduce the actor to words without a body. Thus segmentation and its criteria is of crucial importance for analysis.

The irreversible and positional logic of the process is one of the two important general characteristics which Brøndal ascribes to the concept of discourse. The other he expresses thus:

What above all characterizes this asymmetrical totality that we call discourse is the goal toward which it always tends, its sense or orientation,
its constant will of expression, in a word, its intention. (Brøndal 1943,
55)

Brøndal uses the word "intention" in direct reference to phenomenology,
with a tacit understanding that consciousness is always a consciousness of something, always directed toward an outside world which is simultaneously not
only an object world, but a potential universe of meaning. It is this relation
which is expressed in the discourse's irreversible logic, that which indicates
that language is directed toward something. On the other hand, the introduction of intentionality as a general characteristic of discourse implies that the
manifested textual process cannot be analyzed as a process without *the instances which mark the subjectivity and the referentiality of language and
which belong to the very logic of the process.*

In the embryonic years of structural linguistics, this aspect of the discursive
nature of language went completely unappreciated with the exception of a
few notables such as Karl Bühler, Viggo Brøndal, Eric Buyssens, and Emile
Benveniste. But since then the analysis of speech acts and enunciation has
given the analysis of discourse some dimensions which accentuate the factors
of enunciation (pronouns, for example) and the modalities of language (doubt,
belief, demand, etc.) which have not been completely absorbed by the dominat-
ing assertive form (A is B / A is not B). The accentuation of the discursive
process underlines its connection to the concrete textual process and its situational dependence. By an emphasis placed on the factors and modalities of
enunciation, discourse is anchored in the inventories of the virtual signs and
elements of language. Discourse then is intentional and coded textualization.
At the same time, the analysis of discourse needs to be specified in semiotic
systems other than those of natural languages—in theater semiotics, for example.

The quality of presence in the theatrical event was pointed out above, emphasizing the necessary co-presence of actors and spectators and the simultaneity
of production and reception. We then argued in favor of a specific status for
the processual logic of the theatrical event. However, it is not until the factors
entering into speech acts are foregrounded that this concrete and physical character of simultaneity takes on its true perspective. It is important to emphasize
that the actor and the spectators do not enter into the theatrical event solely
by virtue of their simultaneous physical presence, but also because this presence
means that they, as actor and spectator, become *factors in the discursive dimensions turning the theatrical event into a text.* Thus the spectator—by representing a certain dramatic competence with certain pre-established knowledge,
ideology, imagination, desire, etc.—is an active constituent of the processual
logic of presentation.

While the linguistic (eventually socio- or psycholinguistic) analysis of discourse can analyze a single discursive dimension by emphasizing the subjective

factors (in a discourse in which the constituents of enunciation lie on the same logical level), theatrical discourse is distinguished by the fact that there are *always at least two discursive dimensions*. If a speech-act analysis isolates an everyday conversational situation, a discursive dimension can be delimited. Irony, misunderstanding, and Freudian slips can be analyzed and organized in temporal order or in a logical structure of antecedent and consequent. It is this analysis that allows a homogenization of the implied discursive levels so as to arrange them in a discourse where the factors of enunciation are situated at the same level.

When a line is spoken on stage, it is always addressed *simultaneously* to another character and to the spectator. When a soliloquy or an aside is addressed beyond the footlights, the explicit dialogue on stage is of course disrupted; however, these two types of monologic expressions are still bound to the discursive dimension constituted by the dialogues: the orientation of the scenic discourse toward the spectator will never be eliminated. The murmur also conveys meaning, eventually inviting conjecture on what could have been clearly communicated. These two orientations in the context of theatrical communication are fundamentally different from the situation of everyday communication as they cannot be temporally and logically separated. They are simultaneously and reciprocally interdependent.

Theatrical communication situations are not, however, fundamentally different from other forms of fiction, but in theater they appear in a *radicalized* form. In written fiction, every conversation is filtered through a sort of narrative instance *before* it reaches the reader. In film, a camera and editor sort the events *before* we see and hear them. These active, distance-creating factors are manifested in the text at the time of its reception. In theater, on the other hand, we will obviously have an interpretation, a script, a long series of rehearsals, and so forth prior to performance before an audience, a pre-scenic dimension of the scenic text. But in the actual reception there is an absolute simultaneity between the discursive dimension on stage and the discursive dimension encompassing the stage and the auditorium. The director, stage manager, etc. are active constituents in the text only so long as their labor is transformed to scenic elements functioning in this simultaneity and according to its conditions.

If, in the semiotic analysis of theater, we are to incorporate some of the concepts established by discourse analysis along with those of speech-act and enunciation analysis, then we must be mindful of these specific traits of the theatrical event. One cannot—like Deirdre Burton, for example (Burton 1980) —be content with analyzing the scenic dialogue that has been isolated with the aid of speech-act concepts without considering the conditions generated by the very nature of the theatrical event.

André Green, points in another context to the fact that even though the theater to a large degree is a phenomenon of presence, it is also a phenomenon of signification, because it refers to other things represented in the universe of signs in the theatrical event. He emphasizes that theatrical language is dual and articulates thereby an absence of something giving theater its *signi*ficant character in general and, according to his own optics, accentuates the relation to the unconscious in a psychoanalytic sense:

> The theater takes up the challenge of evoking this absence in the most outrageous way, since nowhere else does language maintain the discourse of presence with such brilliance. Thus, the theater of representation alone is tempted to annul this presence, but is forced to recognize the impossibility of such an attempt. One must seek rather the locus of absence in the theater in the duplication of respoken speech. It constitutes a differential replication of the exchanges of spoken language. The production of the statements that unfold before us has passed through writing, and a theory of writing for the theatre is therefore inevitable. But such a theory cannot afford to forget that this writing is intended to be respoken. Therefore, a dual theory of writing is necessary, that of the writing of speech and that of respoken writing. The specific effect of the theater lies perhaps in the fusion of these two processual aspects. The spectator becomes entirely caught up in the work of decoding what—in spoken language—the actor means. The spectator believes that he has registered the translation of this spoken language, whereas he has encoded his own displacement. And it is by means of this difference, bearing on reduced statements and forming an integral part of an uninterrupted chain, that the absent signified has slipped into his mind. (Green 1969, 243)

This duality of "spoken language" and "respoken language" is an essential point in the discursive analysis of theater. Green stresses that the scenic dialogue as "spoken language," functions in a simultaneous fusion with the "respoken language," constituting the dialogue between stage and auditorium. But the spectator cannot bridge the gap between the two aspects of theatrical speech that Green mentions by rendering respoken language, as the voice of the narrator, superior to "spoken language."

Everyday dialogue, written fiction, and texts lying *outside* a scenic representation or those texts which reflect on it *afterward,* each in its own way possesses the possibility of forming a *linear hierarchy.* In this hierarchy, a fundamental meaning—possibly complex or contradictory—will organize the means of expression, deviations, and misunderstandings in the speech acts, etc. But such an ordering does not exist *during* the theatrical event. The concepts of discursive analysis for the analysis of the ideal speech acts mentioned above therefore cannot directly analyze the simultaneous presence of spoken and respoken language in the theatrical event. But they do allow a more precise evaluation of where the analysis of the theatrical speech can come into play.

Here our interest centers upon the implicit part of the utterance, *presupposed (présupposé) and inferred (sous-entendu)* (cf. Ducrot 1969, 1972, 1978). If, in a melodrama, a young blonde in a white crinoline says, "I am a sinner," the other characters *presuppose,* among other things, "She possesses a certain moral conscience," and this is readable in their verbal and non-verbal reactions. This presupposition holds true even if the heroine denies the self-characterization ("I am not a sinner"), formulates it as a question ("Am I a sinner?"), or renders it in a conditional ("If I can do what I want, I'll be a sinner"). To such *generally* presupposed semantic rules are also attached non-linguistic rules such as genre, the distinction between fictional and non-fictional speech acts, speech acts determined by an institution or ceremony, etc. These codes can also function as *presuppositions.*

But the young woman's utterance can also lead the others to *infer,* "She is honest," "This is a joke," "She is lying," etc. which will induce a multitude of different reactions to the situation. What is *inferred* depends on whether the utterance is formulated positively, as here, or contradicted, and will necessarily be related to the *concrete* situation. This leads to the fact that the use of the selfsame *presupposed* code (e.g., a moral code) can function as a part of the *inferred* code. In the ironic text, or the text understood ironically, the observation that "one utilizes a double semantic code" is a part of the inferred even if each of the codes used belong to what is supposed.

It is this possibility of shifting between verbal and non-verbal dimensions —together with the possibility that the presupposed and the inferred can shift roles in the discursive process—which makes the theory of speech acts relevant for theatre semiotics. This can be expressed as follows: in *stage dialogue* one may analyze the implicit aspects as being respectively "the presupposed" and "the inferred," provided that at the same time we establish the shifts of position in these dimensions within the *dialogue between the stage and the auditorium,* including the total number of non-verbal scenic elements.

If, leaving the actors, we now turn to the spectator, s/he will as a *presupposition* relate the blonde's utterance to a general theatrical convention, "She's the heroine," which is to say that s/he will presuppose certain elements which, on stage, would be inferred. And the spectator *infers* "her moral conscience is presented with irony" from the contrast between the color and the verbal code. And, finally, the use of certain presupposed codes will appear as the inferred; therefore, the spectator sees at the same time that she is the very example of a genre convention: "She signifies honesty." It suffices here to point to the different representations of *La Dame aux Camélias.*

Thus, the entire repertoire of the implied semantic elements may intervene in the *changing discursive positions* and therefore indicate the possibilities of interpretation both for the actors, directors, and spectators. The specific duality of scenic speech is thus the necessary point of departure for an analysis of theatrical enunciation.

6. *The code: position and transformation*

This shift between discursive positions and the meaning with which they are invested is rule governed, which is why in analyzing them it is necessary to institute a *code concept* relevant to theatre semiotics. This concept may point to traits other than those found in a purely linguistic code theory (e.g., Eco 1976, 1977).

In contrast to the general code theory, we shall be only preoccupied with semantic codes. For, where theatre is concerned, we must accept the fact that, on stage, there are no non-significant elements, none independent of all sign relations, for instance, no purely physiological codes. And we accept that we are in a particular discursive universe where the elements have been chosen specifically for the spectator to observe and interpret them during the theatrical event. They enter into two fundamental discursive dimensions (the scenic dimension and the dimension encompassing the relation between the stage and the auditorium). The fundamental sign relation is established before the curtain rises, as all the elements which constitute the representation (words, props, scenery, choreography, etc.) have been pre-selected with a specific goal: the words are, as affirmed by André Green above, respoken.

In contrast to the linguistic code theory, the distinction between a first articulation (one-to-one relation between content and expression, as, for example, in a traffic signal) and a second articulation (arbitrary relations between content and expression, as in the linguistic sign) is of as little importance as the general problem of the sign relation. We presuppose that the elements on stage are already significative and that we are dealing with pre-established sign relations. Again, in contrast to linguistic theory, we cannot accept a single code —the verbal, for example—as being fundamental, but will have to employ a multitude of codes, changes in codes, and levels of codes.

Thus the general definition of the code in theatre semiotics is a *rule for the choice and the combination of already-significant elements*. To be able to specify specific codes, we must operate with various *types of codes* and various *code functions*. Thus we have to combine the code concept with the theatrical event as a dynamic and discursive process.

The code is constituted by the rules through which a set of elements is mutually combined. It will then define an object immanently, by virtue of the particular laws by which the elements are mutually connected. It is obviously possible and, where the objective is descriptive, quite often useful to isolate different aspects of the theatrical event, thus making of them semiotic objects having a relational coding. The colors of the actor's costumes, for example, can be specified as an independent textual aspect by the code combining them. The code is in this sense static and closely related to the structure concept in classical structuralism. One can, in agreement with Umberto Eco, speak of a *code system* or an *S-code*.

The essential is not however the establishment of a series of *S-codes* but rather their reciprocal relations and the change they undergo through these relations. Consequently the *S-code* alone is not sufficient. The *codes proper* or simply the *codes* then, still in company with Umberto Eco, are the transformation rules which exist between at least two objects defined by way of an S-code. They are related and perhaps modified through these transformation rules. But in any case, the static systems—for example, colors as one system, gestures as another—are activated, thereby creating meaning.

The general code definition is thus manifested in two code types: the static S-codes delimiting what belongs in a given context to the pre-given meaning, the dynamic transformation rules or codes simply combining the textual aspects delimitable by an S-code. And, since the theatre operates with pre-invested meaning elements entering into a discursive process, both types of codes will be equally relevant.

It must be emphasized further that the two code types designate not only the qualities of the determined objects, but the *different discursive functions*. Any part of the theatrical event may be delimited through an S-code and thereby serve as the point of departure or the end-point of a discursive transformational process. And any part may also become the bearer of transformation codes. In *La Dame aux Camélias*, white and red are related in an S-code with other colors, expressing different values. But at the same time the change of the white flowers with the red flowers and vice versa creates relations between systems by transforming them (for example, between moral values and corporeal and sexual behavior). Thus, colors may also function as the code.[2]

In the analysis of theatre, we do not place ourselves in relation to the general rules—or to general code-types or general functions of the codes. We here place ourselves in relation to coded significations.

7. *The structure: code and interpretant*

Since the breakthrough of structuralism in France in the 1960s, the concept of structure has been greatly defined, discussed, applied, defended, and rejected. It has proved relevant in the discussion of *epistemological* problems and those encountered in *interpretation theory*. Both these problem areas would, however, be best approached through an application of the concepts we have introduced here.

The structure of an object is usually defined as the internal network of relations defining it, regardless of what elements are in interrelationship (cf. the S-code).

In an extension of the above definition, the ontological status of this concept has been taken up: as an immanently defined set of relations, is it in the final analysis identical with the object's own inherent structure? If the answer is no, then the referent problem is simply put in brackets. If yes, it is taken as given that the referent problem is concerned solely with the object and thus expressible in the so-called assertorial propositions which are univocally true or false (A is B / A is not B). In either case, this concept will not be of interest in the theatrical domain, where the reference problem cannot be discarded but where at the same time it must be understood as a number of relations between several types of reference.

We are thus led to another problem associated with the structure concept, namely that articulated in interpretation theory. Here the structure can be understood as the unspecified presupposition that the given object—such as a theatre performance to be seen or produced—is a cohesive whole, that it is delimitable as a text.

This understanding of the structure concept lacks descriptive content but is tenable if we accept in advance to place an object in a communicative context, implicating it thereby in the concept of the immediate interpretant or the presupposition of an object's interpretability. But, in contrast to the structure concept, the concept of interpretant implies that this a priori hypothesis leads necessarily to a specification of the object in a discursive interdependence of coding processes.

Structure understood as a construction of the object according to specific presuppositions coincides with the dynamic and final interpretants of the text. But what these concepts emphasize (in contrast to the structure concept) is, first, that the construction enters into a continuous interpretation process and that the object (i.e., the theatrical event) must itself be understood as a dynamic exchange between *discursive dimensions and code positions*. Second, it follows from the concept of the contextualized text (as opposed to the concept of structure based on immanence) that the actual delimitation of the object and the minimal units upon which the structure of the text is built depends on *a choice made in relation to the given context*. This is why we here abandon the concept of structure in favor of the concepts of text, discourse, and code. But of what importance are these for theatre semiotics?

8. The code, the text, and the discourse

The code considered as an aspect of the text implies that everything occurring on stage and entering into the theatrical event *can,* in principle, function as a code or S-code. But, at the same time, always in such a way that everything *is not coded* in each concrete interpretation situation. Therefore we shall not simply suppose that the stage production is, as a text, a totality, as would be the case in accordance with the structure concept. Instead we introduce a distinction: on the one hand, the texts contain characteristics which *are coded*, which enter into different, mutually related rule-governed transformation processes. On the other hand, the texts contain a long series of elements which, for different reasons (e.g., technical error, actor forgetfulness, production possibilities overlooked either by the director or the spectator), do not enter into relevant codings which are analyzed via the delimitation of the text. Finally, there is a long series of elements which *principally cannot be coded* in connection with the chosen delimitation of the text (i.e., the actor's body cannot be totally coded in relation to the production; the scenic material and the theatre proper are not completely transformable to the requirements of the individual production). Such non-coded phenomena can influence and interrupt the coded text without it ceasing thereby to be a coded and distinctively delimited text. The characterizing of certain elements as non-coded does not mean they are disregarded but, on the contrary, that they are given status in relation to the coded text, in relation to which they are also efficacious.[3]

An important aspect of this dynamic is the shifting between code positions *within a single production*—from non-coded to the code or S-code positions. It is through such a process that the pre-coded meanings serving as the production's historical foundation are given the impetus to *be seen*. In the version of Büchner's *Woyzeck* beginning with the scene where Woyzeck and Andres cut straw, the knife is a neutral element, a tool whose appearance and gestural presentation need not be subscribed to a particular code. But a subsumation to a code occurs later on during the play (cf. Larsen 1985). It is also possible, by comparing the *different* scenes, to see just how the elements can be adopted or rejected, subsumed under specific codes or treated neutrally. This applies, for example, to the use of the coffee grinder in the first act of *Callers at the Child Bearer* (1723) by the Danish moral philosopher, comedy writer, and man of letters Ludvig Holberg.

If the code concept is to be thus unified with a descriptive analysis (the S-code) and a functional analysis (code), then such an analysis should specify the rearticulation which the existing repertoire of pre-established meanings undergoes in the discursive logic of theatre. Again, the knife in *Woyzeck* can serve as example. A number of characteristics, deriving as much from the knife's role in the play as from its use as a practical tool and its placement in a pre-established but not always well-known symbol structure, can enter into a characterization of the knife's S-code and invite its induction into parallel S-codes in the meaning universe of the given drama. There will, in such an S-code, enter elements from a general historical repertoire of meaning (such as Ad de Vries's *Dictionary of Symbols and Imagery*), including its association as an instrument of revenge, a manifestation of power, a sexual symbol, and a combination of an aggressive and defensive weapon possessing magical overtones. However, elements from the specific text will at the same time also come into play. Hence, particularly in *Woyzeck,* the knife's connection to dance and its consequent association with aggressive and lascivious body language. All these elements exist as open dramaturgical possibilities for a given production. They constitute a part of the written text's sign-structure which can enter into the discourse-dominated transformations with a greater or lesser force dictated by the actual codes responsible for the production of a specific meaning. In the production in Bochum, West Germany (1980–1981) the knife is given such a dominant role that in the opening scene a knife-thrower appears in the market place, with Maria as the victim.

Here we would like simply to emphasize the *discursive* determination of the coding process. In one of the scenes, the captain and the doctor meet Woyzeck in the street before Woyzeck's knowing anything of Maria's infidelity and hence before his murder plans (Büchner 1969, 40ff):

> Captain: Hey, Woyzeck, why are you running past us like that? Stay here, Woyzeck. You're running around like an open razor blade.

You might cut someone. You're running like you had to shave a regiment of castrates and would be hanged while the last hair was disappearing. But about those long beards—what was I going to say? Woyzeck—those long beards. . . Hey? What about those long beards? Say, Woyzeck, haven't you found a hair from a beard in your soup bowl yet? Hey? You understand, of course, a human hair, from the beard of an engineer, a sergeant, a—a drum major? Hey, Woyzeck? But you've got a decent wife. Not like others.

Woyzeck: Yes, sir! What are you trying to say, Cap'n?

In *the dialogue on stage,* the captain's replies are ambiguous: he speaks at one and the same time about Woyzeck's great agitation and his wife's fidelity, with hair and beard serving as the link. And Woyzeck is clueless. Yet it is not an ordinary revelation or jest which the captain delivers here. Normally, Woyzeck understands very well—and has accustomed himself to—the captain's manner of speaking. But here he meets a fatal revelation changing his life. And his understanding does not come until later on. He answers "Yes, sir" yet expresses in the same breath that he understands nothing. In other words, Woyzeck can establish neither the S-code to which the captain refers nor the transformation rules the codes are subjected to so that the mentioned elements can be brought into relation.

Consequently we must take the *inferred* and the *presupposed* into consideration. In any event, "Woyzeck is married to Maria" (which in the play will imply only a relation resembling marriage) and "Woyzeck is a subordinate to the captain" are presupposed. The latter aspect is linked to the situation and expressed linguistically in the spontaneous "Yes, sir," in the use of the title "Cap'n," and in Woyzeck's accepting the boundaries that the captain sets for meaningfulness. The *inferred* in the captain's reply is, among others, "Woyzeck is dangerous," "Woyzeck is dumb" (has not discovered Maria's infidelity), "Woyzeck's agitation is in vain" (has to shave the castrates), "Maria has a relation with the drum major." The indirect character of the utterance, moreover, will cause us to note, "A double semantic coding is being used," and this enters into the inferred. Woyzeck understands this and only this aspect, as his answer shows; he cannot simply connect this duplicity with a concrete content, since the double coding hinges upon the union of these two aspects of the presupposed. The witnessing of this ignorance on Woyzeck's behalf is part and parcel of the captain's intent and an affirmation of his power.

It is precisely the lapse in communication in the dialogue on stage which turns *the dialogue between the stage and the auditorium* into an independent factor. For it is this discursive dimension that the cohesion that is incomprehensible to Woyzeck can be found by virtue of certain dramaturgical *choices* of general frames of the production's semantic universe (in relation to the text's meaning potential). In the brief example provided here, the elements which function as the presupposed on stage are introduced as parts of the inferred in the dialogue between stage and audience. If now in this production we choose an element presupposed in the dialogue, for example "love and social power are mutually related," this lies outside Woyzeck's knowledge (at least at this point in the text), which is why he does not understand anything. An element not belonging to the presupposed in the dialogue between the stage and the audience but, on the other hand, to its inferred, can only be "social power relations can be changed." But the presence of such an element in this and only this dialogue will, among other things, depend upon the use of such S-codes constituted in the knife, so that it enters as a *creator of cohesion* in the dialogue between audience and stage, and it is *there* that a specific S-code can be interjected: the knife articulates the relation between power and non-power since the ultimate manifestation of power (the murder of Maria) is at the same time self-destructive and gives rise to powerlessness (Woyzeck's possibilities for personal and social development are destroyed)—hence the quotation's reference to both the beard and castration. In the position as *code* (i.e., the transformational factors in this process) social power, love relationships, and body language (dance and eye-contact) are particularly prevalent in a *simultaneous* relation in this play (cf. Larsen 1985). In the dialogue on stage, the knife does not necessarily serve this function: it can enter into the verbal and gestural or the practical and symbolic dimension without having to take on a particularly synthesizing role in the scenic inference.

What is important to stress here is that there is a necessary *solidarity* between the presupposed and the inferred in the two discursive dimensions of theatre, owing as much to verbal as to non-verbal elements in the production. Without such a solidarity, there can be no dialogue between the stage and audience (see the discussion of the stage-production universes below). But besides this solidarity, there is a possibility of the presupposed and inferred appearing in one dimension and not in the other, and for the presupposed to appear in the one which is the inferred in the other and vice versa. It is this *difference* which contributes to the dramatical discourse's dual character and the theatrical event's communicative effectiveness.

It is at the same time important to emphasize that the determination of the *distinctive* aspects of the presupposed in the dialogue between stage and audience rests *in certain contextually determined dramaturgical choices*.

Thus, if—in reference, for example, to *Woyzeck*—one gets the idea of letting the knife serve as the cohesion-creating factor in the scenic inferred, then at least two things must be taken into account. We must first consider the relation to the text and the nature of its characters. Will it in general be possible to let the scenic space represent a space wherein the persons can be attributed with a discerning consciousness, or will this run contrary to the semantics of the drama? (See below concerning scenic and narrative space.) Second, we must consider the relation to the efficiency of communication between stage and audience. Thus, in the example of Woyzeck and his tormenters, we have emphasized that Woyzeck's difficulty in establishing the level of the inferred on stage highlights the autonomy of this implicit level in the other discursive dimension.

9. *Object and reference*

We have touched upon the referent of the text in two contexts in the preceding discussion. It has been designated as the "object" of the text in the semiosis model based on Peirce's sign theory, and it has been presupposed in pointing out the intentionality of the discourse, its direction toward "an outside world." The questions concerning the reference of the text, its referential function, or its indexation are numerous and complex, and in the continental semiotics (Saussure, Hjelmslev, etc.) a refusal to face this problematic has dominated. Indeed, Saussure's dictum: "The linguistic sign does not link a thing and a name, but rather a concept and an acoustic image" can be considered the point of departure for the immanent mode of thought which has characterized strutural linguistics up to recent times.

With Peirce, the triadic conception of the sign serves as the cornerstone of semiotics. In this conception, the object is an indispensable element of semiosis (i.e., in the production of meaning) since the condition for the sign's functioning as an interpretant of another sign is that it be conceived of as referring to the same object.

It is however important to emphasize that the designation *object,* at least at first, occupies a *position* in the semiosis, that it is a condition for the production of meaning and *not* a specific ontologically determined collection of objects (such as material objects or fictive objects). The object is therefore related largely to a (common) universe of experiences and actions, the communication partners' so-called *common ground,* the material foundation of the cultural community necessary for the promulgation and communication of meaning.

The reason for these suggestions (and we shall not mention more) of Peirce's conception of the object of the sign or of the text is twofold. First, it seems important to us to point out an alternative to the dyadic conception of the sign; second, the determination of objects plays a decisive role in the conception of the *universe of the text.*

10. *The universe of the text*

That to which a text refers is often called *the discursive universe.* According to Peirce (C.P. 2.536), the discursive universe is first and foremost conceived of as a net of presuppositions giving the text comprehensibility, that comprehensibility which is the condition for the transmission of meaning between the parties in communication.

The definition of the universe as something which can be pointed to, but which can only with difficulty be described, implies two things. First, that the foundation of the universe is constituted of presuppositions which are so basic that only in quite extraordinary circumstances can they be made objects of reflection (suppositions such as reflections on space and time, the relation between cause and effect, etc.). Second, it follows from this definition that the discursive universe is not merely a notion related to the text conceived as an autonomous, context-free entity, nor merely something related to the codes manifested by the text. Peirce's emphasis on indexicality must be understood in this connection; for there are not only deictical elements in the text (pronouns, indicators of time and place, etc.) which delineate a spatio-temporal field within which something happens, but this very delimitation necessarily implies a place and a point in time in relation to which the universe can be perceived. Tempus and modus and the other *shifters* mark the referential and communicative functions at the heart of morphology and syntax.

It seems reasonable to suppose that all the different types of discursive universes which can be produced by human speech emanate from experiences acquired within a living social and material world and that, in the final instance, these various universes therefore become understandable by relating to the interplay between interaction and linguistic communication in social activity, in the interaction of external nature together with actions and interpretations ultimately grounded in our inner nature. In other words, it is through the coupling between *the discursive universe* and *the universe of action* that meaning arises and becomes intelligible.

This conception of the conditions of the appearance of meaning is a fundamental postulate underlying our entire exposition, and it implies several things. It requires, first of all, an interference between two or more expression systems (S-codes in Eco's terminology) and, second, an interference between this interconnection of the semiotic systems and the everyday world within which they receive meaning by virtue of their function as interpretation schemata and rules of conduct. This point of view implies, negatively, a rejection of all attempts at explaining meaning through a reduction to a single function or source, be it the connection between expression or content and form, or a reduction of symbolic signs to iconic signs. Positively, this point of view means that meaning is supposed as a function of the interplay between all five poles of the semiosis model and the internal and external aspects of these. It follows moreover that meaning is a social and communicative phenomenon, something which at least two instances, a sender and a receiver—in principle—can come to an understanding of.

The difference between a text referring to a fictive universe and a text referring to a social and material universe lies in the indices contained in the text or in the situational context. Indeed, it would not be possible to decide whether an ordinary descriptive text lacking clear indexical anchorage in a given space presents a fictive or a historical universe. This means that a minimum of specific information is required in order to determine a text's reference. For example, if we find the expression "Romeo loves Juliet" as graffiti on a wall, without any further information, we cannot in principle determine whether we are faced with a (true) proposition on the fictive persons in Shakespeare's *Romeo and Juliet* (or another fictive work with the same motif) or whether it concerns two neighborhood adolescents, a statement which can be either true or false.

11. *The universe of the performance*

The theatrical performance is characterized by a plurality of universes. In order to define this plurality it is useful to stipulate a difference between the *spectacular* and the *theatrical*. Let us designate the spectacular as *the events which separate the socio-material reality into two partial universes, one comprising the actors, the other the spectators*. Such a halving of our everyday world is not uncommon and most often occurs spontaneously, as for example the ring formed on the school playground by a group of children surrounding combatants. A more formalized version of the spectacular is the sporting event (e.g., a boxing or a wrestling match), where the demarcation between spectator and actor is enforced by a formal authority and, if necessary, by the use of public force. The fight in the schoolyard and the combative sport share a characteristic feature: the attention of the actors and spectators is concentrated on what is happening *right now*. Other spectacular events (such as parliamentary debates or court trials) are also characterized by a separation between spectators and actors. But here the actors' own partial universe is divided into a present space, in which they act, and an absent space, which is spoken of or imagined.

Even though the development of a court case or a parliamentary debate (like the institutionalized sporting event) requires a sharp distinction between actor and spectator, a distinction marked in the construction of the physical room, the spectators are essential for the spectacle's development because in both cases we speak of the ceremonial practice of a social institution's function which, by definition, is public, and this practice will completely change character if this public aspect is left out (cf. court-martial and arcane political disputation). Even though one may not associate anything spectacular with the phenomena mentioned above, they nevertheless possess the essential spectacular characteristic: that of being *a delimited, rule-governed event-process presented by a group of actors and in which both parties (in large part) are familiar with and accept their roles; furthermore, the actors delimit and occupy a specific physical locality which is constituted as an arena, platform, or podium for the duration of the performance process.*

If we turn now to other events which would at times be characterized as spectacular, for instance, the circus or the bullfight, we cannot glean any departures from the criteria we have posited forthwith. Of course from other points of view there are very great differences; among others, that the bullfight is characterized by reproducing at the surface level traces of archaic rituals: they are defined as recreative (just like a sporting event) in contrast to the court-martial and political debate, which represent the organs of legislative and judicial government, etc. It is essential in this context that in each of these cases, the actors act within and refer to the universe to which both they and the spectator belong: a historic, socio-material universe. Given this background we can now add yet another criterion to the definition of the spectacular: The spectacular (in contrast to the theatrical) is *characterized by NOT constituting a universe categorically different from the spectator's.*

The carnival becomes an interesting phenomenon in the above context, as we could imagine: a sort of transition between the spectacular and the theatrical which can ultimately be ceremonial, as in the courtesans' masked ball. Whereas to be an athlete, judge, prime minister, etc. is a part of the actor's social identity, to dress as Harlequin, Mandarin, Domino, etc. (or as a soccer player, referee, or bullfighter, if one is otherwise not one of these) is to claim another role through costuming, make-up, and masking, a role not a part of one's normal social identity. The difference in the carnival experience as opposed to others is that if one meets a person acting in one of the above spectacles, he would, in another context, present himself as a professional athlete, judge, minister of state, etc., whereas the person who has been dressed up as a Mandarin at the carnival the previous evening would hardly introduce himself as "Maurice Dupont, Mandarin"; the person one has just seen in the role of Hamlet in "The Barbican," will not introduce himself as Hamlet but as "NN, actor."

Thus far we have provided examples of spectacular events which were not theatrical and of one event, the carnival, which brought the spectacular and theatrical together. We concluded from these examples that the spectacular was a far more comprehensive concept than the theatrical because the spectacular demanded "only" one of the two, either a dividing of the physical space into two partial universes, the actor and the spectacular, or a pseudo-fictivization of the social interaction which is spatio-temporally delimited (the carnival). *In order for an event to be theatrical, one further characteristic must be added: the distinction between a social and a fictive universe.* In order to better determine the specificity of the theatrical, it will be practical to introduce some diagrams illustrating the relation between interaction and dialogue in relation to space and time. The simplest illustration will be a situation in which two partners in the dialogue are simultaneously present within a well-defined physical space, with their dialogue and interaction reduced to a simple

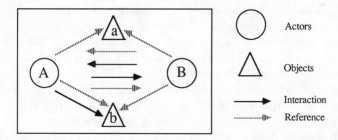

Figure 1

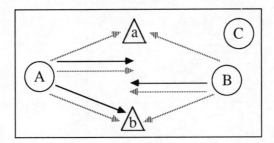

Figure 2

treatment of what is simultaneously present (themselves as they are at that instant, the objects, and the surroundings) (Figure 1).

In this case, which is highly stylized and only rarely occurs, the dialogue and the interaction of the actors is intended solely for themselves and the two elements included in their commonly defined universe. A, however, is not content with a reference to B, s/he interacts with it (s/he refers linguistically or gesturally to a glass of water and then drinks it). It is essential that unless we are A or B we will never, in a historical universe, be able to experience this situation; we will only be informed about it later in the form of an account from one of the actors. We will naturally be able to imagine the action while it occurs (e.g., the jealous husband suffering the pangs of imagining his wife's placid moments with the lover, while she in fact is doing just that), but we are generally excluded from perceiving this situation.

In Figure 2, a supplementary actor (C) is introduced; s/he is marked neither as interacting nor referring, but his/her isolated existence is important because s/he is in any circumstance an observer, and we presuppose that C is not present for A or B—neither in their consciousness nor in their field of perception. We assume the situation of an outside observer, maybe even a spy. If C is present for the actors, their interaction will be influenced and their communication with one another will at the same time be an indirect communication to a "deaf" third. As there is no mention of a sub-partition into partial universes, C will potentially be interacting, and if we imagine several Cs, the diagram can represent the scuffle in the schoolyard which can end in a free-for-all.

If we divide the universe formally into two parts—into a space for interaction and a space for spectators—we have the sporting event, the bullfight, etc. (Figure 3).

The very space of the dialogue and interaction, the space for the actor's physical presence must in everyday communication and interaction be supplemented with a dimension of time, transcending the dimension of the corporeal present in the space of physical interaction. This time must also be tied to a space, and the interaction space must be further supplemented by a simultaneous but not-present space (Figure 4).

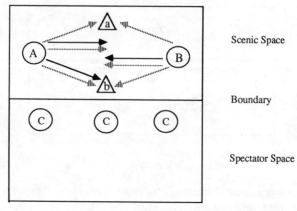

Scenic Space

Boundary

Spectator Space

Figure 3

This figure should present the division of a dialogic discursive universe delineated by two parameters: physical presence vs. physical absence and contemporaneity vs. non-contemporaneity (subdivided into past and future). This representation however is highly incomplete at one essential point, for it most definitely respects tempus, but not modus, it thus represents a discursive universe which is abbreviated to facticity (or to a supposed facticity) and a possible future. An utterance such as "If we had married back then, we would be celebrating our silver anniversary two years from now" can be placed readily enough in relation to the timeline, but it represents an imagined event which cannot be situated within the factual universe and must therefore split the respective space into two *universes,* a factual and a counter-factual (Figure 5).

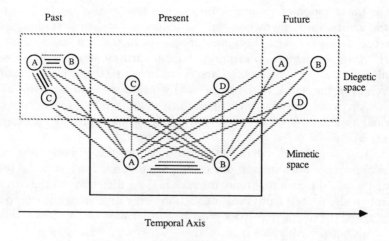

Figure 4

If one asks how it is possible to divide the future into a counter-factual and a possible space, the answer is provided in the latter part of the utterance: ". . . we would be celebrating our silver anniversary two years from now." Here reference is made to a future event which by definition cannot occur; one can therefore maintain this division of the future.

Figure 5 should roughly illustrate a division of the references in the dialogue; the seven localities must not be confused, however, with the discursive universes in the ordinary sense, since several of these localities belong to the same universe (in Peirce's terminology). If we combine Figures 3 and 5, we get a model which could represent the discursive and interactional relations in, for example, a court case or in a parliamentary debate, and it seems clear that the division of the respective space into factual and counter-factual universes is also necessary in these concrete instances where both places are argued contra-factually. Thus the model for this type of communication situation (Figure 6).

With this division we approach the plurality of space and universe that is characteristic of the staging of a theatrical production; but the simple fact that a court case can be (and in fact very often is) presented on the stage (where both actors and audience are represented by actors) points to the fact that this model must be supplemented with yet another dimension in order to encompass the specific character of theatre production. Obviously this is not effected through a mere distinction between "the spectators" in the interaction space and the spectators in the auditorium (a combination of Figures 2 and 3 would exemplify this), for if a person cracks open the door of a courtroom in session we have precisely this situation of a spectator observing spectator and actor, and even if with the help of an infinite number of doors this situation becomes an *endless embedding* which no theatrical event would produce.

Even if the presence of the spectators is essential to the theatrical representa-

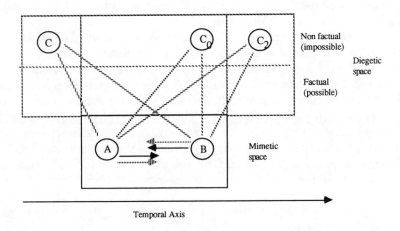

Figure 5

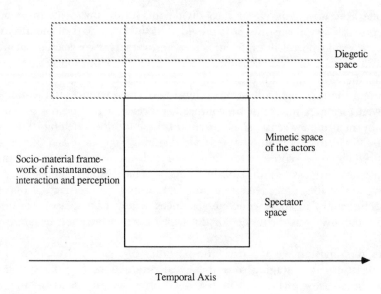

Figure 6

tion for other reasons (see below), the production's *differentia specifica* must
be connected between the stage (mimetic space) and the diegetic space. This
dividing of the diegetic space, illustrated by Figure 6, must also apply to the
interaction going on stage. When at the end of *Hamlet* Fortinbras concludes,
"Bear Hamlet like a soldier to the stage, / For he was likely, had he been
put on, / To have prov'd most royal . . ." (V, ii, 401–403), he refers then
to a non-factual future space in relation to the absolutely identical postulation
of the following hypothetical statement: "If Mozart had lived longer than 36
years, he would have composed more works."

The specificity of theatrical production, distinguished on the one hand by
normal social interaction and on the other by the reader's construction of an
epic or dramatic fictional universe, lies in the uniting elements from both of
these categorically different universes. A more precise description of this cate-
gorial interrelation will begin with the actor's dual presence on stage, the
duality of that real physical presence in conjunction with the spectator in the
auditorium who also personifies or is an incarnation of a character in a dramatic fiction. This ties into the actor's relation to the fundamental definition
of the sign: *aliquid stat pro aliquo.* This has already been hinted at conceptu-
ally in that we did not infer that the actor refers to a character in the dramatic
fiction but instead *personifies* or *incarnates.* The actors playing Hamlet or
Richard III refer not to a fictive or historical person; *they personify them
by virtue of their presence.*

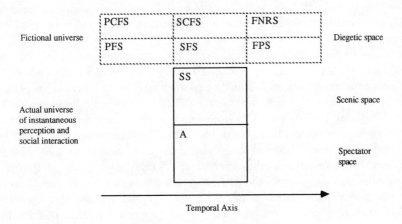

A = Auditorium, SS = Scenic space, PFS = Previous factual space,
SFS = Simultaneous factual space, FPS = Future possible space,
PCFS = Previous counter-factual space, SCFS = Simultaneous
counter-factual space, FNRS = Future non-realizable space.

Figure 7

It may seem unnecessary to take this detour around the diegetic space in order to give a more explicit formulation of what occurs on the stage, but this detour is necessary if we are to distinguish between a pseudo-theatrical event, such as the carnival, and the theatre production as such. The following passage from *Hamlet* should make this clear. Hamlet: "My lord, you played once i' th' university, you say?" Polonius: "That did I, my lord, and was accounted a good actor." Polonius's earlier career as an amateur actor is of course fictive, and through reference to this, the physically present person, Polonius, allows the incarnation of the textual entity in a non-realized fictional universe. As spectators, we are in the same situation as when reading *Hamlet*; if this reference is to be realized it can be only in the reader or spectator's own imagination. Even if the actor's physical presence on the stage can rightly be determined as essential for the theatre, the iconic, cardboard representation of Polonius in a puppet production of *Hamlet* also implicates him both in a mimetic and a diegetic space.

This very distinction between a factual universe and a non-factual universe holds true in the fictional as well, as the latter can also refer to something imagined (cf. Fortinbras's reply). This means that Figure 6, which depicts localities in the spectacular space (constructed with a diegetic space), applies as well to the theatrical production, but with the essential difference that *the diegetic space and the spectator space correspond respectively to fictional and to socio-material universes, whereas the stage is located in both universes. It therefore applies to both action and dialogue on stage: they always assert themselves in two contexts as the communication and the action occurring within a fictional universe and as a performance addressing an audience* (cf. discussion of *discourse,* above). In order to mark this duality of Figure 6, we supply Figure 7.

Thus we get the following five universes: (1) universe of concluded objective experiences (PFS); (2) universe of actual experience (A, SS); (3) universe of contemporaneous events, not directly experienced (perception) (SFS); (4) universe of future possibilities (FPS); and (5) counter-factual universe (PCFS, SCFS, FNRS, and FPS). That FPS both figure in universe five and are marked as independent universes (four) is due to the fact they are possibly not realized, and, until we know this, it must belong thus to a counter-factual universe. Therefore, what specifically characterizes the theatrical production's *plurality of universes* is that *four of the five universes conjectured here are fictional, and that universe number two (the universe of actual experience) is divided so that, even though that which occurs on stage naturally takes place within universe two, it still attains meaning by being seen as part of the four fictional universes.* This also means, of course, that what is produced and narrated on stage needs by no means to respect the conception of what is valid in a historic universe. So, for example, what could belong to a counter-factual universe in association with a historical universe might very well extend to the previous factual space or even the mimetic space.

12. The sign and the object in the mimetic space

The genesis of a theatrical performance is the production of a fictional universe. If we limit ourselves to the staging of drama, the comparison to the construction found in reading can be shown. Here, in the imaginary realization, a connection between non-symbolic (in Peirce's terminology, "icons" and "indices") and symbolic signs emerges. Icons are not particularly natural or purely visual signs but contain conventional elements in such a way that the iconic sign refers through its signifier, among other things, to an object, something which a symbolical sign does not do because of its arbitrary signifier. The similarity between iconic sign and object which is ordinarily attributed to this relation is thus more complex in semiotics than in everyday conception. There is a specific similarity with respect to certain chosen aspects—manifested structurally or qualitatively—so that this selection is ruled by a rational functionality in the relation between sign and object.

In reading, it is possible to relate an infinite number of iconic representations to a linguistic fictional text. But the scenic representation must be one single concretization of the meaning potential of the linguistic text. This more rigorous selection will be governed in part by the material frames of the representation, earlier productions, conventions, etc., and in part by the necessity we have to represent what would otherwise be inaccessible outside the linguistic text, i.e., that which is encoded, uncoded, or not coded, to what cannot be coded (see discussion of codes, above) with the possibility of creating meaning structures which do not agree with the semantics of the linguistic text.

It is in this way that the scenic space, its characters, and its objects are understood as signs, for meaning arises only when the object becomes a sign, that is, when it refers to something else (see introduction to this chapter). This duality of object and sign characterizes our entire life—naturally—the forest floor telling the hunter of a certain kind of animal—or socially—the bureaucrat's imposing desk relating his social status.

It is sometimes asserted that the objects on stage lose their function as objects and function merely as signs. It is an incorrect assertion and a hindrance to a real insight into the complex interplay between sign and object in theatrical representation. The duality must be retained, not only because every prop can be a genuine object, not a stage prop, with a sign function outside theatre (the imposing desk), but because the scenic space and especially its boundaries, its "walls" and entries and exits, will always encompass it: the space of the physical stage is always contiguous with a diegetic space, i.e., a simultaneously fictional and physical space—hallways, stairways, closets, and the spectator space. From a semiotic point of view it is of no consequence what kind of scene we speak of (simultaneous, naturalistic, etc.).

The discontinuity between discursive space and a universe of social action has already been pinpointed as the decisive characteristic of the theatrical (as opposed to the spectacular) production. Another difference, also owing to the sign's *deictic* aspect, concerns the role of the actor, concerns, that is, what is essential in the theatrical representation. When the mercury rises above normal in the sick patient's thermometer, we have a deictic sign because the quicksilver is directly influenced by the patient's temperature. The sign has an iconic aspect because the mercury maintains a relational and proportional identity with body temperature. Finally, the sign possesses a symbolic aspect because the two phenomena are combined in an interpretation owing to a presupposed knowledge and, on the thermometer, to a critical zone.

Another of Peirce's examples of a deictic sign is the lurching gait of the individual, which can be interpreted as an index of his being a sailor, this manner of walking caused by the movements of the ship's deck. The serpentine walk and hesitant slur of the inebriated is likewise an index. If we see a person with a lurching walk or the noted symptoms of inebriation in the actor, we also identify it immediately as belonging to a sailor or a drunkard. Or will we? Because of our knowledge of the drama's fictionality and the theatre as a physical realization of the fictive, we would be more inclined to interpret the person's behavior as an actor playing sailor or drunkard. Then, in the terminology of sign theory, both the actor in the representation and the spectator in his/her reception would be distinguishing the iconic aspect from the deictic. The sailor's lurching walk and the drunkard's behavior are iconic in that they are characteristic qualities which resemble (in the sense that they have a great number of elements in common with) certain qualities of the sailor or the inebriant; and therefore their presence in an individual permits a hypothetical classification of the person as belonging to this or that class. The deictic aspect of the sign, the real relation between object and sign—that is, between the mariner and the tippler and the lurching walk and the drunken state respectively—is, however, absent in the actor's representation of the fictive seaman or drunkard.

We have stressed the differences between deictical signs as they are produced, utilized, and interpreted in a historical universe and on stage: they correspond to Peirce's division of the indexical sign into two types: *designations* and *reagents* (cf. C.P. 8.368). *The designations* are known as *shifters* in linguistics (e.g., personal and demonstrative pronouns, proper names, etc.); whereas *the reagents* are phenomena given sign status by being directly influenced by the object (e.g., the thermometer influenced by the patient's temperature). The reality of the person with the lurching walk or in a drunken state is, or is interpreted as, a reagent, but the actor playing the role is not. What actually occurs in the actor's presentation is not that the indexical aspect disappears —because the character's behavior on stage should ideally still be interpreted as a visualization of a state of consciousness motivated by the character's (fictive) history—but rather that *reagents are replaced by designations*. The difference between the reagent and the designation is, in the former instance, that the object determines the sign by means of an existential influence (sorrow and onions provoke tears) and, in the latter case, that one uses a sign in order to draw attention to an object ("See, there goes Jean"), not so that the sign influences the object existentially, but in such a way that the sign draws the object into the discursive universe. Basically, we most often combine designations with symbolic signs (e.g., language's shifters and deictic expression) but, in the actor's representation, the designations of the dialogue are supplemented by *iconic designations*, and therein lies the actor's art: the very fact that tears of the actor can function as reagents, provoked by sorrow, that the tears of the actor may function as an iconic designation which refers to, or rather is interpreted as referring to, sorrow. The actor has been duly characterized as an *iconic exemplification* in the preceding, and the use of these two types of indices in the analysis has supported this determination. Yet one problem remains to be resolved: An iconic exemplification of what?

We have already rejected the idea that the actor should be an iconic sign if this is to be taken in the sense that he is a reproduction of a copy of an original just as a cast of a copy of the Venus de Milo or drawings by students at l'Académie des Beaux-Arts are exercises in the reproduction of classic works. Surely the actor playing Napoleon can achieve a resemblance to Napoleon through make-up and costuming, which is similar to students' drawings of an original, but—only because it is a specific instance, because there exist iconic representations of characters before the production—this form for iconic representation cannot be essential. It must be asserted instead *that the actor is an iconic representation of the fictive person represented symbolically in the drama*. In the dramatic text, the character is constituted partly through his/her lines, in part through the company. Inasmuch as the actor lends body and voice to the corporeal realization of a process of symbolic signs, he embodies one of the enunciative instances of the text; but, in order to do this he must naturally have read, memorized, and interpreted it, that is, he becomes the *interpretant* of this part of the text. So the actor's role can also be determined as an *iconic exemplification of an interpretation or, perhaps better, an interpretation in the form of iconic exemplification*. The plausibility of this determination can be seen in that whereas it would be absurd to say, for example, that Lawrence Olivier and Derek Jacobi reproduced the character Hamlet in two different ways, it would be reasonable to assert that their roles are two different interpretations of the drama *Hamlet* and particularly the meaning potential of the character Hamlet, interpretations that take on the form of iconic exemplifications.

Two things have been emphasized thus far: (1) that the introduction of objects into the stage's double universe of fiction and physical spatial reality does not mean that they lose their character as objects, and (2) that the transformation of reagent into designation was characteristic for the play on stage. Now these two relations can be formulated more precisely in relation to the actor. To speak of the actor (and the production as a totality) as an iconic exemplification of the character (the drama) is to accentuate the fictional aspect of what happens on the stage. But, at the same time, the actor is also concrete and physically present, and this bodily presence in the same universe and at the same time with the spectators is the *differentia specifica* of the theatrical performance, compared to the realization of dramatic forms in other media (film, TV, radio, etc.). This means that the actor is present for the public in three ways: as a fictive person, as a professional exercising his/her practice, and as a physical individuality. In this latter characteristic s/he is present in his/her own element, so to speak: s/he is his/her own assertion of a bodily reality which cannot be reduced to a vehicle of fiction; and it is precisely this reduction which takes place in the moment that one asserts that objects lose their objective character on the stage and become signs. The actor's bodily presence thus has a triple function: (1) as an incarnation of the textual process (as its dynamical interpretant) s/he makes possible (along with the staging as a whole) a social community of fantasies; (2) as a person exercising his/her profession at a given historical moment, the actor transposes the symbolic process into para-linguistic signs, gesture, mimic, etc., based on a theatrical code which renders them meaningful; and (3) as a constant bodily presence, s/he functions as the anchor point for the spectator's libidinal preoccupation in the fiction (see the section on identification). Precisely because the actor has the world in common with the spectator, his/her physical presence on the stage seem to promise or, rather, mirror the possibility of transcending the limits of social existence by passing into the fictive universe. But the contrary is equally valid, as the actor also manages to go beyond the fiction, to achieve interaction in the world s/he has in common with the spectator; s/he is therefore viewed as bringing the aura of the spectacle and the apparent inexhaustibility of the theatre with him/her.

13. The identification of the spectator: the divided subject

A character in one of Jorge Luis Borges's short stories naïvely questions the true legitimacy of the theatre, since "a good narrator can express anything, regardless of how complicated it is." According to this point of view, there is no difference between the experiences of the reader/listener and those of the spectator; theatre strikes this character as a kind of superfluous "translation" of the story. In this attitude—which, in trying to deny theatre its specificity, refuses to abstract from a specifically literary way of thinking—one not only recognizes the restrictive but blatantly *anti-theatrical aesthetic* we meet in Plato, who at least knew what theatre was. For him, its danger lay in its ability to provoke an identification among the spectators, whom he thought should be controlled and manipulated through a sort of repressive tolerance.

The notion of identification is a constant which reappears in dramatic criticism under different names at different times. It is particularly in periods when a new dramatic aesthetic confronts another that the question arises: What happens to the spectator's identity after the performance? Does s/he turn into a socialist/terrorist/homosexual, etc.? Does s/he become another person? The question can be formulated in many ways, all according to the situation and the dominant preoccupation at the time, but in any case it is clear that in every age the theatrical genre has been deemed as having, among other things, the potential to change people and their reality, a quality shared naturally with all artistic genres, but which shines out in a particularly direct and urgent form in theatre.

As a technically simple genre (compared, for example, to film), theatre lives by virtue of the characters who carry the action forward and who at the same time are models of all the men, women, and children we can/could/would (have) be(en). We will not contend from this, however, that identification with the character is a theatre-specific phenomenon, nor that the character is the sole object of identification, but only that here the character constitutes the central sign in the complex, polysemic experience of the theatre-goer. The encounter with the "other-worldly" aspect of the play is concretized for the spectator in the character, who obliges the former to define or identify himself.

It must be confessed that the word *identification* is a vague term, banalized by everyday usage and by dramatic criticism in general. Nevertheless, we will not give up using it, because it is perhaps this same obscurity that best allows us to clarify the peculiar ambiguity of dramatic reception. We shall be using this term in the two determinations given it by J. Laplanche and J. B. Pontalis in *Vocabulaire de la Psychanalyse*:

1. as a general, non-specific psycho-analytical notion of "recognizing as identical / determining one's own identity."
2. as a specific psychoanalytical notion of "being identical with another."

Laplanche and Pontalis distinguish between these two meanings by applying the linguistic term "transitive" to the former and "reflexive" to the latter. Yet this terminology can give way to misunderstanding. These two linguistic terms are not mutually exclusive since reflexive action must be conceived as a subcategory of transitive action. Just as one can define another's identity, so can one identify or define oneself through an action which is transitive *and* reflexive (subject = object) without implying thereby an identification with another. One can identify oneself positively with another by "being identical" with him or, negatively, by perceiving a difference from him.

We shall appeal to these designations of positive and negative identification in the following. Theatre reception, as shall be seen, is characterized precisely by the interplay of these two types of identification.

A. THE SPECTATOR AND THE CHARACTER

During the performance, the spectator is bombarded incessantly with images offering the possibility of either a positive or negative, conscious or unconscious identification. At the same time s/he identifies negatively with the character, thinking, "I am not like that person—selfish, cowardly, weak, etc.," s/he can also identify unconsciously with those qualities which, to him/her, and to the society in which s/he lives, are unacceptable. On the one hand s/he is able to sympathize with those who take rightful revenge on Don Juan while, at the same time and in utmost secrecy, s/he admires and envies his lawlessness and brazen disdain for the social norms.

In this situation, the spectator is not simply a witness to the conflict which unfolds on stage between duty and desire. The conflict is extended in the spectator, splitting him/her in two and begging him/her *to choose*—Is s/he Don Juan or Elvira?—confronted with a series of events leading inevitably to death for one and victory for the other.

In his famous article on dramatic illusion, Octave Mannoni defines *the theatre as the place of the return of the repressed, a return made possible through denegation, that is, through the spectator's consciousness of being at a theatrical play and not in a scene from real life* (Mannoni 1969). The spectator identifies with the character; of course not in the sense of assuming the character's place, which would be a precise denegation of the negation. But in the sense that the viewer receives his/her repressed identity, so to speak, through the image given of the other.

In the following we will add some reflections to this idea which, since its appearance in 1969, has been an essential source of inspiration for dramatic criticism.

In his treatment of the fundamental idea that the liberating power of theatre lies in denegation, Mannoni treads too lightly over the *complexity*, which, in our opinion, is essential to *dramatic reception*. If the spectator's repressed "I" is freed by the images on stage, then this occurs only through a struggle with the conscience from which in any case s/he will be unable to completely free her/himself. In spite of all the theatrical artifice tending in this direction, denegation does not imply absence of consciousness. On the contrary, denegation is the product of the consciousness, a defense mechanism which allows the spectator to reunite with the repressed "I" in its negated form.

Regardless of the difficulty of illuminating theatre's liberating force, one must not fail to consider *the spectator's ambivalence,* split as s/he is between the powers of the conscious and the unconscious which, in a sense, divide the character into "hero" or "villain"—just like a well-known Little Red Riding-Hood doll whose skirt is transformed (with a simple movement of the hand) into the wolf's furry coat.

By *conscious identification* we mean the identification which confirms individuals in their conception of their own identity in their social, political, and cultural conditioning. This identity is not necessarily in complete accordance with the person's social identity as it is manifested in working life, family life or engagement for example in politics or union work. Rather it is his/her self-definition, that opinion s/he has formed of her/himself, regardless if this corresponds to his/her external identification. Through this identity, perhaps unrealized, perhaps recognized by the individual her/himself as a contra-identity, s/he confirms her/himself as being somebody, as a entity in the middle of the stream of events. The conscious identification is tautologic: *I am like him/her because I have told myself I am like him/her.*

Unconscious identification entails confrontation with everything having been repressed by the individual in constructing an effective identity, at least in his/her self-understanding. This is the very point at stake for self-understanding, the theatre's somewhat malicious challenge to the spectator if not to surrender his/her conscious identity, then at least to reflect upon its arbitrary nature.

Figure 8 depicts the spectator's possible identifications (A, B, C, and D) with the character.

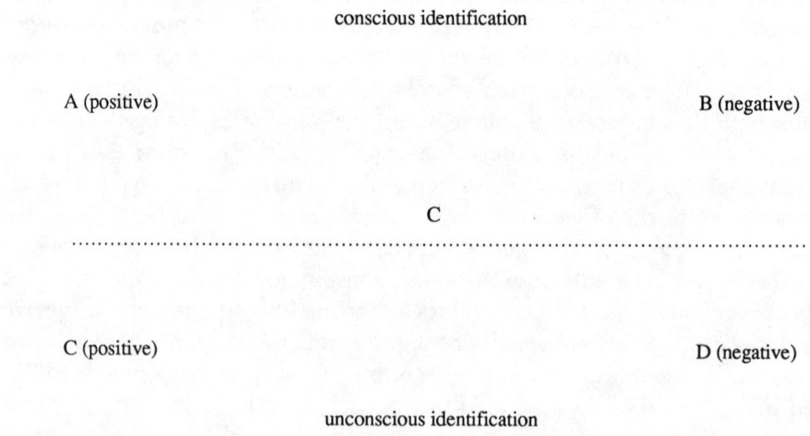

conscious identification

A (positive)   B (negative)

C
....

C (positive)   D (negative)

unconscious identification

Figure 8

Establishing the four poles offers the possibility of the dichotomic combinations A = D or B = C; positive identification at the conscious level corresponds to negative identification at the unconscious level and vice versa.

Let us take as an example the character of the mild, resigned mother. The female spectator can consciously identify here: "I am like her" or "I am not like her." But her identification can also be of a complex and completely illogical nature, split between the conscious and the unconscious: "I am like her, BUT I am not like her" or "I am not like her BUT I am like her." These two negative and positive reactions to the identification object can take place at both the conscious and unconscious level, depending on a number of factors stemming from the socialization of the spectator who, in attempting to defend her/himself, cannot do so without self-contradictions:

1. I am like her. She corresponds with my ideas of a good mother who lives for and through her children. I am tired of "the modern woman." I have no desire to go to work and participate in social life. I want to stay home and play with my children (A or C).

BUT

2. I am not like her. I am tired of "the good mother," I have no desire to stay home and play with my children. I want to go to work and participate in social life (B or D).

Other investments of the characters could be the dutiful revolutionary who awakens "bright and early," ready to contribute to the reconstruction of his/her country, the tolerant husband who leaves his wife in peace with her lover, the old woman who gracefully accepts her declining beauty, etc. All these characters, as if by a diabolical mechanism, open the possibility of their own negation and thereby of a dual identification—often, but not necessarily concretized in an antagonist: the sybarite, the jealous husband, the eternally repressed woman—just as the presence of these same characters would. In a way, we could say that the dialectic which is established and visualized through Brecht's distancing effect, is always already present as an innate characteristic of theatre.

The theatre is not a simple representation of stereotypes, frozen images, but of an action—perhaps an action rendering the character's identity problematic—and the spectator's task lies in following this action. But in theatre "to follow the action" is also to pursue oneself, to discover oneself in contrast to and in the characters, to ask oneself: Am I or am I not like him/her? Would I do the same thing given the same conflict? And is this conflict true or false for me? Have I ever wished to be a revolutionary? Or a sybarite?

The spectator, in his conscious and unconscious identification, represents an opposition, a certain inertia, in contrast to the logic which is established in the development of the scenic events. This resistance to abandoning oneself to the fiction's premises is not specific to theatre, but it is in theatre that it is most strongly manifested because at every moment the spectator is confronted with a virtual model of his/her ego.

The darkness of the theatre (in which we can nonetheless make out our own hands, together with the heads and shoulders of other spectators) does not institute, as by some magic spell, the realm of the unconscious, but an interregnum between the conscious and unconscious. That liberation which the theatre offers the spectator rests in our opinion not in the reawakening of the repressed as in a sort of generous dream-state rendered by denial. It rests rather in the confrontation between the repressed and the conscious identity which is deposited in the pocket of an overcoat in the cloak room. The person setting himself down to assume the role as spectator carries out a courageous action, placing himself at the mercy of a ping-pong game with identification, not knowing the result.

The theatre is not—as Plato opined, and as Mannoni seems likewise to believe, albeit in a more sophisticated and fascinating manner than Plato did—the place of identification, but rather *the place for the struggle of identifications* which, through a sort of neutralizing effect, establishes a free-zone, a space of non-identity, where nothing is yet defined once and for all.

In this no man's land created by the characters, the spectator is finally absolved of his own contradictions.

B. THE SPECTATOR AND THE ACTOR

Until now, we have treated dramatic identification exclusively in connection with the character, the genre's dominant sign. We have distinguished the character from its substratum, the actor. Before we treat this "other half" of the stage's human element, we will, in order to avoid misunderstanding, explain this crude distinction.

Whenever we speak of the character, we refer to the totality of the signs generated by the actor and which constitutes for the spectator a human entity in the fictive universe. The actor is not merely a "channel" or a "material" through which the dramatic text's character is transmitted, but the incarnation —in process as well as product—of the character, with its multiplicity of signs, of which, among others, are included speech acts (Ubersfeld 1981).

The actor's physical presence then is inseparable from the constitution of the character. A part of him/her is absorbed, rendered so to speak invisible by the character, whereas the other part—the character's utterances—remains visible to the spectator, who is aware that that which s/he views is *theatre*. This leads now and again to the actor's physical presence implying *a reinforcement of identification with the character* as compared to the other genres. We will not reject this tempting thesis, but instead of venturing into an uncertain domain, examine *the relation between the spectator and the actor*.

The co-presence of actor and spectator in the same physical space is an indispensable condition when speaking of theatre—but not the only one. It is just as necessary that the spectator be conscious of the *situation's fic-*

tionality, that s/he recognize his/her own status as spectator. For this reason a phenomenon such as a happening cannot, in our opinion, be included in the theatrical genre, because it is a staging that negates itself as such in working without a "frame" (in Erving Goffman's sense of the word) and in calling for the participation of the spectator, who, in this case, ceases to be a spectator. Such a staging is difficult to distinguish from many other real-life stagings which one would most likely hesitate to call "theatre" (Schwanitz 1977).

It is precisely the spectator's consciousness of *witnessing a fiction*—a little slice of life—which, associated with the actor's *actual* presence, embodies the distinctive trait of dramatic reception. The physical presence of a living body in the aesthetic object may reinforce identification with the character, but, in our opinion, its most obvious effect is the transformation of the aesthetic object by constituting itself (the living body) as an aesthetic object and as an object of identification. The play on stage is split in two, *the played reality and the real play,* which leads to a dividing of the spectator's ego, split between two objects of identification, a splitting further reinforced by the conflict between the conscious ego and the unconscious.

The circumstance of theatrical reception implies for the respective spectators a *renunciation of all external activity* except for the codified utterances (laughter, whistling, applause, etc.) which accentuate his/her position as a spectator. Apart from these utterances, the spectator is non-existent, has so to speak no share in physical existence. S/he suppresses the need to cough, and if s/he gets up and leaves the theatre, it is with a shameful feeling of having broken the law. The darkness of the auditorium and the light on the stage divide the room into two zones, of which one is characterized by the possibility of infinite and unforeseeable actions and the other by the exact contrary. The cultivated spectator who sits placidly observing the rules for good behavior in the theatre has deliberately chosen this situation in which s/he is forbidden to speak, move, or exist for a few hours, except as witness to a series of events from which s/he is excluded from the start.

In this respect the situation of the theatrical spectator resembles that of the movie-goer, but differs from the latter in that there is a body in the same room which is just as alive and actual as the spectator, but which is *simultaneously* inscribed in another universe. The actor lends his/her body as a sign of the fiction by assuming the body of the character, while at the same time exhibiting her/himself as a body belonging to the real world facing another body of the real world.

Besides the task of identifying with the character, the spectator contracts a relation of identity with the actor, determined by their common affiliation in the real world and by the contrast between speaking and not speaking, doing and not doing. The spectator is conscious of the fact that what happens on stage is a fiction but, at the same time, knows that *this fiction is a part of real life* and that the liberating of his/her potential for identification is dependent upon a *player.* This fact is incessantly reinforced by the speech on stage, words which (as in real life, precisely because of the mimetic character of dramatic fiction) are strongly marked by deictical signs (I, you, here, now, yesterday, this, etc.), which have meaning only through their reference to the sender, the physical source of the message. Without the mouth pronouncing these words they are but a series of meaningless sounds. The theatre's "I" is not only *spoken*, but is at the same time performed, and every "you," "here," and "now" is organized around this visible 'I.'

The division between character and actor in the spectator's identification is reinforced by the profusion of deictical entities which swarm him/her from the stage and thereby highlight the dual dimension of the theatre's "here and now" that of enunciations inserted in speech acts. The "you" expressed by the character never addresses the spectator, and the latter may not come on stage to become the object of this "you."

Even in the instances where the words on stage are directed to the audience, the spectator is well aware that this is not a summoning of his/her real self, but of his/her character, which is preconceived and determined by the play, and that the entity apparently addressing him/her does so neither as an actual "I," but as the character registered in another modality, that namely of the play. It is not the actor who is speaking to him/her, not the living being of flesh and blood, which breathes the same air as him/her, but a character which has been produced by an actor. It is perhaps just in this case of "going beyond the limelight" that the spectator is most strongly confronted with the theatricality of theatre, rejected by the fiction and referred to his spectator-reality.

If the theatre, through the effect of denial, offers the spectator a possible freeing of his/her identification potential, it also reminds him/her constantly, through the confrontation with the actor, of his/her place in the world, of his/her identity, whether this identity be imposed by others or self-imposed as protest, defense, or self-confirmation. In this way the theatre reinforces in the spectator the very concept of identity in everything it implies for the individual concerning stability, immutability, and continuity, even the demand of being somebody, being ONE all the time.

While theatre gives the spectator liberation and relief, it at the same time points out the prison of identity, showing him/her human beings who transcend the limits of their own identity.

We will not, however, assert that the actor should enjoy a greater liberty than the spectator in the concrete theatrical event. Both are responsible for keeping the theatrical contract, the actor more so than the spectator since the actor cannot leave the theatrical event. But whereas the spectator's situation physically reflects the notion of identity, the permission to view "the other world" and simultaneously prohibition on creating it, the actor is the living embodiment of the transcending of this law. The liberating potential of the play is contradicted by the reality of the theatrical event, where the actor and the spectator acquire status as a sign, as protagonist and antagonist in the spectacle of "to play or not to play."

The spectator's identification with the actor is a complex and disturbing experience. Even if s/he recognizes her/himself at the unconscious level in the actor, thinking, "I am basically like him, multifarious, acting, experimenting with my Richard III, my Dame aux Camélias, my vagabond, waiting for Godot," s/he is immediately thrown back into his/her fixed, frozen identity and to the nostalgic reminiscing on a distant time, wherein it is still allowed to act "another." In the actor's body, which adopts the character, s/he sees the victory over the tyranny of identity as s/he recognizes his/her own reality, the ego, the little straw which s/he clings to like one drowning. The old metaphor of "All the world is a stage" is given an ironic twist, and the spectator is sent back to his place in a world which will not be theatre, except when people hide their own confusing complexity under the masks of identity.

Perhaps the spectator goes to the theatre intending to "drown his/her ego" in order to be free, to find an alternative identity because, as Mannoni says in a quotation from Freud "nothing ever happens to him," and maybe to rediscover her/himself at the level of the story, in identification with the character, a repressed identity.

But the actor presents him/her with quite another project: the play, discontinuity, and identity's anarchy, pointing all the while to the inertia in the spectator's life, his identity—a repressive, mediocre, and mundane existence, but not the only one, nor perhaps the final one.

NOTES

1. Peirce's manuscripts are indicated by the numbering found in *Annotated Catalogue of the Papers of Charles S. Peirce* by Richard S. Robin, University of Massachusetts Press, Orcester, Mass., 1967. The pagination follows that of the manuscripts of *The Institute for Studies in Pragmaticism*, Texas Tech University, Lubbock, Texas (e.g., MS 634, 1909. ISP 18" indicates Robin, ms. no. 634, written by Peirce in 1909, page 18). The manuscripts have been microfilmed (see bibliography).

2. Eco himself invites such an interpretation when—in the chapter on visual semiotics in the first edition of *La struttura assente*—he distinguishes between analytic and synthetic codes, hence indicating different discursive positions which can be invested in the same code (Eco 1979, 35f.).

3. One might take the liberty of seeing in Eco's distinction between strong and weak codes a distinction between codes within a limited (strong) text and codes which cannot be precisely determined in relation to the given textual demarcation, consequently acquiring the status of a non-coded phenomenon which, nonetheless, has an effect in the coded (weak) text (cf. Eco 1981, 652f.).

BIBLIOGRAPHY

Jorge Luis Borges, 1974, "La busca de Averroes," in *El Aleph*, Buenos Aires.

Viggo Brøndal, 1943, "Langage et logique," in *Essais de linguistique générale*, Copenhagen, Munksgaard.

1950, *Théorie des prépositions*, Copenhagen, Munksgaard.

Georg Büchner, 1953, *Théâtre complet*, Paris, L'Arche.

   1969, *Woyzeck,* New York, Avon Press.

Deirdre Burton, 1980, *Dialogue and Discourse,* London, Routledge and Kegan Paul.

Oswald Ducrot, 1969, "Présupposés et sous-entendus," in *Langue Française,* 4.

   1972, *Dire et ne pas dire,* Paris, Hermann.

   1978, "Structuralisme, énonciation et sémantique," in *Poétique,* 33.

Umberto Eco, 1970, "Sémiologie des messages visuels," in *Communications,* 15.

   1976, *A Theory of Semiotics,* Bloomington, Indiana Univ. Press.

   1977, "The Code: Metaphor or Interdisciplinary Category," in *Yale Italian Studies 1,* 1.

   1981, "Segno," in *Encyclopedia Einaudi,* 12, Turin, Einaudi.

Erving Goffman, 1974, *Frame Analysis,* New York, Harper and Row.

André Green, 1969, *The Tragic Effect,* London, Cambridge Univ. Press.

Louis Hjelmslev, 1966, *Prolegomena to a Theory of Language,* Madison, Univ. of Wisconsin Press.

Roman Jakobson, 1956, *Fundamentals of Language,* The Hague, Mouton.

   1963, "Deux aspects du langage et deux types d'aphasie," in *Essais de linguistique générale,* Paris, Minuit, 43–67.

A. Kondratov, 1966, *Sounds and Signs* (trans. from Russian by G. Yankovsky), Moscow, MIR.

J. Laplanche et J. B. Pontalis, 1967, *Vocabulaire de la psychanalyse,* Paris.

Jean Laplanche and Jean Baptiste, 1973, *The Language of Psycho-Analysis,* London, Hogarth.

Svend Erik Larsen, 1985, "The Symbol of the Knife in Büchner's Woyzeck," in *Orbis Litterarum,* 40.

Octave Mannoni, 1969, *Clef pour l'imaginaire ou l'autre scène,* Paris, Seuil.

Charles Sanders Peirce, 1931–1958, *The Collected Papers of Charles Peirce,* I–VIII (ed. Chr. Hartshorne, P. Weiss, and A. Burks), Cambridge, Harvard Univ. Press.

   1966, *The Charles S. Peirce Papers* (microfilm edition, thirty reels, with two supplementary reels recently added), Cambridge, Harvard Univ. Library Photographic Service.

   1977, *Semiotics and Significs: The Correspondence between Charles S. Peirce and Victoria Lady Welby* (ed. Charles S. Hardwick), Bloomington, Indiana Univ. Press.

Plato, 1963, *The Republic,* III, X, Cambridge, Harvard Univ. Press.

Dieter Schwanitz, 1977, *Die Wirklichkeit der Inszenierung und die Inszenierung der Wirklichkeit,* Meisenheim am Glan.

Anne Ubersfeld, 1981, *L'école du spectateur,* Paris, Editions Sociales.

Ad de Vries, 1976, *Dictionary of Symbols and Imagery,* Amsterdam, North-Holland (1st ed. 1974).

IV.
Pedagogics of theatre

"Reading" the text

It is an obvious fact that any spontaneous "reading" of a dramatic text and its performance in the theatre will be made in accordance with the interpretive code which the reader-spectator has been taught. Thus in former ages opera-goers paid particular attention to the technique and vocal feats of the singers. If one asks high-school students what they have found of interest in a theatrical performance, they will reply: the psychology of the characters. They may not believe a word of what they say, but that is what they are expected to notice in virtue of the code they have learned.

For this reason, it is useful to teach a different method of "reading," one which opens up an understanding of the dramatic text as an artistic object, the product of an act of writing, and of the performance as a second text, the product of complex stage practice. The assumptions underlying the semiotic approach have the advantage of presenting the text as a set of (linguistic) signs and the performance as another set of (linguistic and non-linguistic) signs, sets of signs which not only interact, but can also be applied one to the other in accordance with laws which are, however, too complex to be considered here.

We are well aware of the fact that the majority of the reading strategies envisaged in the pages that follow are *structural* procedures which, accordingly, are subject to the inherent weaknesses of any structural method: putting all the elements on the same level without taking into account either the hierarchy of the signs, or the referential worlds of the transmitter and receptor respectively. It will therefore be necessary to consider these procedures as a *preliminary* exercise to analysis proper, indispensable but requiring to be both interpreted and corrected: interpreted in the light of the relationships to be established between the various patterns of the text (text in the broadest sense of the word), corrected in accordance with the conditions of transmission and reception and with the referential worlds of the writer and the reader-spectator.

The starting point

The first question that arises is "Where to start?" At once we are faced with a difficulty: the analysis of the text and that of the performance cannot be superposed. Reading the text means a linear reading of details in which it is always possible to go back; following the performance implies a global, polyphonic form of reading which inevitably highlights the succession of events that make up the fable. Paradoxically, what is overlooked in the reading of the written text is precisely what is not overlooked by the spectator, that is, the fable and the main conflicts; on the other hand, the reader registers the details of the discourse without perceiving the totality of the overarching structures.

The reader should therefore start by analyzing the overarching structures, which alone make the discourse "readable." It is well known that the dramatic text normally has the status of unreadability. Whereas the *conditions of enunciation* underlying the discourse are perfectly and effortlessly apparent to the audience in a production, a reader, on the contrary, is obliged to reconstruct (or construct) these conditions. Hence the need first to study the fable and the actantial model.

Conversely, the spectator who knows the fable and who is aware of the conflicts, should proceed from the diachronic reading of events to a synchronic reading of theatrical signs; and what will be foregrounded in his/her reading are the composition of the stage space, the utilization of the space by the actor, and the use of light; in other words, all the synchronous signs of stage practice.

In the first case, the analyst grasps the discourse as a *mise en signe* of a fable and a conflict (this is a dramaturgical activity); in the second , s/he studies a network of visual-auditory signs as conferring meaning upon a narrative (a *critical* activity).

1. Analysis of the text

A. Reading the text

In order to elucidate the detail of the didascalia and dialogue, the reader should begin by constructing the fable and the actantial model, or rather models.

(A) THE FABLE

Following Brecht, one can say that the *fable* is the diachronic sequence of the events presented by the dramatic text, regardless of the order in which the text presents them.

1. The first procedure might be to establish the initial and final state of affairs—a particularly interesting exercise, in that it enables one to determine the *change* brought about by the dramatic action: thus, for example, the dénouement of *Phèdre*, by a process of subtraction, demonstrates the elimination of both the subject and the object of the adulterous passion and at the same time that of the two *outsiders* (Phèdre and Hippolyte); conversely the seal is set on the reconciliation of the two representatives of legitimacy, Thésée

and Aricie. Many of Shakespeare's plays by differentiation between an initial and a final point mark the passage from feudal anarchy to equitable, centralized monarchy (*Henry VI* and *King Lear*).

2. A second procedure, related to the first, which is pedagogically most rewarding is to make a summary of the action in one sentence: a single sentence with a finite verb (it is not therefore a matter of supplying an alternative—fuller or cleverer—*title*). This necessitates the selection of one principal character (the actantial subject) and one main action. The relatively arbitrary nature of this procedure helps the student to realize (a) that any procedure is always a *construction*, never the discovery of something given, and (b) that any reading of a text, and particularly a reading of it by a producer with an eye to performance, inevitably means exercising a preference: thus, in the case of *Le Misanthrope*, it is not impossible to construct a sentence, with Célimène instead of Alceste as *subject*, showing the triumph and defeat of a kind of female Don Juan.

The possibility of constructing *several* sentences summarizing the action is by no means to be excluded; on the contrary, this may help to elucidate the various explicit or implied conflicts.

3. As for the construction of the *fable* itself (in the Brechtian sense of the term), this implies making up a story, a kind of micro-novel constructed from the episodes that compose the action, narrated in chronological order. This procedure has the advantage of highlighting the *logic* of the events and of rearranging the dramatic discourse as a coherent story; it also facilitates taking into account the past events from which the action flows; lastly, it makes it possible to situate the characters in their socio-historical context (this, for Brecht, was the point of the exercise). In certain cases (where the temporal sequence of the drama is broken by anticipated or simultaneous action) the construction of the fable encourages awareness of the way time has been handled. On the other hand, there are instances (ancient tragedies of the static kind, such as *The Persians* or *Prometheus Bound,* or modern works of the "muscial" species) in which constructing the fable is not a very rewarding procedure.

One practical difficulty is how to determine the *starting point* of the fable (a point which does not necessarily coincide with, and may precede or follow, the beginning of the play); in most of Racine's tragedies, for example, the event that gives rise to the disequilibrium from which the action stems has already occurred before the rise of the curtain, and it is worth while tracing it so as to pinpoint what causes the imbalance and engenders the tragedy. Conversely, in many of Shakespeare's works (*King Lear, Macbeth*), the starting point is subsequent to the opening of the play.

(B) ACTANTIAL STRUCTURES

It is not possible to summarize here, even in general terms, Greimas's theory of an actantial model;[1] suffice it to recall that what he proposes is a syntactical

model deeply anchored in both grammar and anthropology. The supposition
is that there is a *subject* of the action, whose *desire* propels him/her actively
to conquer an *object* (syntactical structure: subject, verb, predicate). The action
may be aided by a *helper* and/or hindered by an *opponent* (who may be sufficiently important to be the *subject* of another actantial model, an *anti-subject*).
It can be seen that almost by its very nature, all theatre, and in particular
all theatre based on conflict, may be read in the light not only of one, but
at least *two* actantial models.

The quadrilateral of subject-object-helper-opponent is not, however, sufficient. The subject is not alone in the world, s/he is caught up in a social
network: if s/he goes forth to conquer his/her object, it is because someone
or something is inciting him/her to do so; behind him/her, there is a *sender*
(his/her social group, the political and familial worlds, or even Eros, though
in the shape of an already socialized desire). Secondly, the action may be undertaken for the subject's own gain, but it may equally well be for the benefit
of a group, an environmental world, or a community. These constitute the
receiver with a whole range of possibilities from the individual (even the anti-
social) to the multiple and social.

It will be seen that the actantial model with its appealing simplicity and
clarity is, in fact, far from easy to construct for a variety of reasons:
(a) the possibility of motivations on the part of the *subject* and the *sender*
as well as in the relationship between the two, and the necessity of a socio-
political analysis, without which one falls into sterile formalism;
(b) the difficulty of making a correct analysis at the first attempt, whence
the need to adjust the model by means of a fresh analysis, *after* all the other
procedures have been carried out;
(c) the plurality of possible models and the need to link these opposing models
to each other;
(d) the possible modification of actantial roles during the course of the action
(the helper who becomes an opponent, or the reverse; a change of subject,
etc.): hence, the need to make a careful analysis, sequence by sequence.

The following is a possible order of procedures:
(a) determine the actantial subject(s) of the actantial model(s), with the arrow
of desire which impels them toward their object;
(b) analyze the play of antagonistic forces (helper(s) and opponents(s)) directed
against either the subject or the object;
(c) determine the complex forces (whether personalized or not) which figure
in the actantial role of *sender* and through which, consequently, the action
is linked to the whole socio-cultural context implied by the text (Corollary:
identify the receiver of the action);
(d) *show how the actantial positions evolve in the course of the action:* a
change in the principal subject, substitution of an "anti-subject" for the subject, changes in the actantial roles of the helper or opponent, a change (less
frequent) in the object or receiver, or a change of sender (for example, substitution of the monarchical order for the feudal order in *Le Cid*).

The *point of the operation* is to show the dramatic action as a complex and mobile, basically conflicting, interplay of forces; to reduce the play of psychology to the one arrow of desire; to establish the links between the action and the referential world of the author as well as with the relevant fictional world; and, finally, to construct an intelligible model which, if limited, is nevertheless usable and generally clear.

B. *Conditions of enunciation*

Obviously our concern here is with an enunciation which is that of the *text,* not of the performance, and the conditions of enunciation are *fictional:* in other words, the space and time of the dramatic discourse are those of *fiction,* not of the stage.

(A) DIDASCALIA

1. Space as inscribed in the dramatic text is indicated in the first place by the *didascalia.* Let us recall that the didascalia form the only textual layer of which the enunciator is expressly the writer her/himself: it is the author X who addresses the practician (or the reader, a potential practician), enjoining him/her to construct such and such a set of spatial conditions of enunciation: "a hall in the palace, a lounge, a kitchen, a street. . .". The didascalia therefore construct an imaginary *location* conditioning the action. But this is not their only spatial role: often they specify the way the space is to be utilized by the characters: occupation of the playing area, movement within it, and gesture; a whole fictional space is brought into being.

2. The above concerns the *explicit* didascalia, which frame the dialogue; there is another kind, customarily called *internal* didascalia, which may be extracted from the written dialogue itself. Most of the didascalia in editions of Shakespeare are simply taken from the dialogue. The interest of the *internal didascalia* lies not only in the fact that they greatly enrich (when they do not entirely constitute) the sum of didascalia in the text; they encompass both the spatial indications stipulated for the concrete stage and the entire *spatial universe* of the play, including what need not necessarily be represented: for example in *Phèdre,* not only Troezen (where the action takes place) but also Athens, Crete and the Labyrinth, the Empire of the Dead, and the shore where the Monster appears.

3. *Space as icon.* The paradigmatic whole which may be built up with the aid of the lists mentioned below enables us to create an image of an actual location, but it can equally well be the image of a psychological structure, the Freudian *other stage,* whose divisions may reproduce, so to speak, the spatial structure constituting instances of the psyche. A good example is Maeterlinck's *Intérieur.*

More commonly, space so constructed reproduces social divisions or class oppositions (such as servants' space opposed to the masters' space in

Beaumarchais's *Le Mariage de Figaro*); in Musset's *Lorenzaccio,* the space created is a sort of figuration of the *city,* that is, of a whole society; a list of the spatial indications proves this to be the case. More subtly, the way space is handled can impose an image which is like a figuration of the text itself as a whole (Ubersfeld 1977, 153–164).

Finally, in many instances the kind of space which emerges from the text relates to a referent which is not (or is hardly) a place in the real world, but the stage itself: in this case *the space becomes theatre;* this covers not only instances in which we have a play within a play as in Corneille's *L'Illusion comique,* but also all those cases in which what is represented can be nothing else but theatre. One could perhaps cite all the plays of Racine and, among modern plays, Genet's *Les Paravents (The Screens)* or *Les Nègres (The Blacks).* In this case, as we shall see, the stage should be set up as a platform.

4. *The poetics of space.* It will be found that some of the lists mentioned below result in the creation of literally *imaginary* spaces. Thus the reiteration of the word *bord* ("edge," "limit") in Racine's *Phèdre* (Ubersfeld 1981) functions as a nodal point of the imagery, an imaginary center. The spatial lexicon (which forms a paradigmatic whole) is thus linked to the totality of the syntactical structures derived from the actantial analysis previously mentioned.

The internal didascalia contain a specific textual layer—that of verbal spatialization—comprising predicates of place and verbs of movement which can help the reader to construct the space of the dramatic text.

(B) SUGGESTED PROCEDURES

1. From the foregoing one can deduce the preliminary procedures for constructing such a space:

(a) make an exhaustive list, *following the order of the text,* of all spatial information given in the didascalia;

(b) make a similarly exhaustive list, again following the order of the text, of the spatial information *in the dialogue,* without making any distinction between what can be represented on the stage and what cannot: it is impossible to foresee exactly what will be represented in a particular production. To prejudge the issue by attempting to make this distinction at the outset is just bad methodology; include, therefore, *every* piece of spatial information;

(c) make an exhaustive list (however long it may be) of all the predicates of space and all verbs of movement, even if this procedure does not seem to be of any immediate utility.

One will thus have at one's disposal three lists which will probably be rather long and confused. (While they may be simple and clear for a certain number of texts, such as those of Racine or Beckett, they are likely to be complicated for those of Hugo, Claudel, or Genet.) In any event, they will not yield any useful result until they have been processed in various ways.

2. *Space as text.* What these lists provide is a spatial lexicon which makes it possible to produce a number of patterns or significant oppositions. In other

words, what can be established in this way is a textual space which functions both as a sign (or icon) of an actual location and as a complex text referring to psychological space, social structures, the whole of the textual space—but a text whose structures are autonomous.

The dramatic text allows the reader to construct a whole series of significant oppositions: on stage / off stage, near/far, open/closed, etc.; it also allows for the construction of spaces reserved for particular characters. But perhaps the most important thing to look for is spaces in opposition/conjunction which represent at once two zones in potential conflict with each other and a constantly fluctuating relationship between modes of signification, such as the opposition between *space of incorporation* and *space of non-incorporation* which runs through the entire dramatic literature of the nineteenth century: here poetics and meaning intersect, and the inventory of spatial elements is a decisive procedure.

Needless to say, taking the same inventories as a point of departure, a plurality of readings can and ought to be attempted. This follows from what has already been said: separate readings or confrontations of different readings allow for a variety of spatial constructions on the stage and leave room for the creative imagination of practicians, scenographers, and producers.[2]

C. The object

Space should not be thought of as empty form: to the different inventories already mentioned must be added an inventory of *objects,* discrete signs occupying space in competition with the actors. What is a theatrical object if not something that can potentially be manipulated, figuring both as a lexeme in the text and as something that can (or could) find its place in the stage space? More than a sign, an object in a dramatic text is already a semiotic whole and, as Umberto Eco says, a "text." By its very nature every "thing" in a dramatic text is called upon to become an object (signifier).

(A) PROCEDURES

1. The first procedure as regards objects must be to make an exhaustive list of them, in the order in which they appear in the text (including those "objects" which can hardly be handled or detached, like parts of the human body or distinct elements of the set). Nothing should be omitted from this list, which may be extremely meager (Racine) or astonishingly rich (Shakespeare). No distinction should be made between what is meant to be represented on the stage and what cannot be. As staging is not a *translation,* it is important to note the often rich semio-lexical paradigms which speech may be sufficient to convey but of which the staging could or should, perhaps, take account by other means: thus, for instance, the incredible plague of repug-

nant small animals that punctuate the text of *King Lear* (mice, rats, cock-roaches, dirty or stinging insects).

2. The second task of the reader is to construct semio-lexical sets, noticing how they change in the course of the text: hence the need for the list to *follow the order* of the text. It is impossible to determine in advance what the pertinent semio-lexical fields will be. This operation is no more mechanical than that relating to the analysis of textual space; this is particularly true in the case of an older text, in which the connotations will inevitably have been modified by the course of history. One may, for example, note the importance given to the lexical fields relating to the parts of the body in Racine, to clothing and finery in Marivaux, or to food in contemporary writers (Beckett, Vinaver), sometimes including the pertinent opposition raw/cooked (nature/culture).

3. It remains for us to identify one or several objects characteristic of a text or an author: the mirror in Marvaux, or the significant constellation of silver coins, coats of arms, torches, and moon in Hugo.

(B) FUNCTION OF THE OBJECTS

The task of the analyst is to determine the function of these objects:

(a) They may be basically functional (a sword if there is a duel, a tumbler if there is drinking).

(b) The object may indicate an actual location or situation: ovens and cooking utensils will indicate a kitchen, particular furniture will provide information of a spatio-temporal nature. A textual object can both create an impression of reality and perform a referential function.

(c) The object may symbolize aspects of reality or people; thus the moon may be a symbol of death; the crown, like the sceptre and the throne, is a traditional symbol of royal authority; consequently, in a dramatic text, it can be argued that the words "throne" or "crown," even when used in their "derived" or "metaphoric" senses,[3] do indicate *an object* (which may or may not appear on the stage).

(d) In a more general way, and more interestingly, one can say that any object in a dramatic text is caught up in a poetic network: it is a metonymy of this or that element of reality (a bunch of wild flowers for the country, a bottle for the drunkenness of a protagonist), or a metaphor (a black costume for "blackness" of soul; the moon, a metaphor of death). Beyond such self-evident examples, an entire rhetoric, an entire poetics, comes into being thanks to the objects in the text, far beyond what can be materially represented: for example, in Racine's *Phèdre*, the astonishing recurrence of parts of the body prefiguring the scattered limbs of Hippolyte in the dénouement. If dramatic poets are indeed poets, they earn this title with the aid of a network of objects whose components and often complex interplay must be laid bare.

This analysis of the poetics of the object also serves to elucidate the poetics characteristic of the playwright: an elucidation both of a poetic lexicon and of the way the text functions.

D. Time

(A) DURATION

It is obvious that whereas space is always, or almost always, precisely delineated, the temporal dimension is almost always blurred; with the exception of classical tragedy (in which the duration must be specified because of the twenty-four hour "unity" of time) the duration of the action remains imprecise, all the more so since one does not *see* time on the stage (the signifier of time on the stage is always spatial) and since, with very few exceptions, the time of the fiction greatly exceeds performance time. However, it is important for the reader to take precise cognizance of the supposed duration of the action, and especially, perhaps, of the pauses in the action, for it is the latter (more or less loaded with events) that establish the temporal rhythm of the text. The total length of the action depends on these pauses, and the reader should undertake an *exhaustive listing* of all the references which may assist in constructing this duration of the fiction.

(B) HISTORICAL TIME, MYTHICAL TIME

Any dramatic action can take place either in accordance with progressive, irreversible *historical* time, or with circular, recurrent *mythical* time. The reader should endeavor to pick out the signs enabling him/her to see in the story, for example,
(a) a closed fable, mythical time;
(b) a fable in which the future is already written into the present in the form of announcements, prophecies, dreams, etc. (for example in Racine or in Shakespeare's *Macbeth*);
(c) possible indications of circular (carnivalesque) time or a sacred rite.

Conversely, the logical, continuous, irreversible progression which denotes *historical* time, can be found in Shakespeare's chronicle plays or in Corneille's *Le Cid*.

An important element that must always be taken into account in the analysis of time is the *ending*. Does it mark the completion of the action in the closed circularity of myth, or remain open to a historical future? Or, as is fairly often the case, does it bring into play theatrical time, that of the performance itself? There is sometimes hardly any point, however, in making a radical distinction between these three possibilities, as they are, at times, combined: the dénouement of Beaumarchais's *Le Mariage de Figaro* is both open and theatricalized. Likewise, the ending of *Hamlet,* which is of the historical kind, is not without elements of a specifically mythical circularity.

(C) INTERNAL RHYTHM

An extremely important analysis to be made is that of internal rhythm:
(a) the succession of sequences: major sequences (acts of tableaux) with numer-

ous subdivisions giving an internal succession of minor sequences, or, on the contrary, major sequences sparsely punctuated and containing continuous developments, giving the impression not of a rapid succession of events but of static duration. One of the features of contemporary theatre is the succession of short sequences separated by a blackout, creating an impression of discontinuous time, a disjointed kind of life, but also suggesting the passing of time, the days going by;

(b) within each sequence of medium length (or scene), it is important to notice the rhythm of the dialogue, whether it is made up of long tirades and set speeches or, on the contrary, of rapid exchanges, or even stichomythia.

In this way a precise impression is gained not only of the general rhythm which a particular author gives to his texts, but also of the specific rhythm(s) of a particular play, or even a particular episode.

(D) THE MOMENT

It is worth while, where relevant (as it frequently is) to note the exact moment of the action or actions and, in particular, the time of day: for instance, the morning of victory, the triumphant dawn of the last two acts of *Le Cid* after the nocturnal roaming of Act III. Likewise, in Hugo's theatre, the succession of nights in *Angelo,* or the way the successive acts of *Ruy Blas* make up a kind of day (from morning to midnight), though their "objective" duration is different; or the succession of days and nights in *Hamlet* or *King Lear.* This type of research is an important preparation for the visual and psychological climate of the performance.

(E) THE HISTORICAL MOMENT AND THE REFERENT

The writer by means of his/her text constructs a *possible* world; this world exhibits two systems of reference, the world of the time of the action and that of the writer her/himself. It can happen that these two systems coincide, if it is his/her own world that the writer is evoking; but more often there are two different *moments* within the same text, that of the fiction and that of the writing, even though they may be very close.

It must be emphasized that referential worlds comprise a temporal component; there is a whole spatio-temporal complex operative within the dramatic text, which the reader must analyze.

S/he will therefore have to list the textual elements which refer to a specific historical moment, as well as those which pertain to the "present" referential world of the writer. This is not always easy, as the author often takes pains to cover up the traces of his/her own moment in time. But s/he cannot prevent these traces from showing up somewhere, in the form of intentional or unintentional anachronisms (or achronisms), which are all the more important to note as they give the text its special "relief" and its meaning. Thus when Shakespeare writes *Antony and Cleopatra,* trying as he may to follow Plutarch faithfully, he actually gives us a reflection of feudal struggles; and, in *Othello,* love as it is dreamed and lived by Desdemona has nothing Mediterranean about it; it is the courtly love of the North.

E. *The character*

It has been possible to maintain, without being too paradoxical, that the real semiotic unit in the theatre is the character. This is a view which perhaps does him/her too much honor, inasmuch as one of the features of the stage character is to be in some way *indeterminate;* otherwise s/he could not be impersonated by a potentially unlimited number of actors. How indeed can one define the stage character and how can one characterize him/her? By a name, but this is hardly true: a character with a speech to make may still be anonymous. The best definition might be that s/he is the *enunciator of a discourse* (or an action in the case of a silent character who is required by the didascalia to perform it). S/he is characterized in the first place by a certain number of speech acts, the enunciation of which s/he is said to be the subject; to this may be added a certain number of distinctive traits indicated by the didascalia or contained in the dialogue. This is all one can say in the abstract about a character in drama.

The ambiguity of the character's status derives from the fact that a reading habit inculcated mainly at school turns the character into a substitute for a real person (hence the unfortunate metaphors used to speak of him/her as a "living being"). And so the habit is formed of searching the didascalia and the dialogue for all the details that enable the student to reconstruct the charac-ter's personality and the story of his/her life—as if the main task of dramatic literature were to create or recreate imaginary "persons."

(A) HOW TO READ/CONSTRUCT THE CHARACTER

In fact, the procedure by which the character is analyzed should be exactly the reverse: one ought not to be looking, in the dialogue particularly, for a supply of information that will allow one to decipher the character's personal-ity, but rather, given the discourse/actions attributed to the character, with all his/her indeterminacy, look for whatever may elucidate his/her discourse, in other words, the conditions that govern the character's speech. The proce-dures for reading the "character" will then not lead to the construction of a complete, autonomous person, not even a complete enunciatory subject, but to a certain number of elements which are meaningful only in relation to the dramatic action and the discourse of which the character is the enunciator.

(B) ACTANTIAL POSITION AND DISTINCTIVE TRAITS

The first investigation to be undertaken concerns the character's actantial position within the pattern of forces written into the dramatic text: What are X's actantial position and role? And as a corollary, what are the distinctive features that characterize him/her? The link between the two aspects is clear: just like the character's sex or age, his/her position as actantial subject or object is a *predicate* of X, who is also the enunciator of a discourse. In other words, character X can be studied according to

(a) his/her *actantial position* and actorial role;
(b) the *distinctive features* that characterize him/her;
(c) the *discourse* of which s/he is the enunciator.

These three modes of analysis are, naturally, linked with each other and convergent.

To analyze a character is, in the first place, to investigate his/her position in the general syntax of the text and to consider whether this position remains fixed or how it changes. Note, for example, how in *Le Cid* Chimène takes over Rodrigue's position as actantial subject, while in *Cinna*, it is rather the other way round, the male subject stealing the show from the female subject during the course of the action; or how Macbeth, during the course of the play, reassumes the position of actantial subject which his wife had temporarily usurped.

(C) THE ACTORIAL "PROCESS"

Besides his/her actantial position, the character has an actorial "role": the valet's *role* is to *serve* (*I-valet serve*), in the same way that the fundamental *process* of the lover is *to love*. Analysis will demonstrate the relation between the actantial position and the main *process* of the character, with the possibility of *conflict* between processes: for Rodrigue in *Le Cid*, conflict between the actorial role of Lover and that of Avenger; likewise for Macbeth, opposition between the role of King (process: to rule) and that of indiscriminate murderer. Successive roles, conflicts between roles, within the same character or from character to character—analyses of all these are required to construct the syntactic configuration of the text.

Futhermore, there is a direct relation between the main process of the character and the coded nature of his/her role: the more readily the character can be defined by his/her process, the more s/he appears as *coded:* a stock type, such as Harlequin in the traditional Italian comedy, is defined by a certain number of processes (as well as of fixed, distinctive traits); likewise the Matamore, or in the old Latin comedy, the Slave or the *leno* (the go-between, characterized by the fact that he "plays the go-between").

(D) DISTINCTIVE TRAITS AND COMPONENTIAL ANALYSIS

A stage character is generally not alone, and even if s/he were, s/he would still be opposed in imagination to the rest of mankind. A particularly fertile mode of analysis is the one that makes it possible to define the "stock" of characters in a dramatic text by a certain number of distinctive traits in conjunction/opposition, from the most elementary (sex or family status) to the most particular (such as belonging to a very specific social group). Even so, it is necessary to select the *relevant traits*: reflection and choice are no less necessary for this mode of analysis than they are for any other in the field of theatre. It is, for instance, not difficult to see that all the characters in *Le Misanthrope* have the same distinctive traits; they are all young, unmarried, apparently with no family ties—they have neither parents nor children—they are rich and (probably) noble (in any event, in a position to frequent the court). There is thus no opposition between Alceste and the others: they all belong to the same clan of "golden youth"; the only split within the group is between those who go to court and those who do not.

A componential analysis of *King Lear* would reveal the two characters Lear and Gloucester as doublets with practically the same distinctive traits, except that of royalty.

Concerning the choice of components, it may be remarked that, whereas in the tragedies of Corneille the element of *royalty* is essential, in Racine the decisive question is *power,* and the key opposition, working in conjunction with the secondary oppositions *loving / not loving, loved / not loved,* is *powerful / not powerful.* The important thing for the analyst is to identify the oppositions that are relevant.

One can then construct a componential table, marking the distinctive traits horizontally and the characters' names vertically. Figure 1 is a particularly simple example, that of *Bérénice.* We can see at a glance that simple as it is, this table rids us of certain false problems, in particular, having to ask ourselves if Titus is not perhaps seeking to be rid of an unwanted mistress: it is quite evident that the real problem is that of the incompatibility of passion and power.

(E) SPEECH DISTRIBUTION

1. Another necessary investigation relates to the exact quantity of speech given to a character. Surprising or illuminating results are sometimes obtained: in Racine's plays, with the sole exception of *Phèdre,* the title roles are the ones that have the fewest lines; in Molière's *Le Misanthrope,* Alceste talks as much as all the other characters put together; he is literally a *master of words.* It is consequently important to *calculate* the quantities and proportions of speech allotted to the various characters.

	loving	loved	powerful
Bérénice	+	+	−
Titus	+	+	+
Antiochus	+	−	−

Figure 1

2. Furthermore, it is interesting to show how a given character's speech-allocation is apportioned between different points in the action, and the different forms it takes: for example, Don Juan may appear not to talk very much because his speech is reserved for certain moments in the action and because he hardly deigns to reply to the other characters, but he does express himself in compact masses of discourse, generally addressed to Sganarelle.

It is thus important to examine the total distribution of speech among the characters in order to understand not only the way the character functions, but also his/her differential role in the text.

(F) A CHART OF THE PLAY

It is worth while to construct a picture of the text as a whole by drawing up a kind of chart in which the proportion of speech allotted to each character is shown in the form of differently colored rectangles of quantitatively proportionate length, one line being given to each of the sequences of medium length —indicated by the segmentation (*découpage*) of the text[4]—which make up the major sequences (acts or taleaux). In Figure 2, bands 1, 2, 3, 4 are the first four sequences of the major sequence I, and A, B, C, D are the characters. In this way one can obtain a general view not only of the relations between the characters, their degree of presence and co-presence, but also of how their speech functions; naturally the information so obtained has to be weighed in the light of what has been learned from other procedures.

F. Dramatic discourse

(A) THE DOUBLE ENUNCIATION

We shall not repeat the classical definitions of discourse here; let us simply recall the cardinal fact of writing for the theatre, which is that it involves a *double enunciation*: the enunciator of dramatic text taken as a whole is the writer; s/he is the speaking subject of all the utterances that occur in the

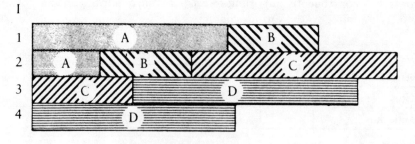

Figure 2

text (didascalia and dialogue); but s/he delegates his/her speech to other, mediate enunciators, who are the characters: when character X speaks, it is s/he who speaks, and at the same time it is the writer.

There are thus two possible modes of analyzing dramatic discourse, one of which considers the text as a whole, the enunciator of which is the writer. This mode of analysis is not restricted to the theatre: studies of Racine's "style" or the philosophical content of his work are not fundamentally different from those which could be undertaken on the works of La Fontaine. This kind of stylistic or semantic analysis of *content* bears on the text as a whole, not taking into account the distinction between dialogue and didascalia or the division of the dialogue among different speakers.

(B) THE CHARACTER AND HIS/HER ENUNCIATION

The above does not apply to the character's enunciation, which requires a *specific* analysis: an utterance placed in the mouth of a character has strictly no meaning apart from the conditions of its enunciation. This is the case of human speech in real life: if the theatre has any mimetic function it is not in regard to conditions of existence, but to conditions of speech.

The task of the analyst will be to pinpoint the conditions of enunciation of the character's discourse, remembering however, that these conditions are imaginary, *fictional*.

The conditions of enunciation are:

(a) place and time (see above);

(b) the *situation* of the character in relation to his/her world as well as in relation to other character-speakers: for example, Cinna in Corneille's play of that name is both friend and counselor to Auguste (as well as being the leader of the conspiracy plotting his death) and in love with Emilie (who is the soul of the conspiracy)—a sociological and psychological situation in relation to the other characters. Componential analysis is clearly of direct use here.

(c) the moment and more specifically the new situation created by every former part of the dialogue.

(C) ANALYSIS OF THE CHARACTER'S DISCOURSE

Two methods are available:

(a) analysis of the signifier: rhythm of the discourse, vocabulary, syntax, rhetoric of the character; for instance insults, injuries of Alcest in *Le Misanthrope*.

(b) analysis of *content*: the recurrence of themes and the frequency of keywords or expressions characteristic of a particular group or formative background (Pécheaux 1975); thus the vocabulary, turns of phrase, themes and images used by the little painter Tebaldeo in *Lorenzaccio* are characteristic of the reactionary *idéologues* of the beginning of the nineteenth century (Bonald and Joseph de Maistre).

These two types of analysis are not peculiar to the theatre, but can be illuminating when applied to a specific portion of the text, namely one which, having a character as enunciator, will necessarily enter into a relationship of likeness, difference, agreement, or conflict with parts of the text attributed to some other character.

(D) THE UNSAID *(LE NON-DIT)*

A third mode of analyzing a character's discourse is, perhaps, more important and more specific: this concerns the "unsaid" layers of the discourse (it being understood that what characterizes the unsaid is that it is said nevertheless). It involves:

(a) identifying the *implied meanings* of the discourse; that is, everything the characters understand from their mutual discourse without anything having been directly stated, and which is therefore potentially ambiguous to the reader "listening" to the discourse;

(b) identifying the *presuppositions*: a presupposition is an unformulated utterance underlying the discourse, which remains true even if the formulated utterance is denied or questioned; for example, the utterance "My brother is ill" presupposes that I do have a brother and, if my interlocutor replies "No, there's nothing the matter with him," this does not call into question the existence of my brother. Now all theatrical dialogue, all communication between characters is conditioned by a whole battery of presuppositions, some relating to historical or fictional facts (such as the Trojan War or the enmity between the Montagues and the Capulets), others depending on the referential or ideological worlds of the protagonists (for instance, the aristocrats' right to live without having to work in Chekhov's *The Cherry Orchard* or, for Shakespeare's characters, the imprescriptible majesty of kings). The presuppositions underlying the world of Marivaux's characters constitute a particularly stimulating field of investigation.

(c) analyzing, in the light of both what is actually said and its underlying presuppositions, the *discursive position* of the character-speaker (a position of power or weakness, of attack or defense, of entreaty or demonstrative assertion, etc.)

(E) SPEECH ACTS AND DIALOGUE

1. The discourse of a dramatic character, then, ceases to be ambiguous once we are aware of

(a) the context of the enunciation;

(b) the underlying presuppositions and implied meanings.

However, it is not only the sum total of a character's utterances that needs to be clarified, but also the way in which the dialogue works; and the latter depends on the interplay of forces established between the speakers, to which language is the key. We now know that the rules governing particular languages are not the only ones, and that there are also rules governing the way language functions in speech.

The basic hypothesis (which is that of the linguists of the Oxford school: Austin, Dearle, Ducrot) is that speech is *saying,* well adapted for conveying information to the interlocutor, but that speech is at the same time *doing,* since

(a) it *acts* upon others, and that is its goal;

(b) at every moment it establishes a *contract* with the interlocutor—a contract that creates, modifies, or maintains a certain relationship between the speakers. *Actions, contracts,* and *relationships* are the very basis of dramatic dialogue and it is by studying them that we can understand it.

2. *Illocution.* If we recall that any utterance can be analyzed according to three components—a *locutionary* element (the totality of the signs making up the utterance itself), an *illocutionary* element (the *force* of the utterance itself), and a *perlocutionary* element (the *effect* it has on the interlocutor)— it will readily be understood that the essential thing here is *illocutionary force.* We know that there are verbs (the performatives) which, by their nature, enact what they describe: one cannot say *I promise* without promising, *I curse* without cursing, and even *I deny* without denying. But *performativity,* that is, the power of enactment through speech, is not restricted to performative verbs. One can say that any utterance contains a performative component; this is obvious in the case of an utterance with a *conative* function (in Jakobson's terminology) such as commanding, advising, or requesting, but hardly less so in the case of assertive utterances. Let us take the example of a question: the implication is that the speaker has taken up a position in which s/he has the *right to ask a question,* the interlocutor remaining free to answer or not, that is, to accept or refuse the linguistic *contract* proposed. It can thus be understood how any speech in a dramatic text establishes, modifies, maintains, or destroys a contract between the contractors.

This mode of analysis is extremely useful and illuminating. For example, in Racine's *Britannicus,* Agrippine—stripped of her power by her son Néron —summons him and, with her first words, tries to establish a linguistic contract which will ensure her superiority: "Asseyez-vous, Néron, et prenez votre place" (Sit, Néron, and take your place). The addressee is required to submit—or to respond with a blatant refusal.

3. Procedures:

(a) The reading of the dialogue should, therefore, following the order of the characters' speeches as they appear in the text, take account of the nature of the successive speech acts as well as the linguistic contracts proposed or entered into, thus making it possible to grasp the movement of the different scenes and of the action, and to identify *micro-sequences* within the scenes in the light of the changing nature of the speech acts.

(b) It will be appropriate to show the relation between the propositional content of the utterances and the functioning of the speech acts (between the semantic and the pragmatic).

(c) The *perlocutionary* component must not be overlooked, that is to say the effect on the interlocutor and, indirectly, the anticipated effect on the audience (emotion, laughter, tears).

(d) These analyses leave out the *poetic* element, which should be the object of yet another analysis (which we cannot provide here).

2. Analysis of the performance

A. A *few preliminaries*

(a) It must not be forgotten that the *text of the dialogue* figures *as part of* the performance, in phonic form, that it is *heard* and must be taken into account in analyzing the performance, but that, for this very reason, the performance must never be thought of as the translation of a text which it contains.

(b) Whereas the text consists entirely of "digital" (linguistic) signs, the performance consists of both digital and "analogical" (non-verbal) signs.

(c) Consequently, the modes of analysis will be different: analogical signs exist in only one form and so are more difficult to analyze.

(d) An important fact: the spectator (at least in the more familiar forms of theatre) is sensitive to the fable, the story which s/he can easily grasp; the diachronic, horizontal dimension is something s/he takes for granted, and this also includes the *people in the story*. The natural inclination of the spectator will therefore be to take an interest in the story that is told and in the feelings of the characters. The task of the analyst will be to make him/her aware of the "vertical," tabular aspect of the performance. Whereas in dealing with the text, we start with the fable, obscured during reading by the details of the discourse, when it comes to the performance, we have to start with the materiality of the visual-auditive signifier (space, objects, music).

B. Space

Analysis of the performance should doubtless begin with space and the work of the scenographer.

(A) PLAYING AREA AND SPATIAL MODE

The first question concerns the relation between the space allocated to the audience and the space of the theatrical performance. We shall ignore the problem of the relation between theatrical space and the space of the world outside. But the form of the stage space is an important element, fluctuating between the Italian-style frontal form and the platform stage with its various possible configurations (rectangular or circular, centered or placed to one side). As has been shown (Ubersfeld 1982, 56–58), the Italian-style space implies a rupture with the public and lends itself to performances directed toward imitation (with representation of a fictional location), extending in imagination beyond the limits of the stage and so implying a stage space homogeneous with the real world. The platform stage on the other hand implies less importance attached to the fiction and more to the performance, the element of play and the materiality of the stage. It is interesting to study all the *mixed* or composite forms, intermediate or multiple in relation to the two main types; these mixed forms are precisely those found in contemporary performances.

(B) COORDINATES OF SPACE

The concrete stage space offers a number of alternatives, and it is important to study the choices that have been made: closed space or open space; shallow or deep; a vertical dimension or not; furnished or empty space, continuous or broken, homogeneous or subdivided, imitative or neutral, ordinary or theatricalized. All these options have precise connotations, and the extent to which they agree or conflict with what is in the text will be significant: a strange effect could be produced, for example, by performing a naturalistic play on an empty stage.

(C) REFERENCE

The audience looking at the stage does not do so naïvely: it is not devoid of culture, and the scenographer's work serves to establish contact with the culture of the audience. The stage space may, for example, make reference to the contemporary world as in the *Athalie* staged some years ago by Planchon, which evoked the Sinai War; it is almost impossible to conceive of a production that does not refer in some way to the present world of the spectator, and it is important to examine the use of space which ensures this reference.

Culture: The observer must note the various cultural references, for example the figuration (set, depth, costumes) borrowed from Paolo Ucello by Yannis Kokkos for the version of *Hamlet* staged by Vitez. Connections with the decorative arts of our time or with artists of the past are always worth noticing.

Finally, there is a third type of reference: that pertaining to theatrical forms and in particular to the types of stage used in earlier times or in other places —to the Elizabethan or kabuki stage, for example.

In all cases the observer must note not only the reference itself, but also the way it is conveyed in a particular performance, and the meaning taken on by both the reference and its manifestation on the stage.

(D) POETIC FUNCTIONING OF SPACE

In the first place, the use of stage space is a creative activity involving in particular the creation of a *stage form* which the student must not only describe, but also relate to the action (that is, to the totality of relevant indications in the text), and so demonstrate its meaning, whether simple or many-sided.

Stage space may function in a fundamentally *metonymic* way; in this case one must show not only the connection with such and such a place, but also how the metonymy works: by a selection of samples, by an accumulation of details that make it possible to identify a particular place, or by indirect allusion. A single glass can be used to represent a café (an example of synecdoche), but one could also use a counter with its whole stock of bottles: this too would be a metonymic image, but a different one.

Metaphors: Space can also be made to function in an infinitely more complex way, as a metaphor of aspects of the world or of the mind. Metaphor implies the confrontation and conjunction of different elements to form a new reality, in this case a stage reality. The analyst will have to try to show both the way different elements work together and what their metaphoric conjunction adds to the performance. For example, in a particular Kantor production, the door at the back opens onto what is at one and the same time the vestibule of memory and the railway carriage taking prisoners to the concentration camp: a completely *new* place, created by an operation which is typically poetic.

It can happen, too, that the metaphoric effect is achieved by juxtaposing several different spaces which are simultaneously present on the stage.

(E) MULTIPLE SPACES AND THEATRE WITHIN THE THEATRE

This leads to another question: Is there just one single space or is it broken up? And, if it is divided, separated into compartments, is it just temporarily made to function in that way, or is it so by "nature," so to speak, from the beginning to the end of the performance? And what, in either case, is the particular function of each sub-space? Or, on the contrary, is the space polyvalent (as it was, for example, in the Molière plays staged by Vitez)?

A particular case is that of theatre within the theatre: in certain instances (which may or may not be provided for in the dramatic text) part of the stage is occupied by an *internal* audience of performer-spectators, who—by mirroring the status of the real audience—paradoxically give what happens on the inner "mini-stage" the value of truth. Such cases may or may not be obvious and need to be picked out by the analyst.

(F) THE PLAYING AREA

Another important point, linked to the study of the actor, is the use of space for acting and the relation of space to the actor's body. It is useful to consider the stage space not only as offering an aggregate of signs to be looked at and understood, but as providing a *place for a certain number of activities* which pertain to the actor. A space may, for example, imply a specific activity for which it seems to be expressly designed and yet, at the same time, be shaped and transformed by that activity. Thus the classical drawing room of bourgeois theatre, devised for conversation, or the vaudeville bed where people will change partners, or the area left clear for fighting. But equally, a crowd of supernumeraries can transform an intimate setting into an arena.

(G) TRANSFORMATION OF SPACE

An essential procedure is to list the spatial transformations which occur during the course of the performance, linking them to the development of the action and dialogue, and noting the nature and number of the transformations deriving from:

(a) modifications in the *shape* of the space: changes of playing area, extension or reduction of the surface used, substitution of a different principal acting space, or even changes in the positioning of the audience (movement of the audience during the performance, for example in Mnouchkine's *L'Age d'or* or Engel's *Dell' Inferno*);

(b) changes of lighting which can alter not only the "atmosphere" of the stage but the shape of the playing area itself. A striking example was the simple set constructed by Yannis Kokkos for Vitez's *Hamlet,* which was modified not only by the use of curtains and an interior partition, but by a variety of lighting effects indicating not only the time of day, but also changes of scene.[5]

(c) sound effects and *music* making for a change in the stage space, by conjuring up, for instance, extra-scenic spaces or suggesting a change from indoors to outdoors (for example, the heath in *King Lear* suggested by the sound effects of a storm).

The list of transformations makes it possible to construct *spatial sequences* which can be related (noting the degree of conformity or difference) to the segmentation of the text.

C. *The stage object*

If there is any element in the performance which lends itself to semiotic analysis, it is surely the stage object, with its characteristic finiteness and semic richness, its discrete nature, and the relative ease with which it can be picked out.

(A) PROCEDURES

It is fairly simple to make:

(a) an inventory of objects present together on the stage;

(b) a list of the successive appearances of objects during the course of the performance;

(c) possibly also, a comparison with the corresponding lists derived from the text.

Here again we have elementary procedures which make research and analysis possible, but which can never be an end in themselves.

(B) ORIGIN AND NATURE OF THE OBJECTS

The next investigation will involve:
(a) a typology of the objects according to the same type of semantic classification as that used for the objects named in the text (nature/culture, etc.);
(b) noting the *origin* of the objects (including their immediate provenance): new or second-hand; purchased, borrowed, or made;
(c) a classification according to *material* (natural materials such as stone, wood, leather, wool, and silk—or synthetic and artificial materials such as plexiglass and synthetic fabrics);
(d) a sociological classification, which may or may not overlap with the previous ones.

These investigations will yield a kind of chart of the concrete world that emerges from the performance, building up a *possible world* which the spectator cannot fail to compare with the world of his own experience.

(C) FUNCTION OF THE OBJECTS

The prime function of objects is utilitarian: objects are necessary for the action and, in this sense, are purely denotative; one might expect them to be indicative of nothing but the use to which they are put, a glass for drinking, a dagger for killing. In fact, as we know, this is not the case, and the preceding investigation will show clearly that the dullest utilitarian object forms part of a meaningful semiotic whole.

The object is thus always a source of both metonymy and metaphor: metonymy of a particular physical or sociological space, metaphor by conjunction of semes, of distinctive traits pertaining to different entities. On these various points, the analysis of the object on the stage is not fundamentally different from that of the object in the text.

(D) TOWARD A SEMIOTIC ANALYSIS OF THE STAGE OBJECT

1. To start with, the object is not a sign; it becomes one on the stage through its function within the totality of signs in the performance. From the very fact that it does not serve a purpose in the real world, it becomes a *sign* of the real world.
2. Because of this, it acquires a double semiotic status. As a sign of an object in the real world (standing for an object in the world), it is an *icon* of that object, and has a more or less mimetic relationship with the object it represents (in other words, it resembles it more or less); but, as an element of the performance, it has an autonomous existence: an *aesthetic* value within the performance, and a *semantic* value in the building up of meaning in the performance.
3. By a kind of extrapolation, one may consider the stage object the visual, concrete equivalent of a *lexeme* in the dramatic text. In fact, its structure is much more complex than that of a lexeme.
4. From a more strictly semiotic point of view one can regard a stage object

as a sememe, that is, an organized body of semes (one or more semes correspond-ing to a distinctive feature). For example, a chair does not only have the distinc-tive features of any chair (a seat with backrest, etc.), but it also has the features relating to *material* (wood, metal, plastic, etc.), features of *style,* of *state* (new, used), etc. (the list is unlimited).

(E) OTHER POINTS

1. One can examine the degree of *iconicity* of the object, that is, the way in which it resembles the object for which it stands (duplicate, replica, or simply a stimulus, such as a drawing of a horse in relation to the real animal); the degree of iconicity tells us something about the mode of performance (Eco 1978).

2. One can look into the status of the object as a lexeme, that is, its relation to other object-lexemes, to form a tightly woven text; one can thus consider the object-lexemes something like *words* in the great "text" of the perform-ance: one can study their syntactical organization (functioning as predicate-object or instrument) and their rhetorical and poetic effect (see above, C, c).

3. As sememes composed of semes, objects can form part of several *sets,* which they help to constitute and organize: for example, a jar of caviar on a table forms part of the set *food* and also the set *luxury goods;* if it is a present from a rich young man to a young courtesan, it will be part of the set *objects of corruption;* it could even possibly form part of the set *Russia* or *Iran.*

4. It is useful to ask *who* (which character and also which actor) is the enunciator of the object, who picks it up, handles it, uses it; in this way we construct a paradigm of the objects linked to this or that character.

5. Finally, it is appropriate to study the *transformations* of the stage object throughout the performance; proliferation, reduction in size, appearance-disappearance-reappearance, change of color, shape, or use; wear and tear, deterioration, or replacement by another which is newer or of better quality.[6]

(F) THEATRICALITY OF THE OBJECT

One of the most interesting aspects to study is the polysemy of the object and—by the way of corollary—the different images it can present: a famous example is the ubiquitous stick and suitcase, put to all sorts of unexpected use, in the Molière plays staged by Vitez.

An important aspect of the actor's work which can be noticed is the way s/he handles the object (see below), using it, transforming it, or being trans-formed by it.

Finally, it is important to notice those objects that contain the seme *theatre* or *show* (mirror, make-up, mask, etc.) or that have been used in this or that theatrical form and are thus part of the *code* of that particular form.

If we make a synthesis of the system of objects used in a particular perform-ance, we see that it will give us a fairly complete impression of the mode of representation: "realistic" or symbolic, concrete or abstract, theatricalized or not. It is useful to show in the final resort, but only as a complement, what the use of an object is in the performance as compared with its use as envisaged in the text, not at all from the (absurd) point of view of measuring the extent to which the production is faithful to the text, but to show what solutions have been found here and now, compared to other solutions that have been previously suggested or worked out.

D. The actor

The most important and the most difficult field of analysis is the one pertaining to the actor. The most important, because on him/her depend the fable, the dialogue, the fiction, and the performance of which s/he is mediator. The most difficult, because of the arbitrary and uncertain nature of the notation available, the mobility of the details to be noted, their variability from one performance to the next, and the multiplicity of codes operating simultaneously (voice: diction, prosody, and intonation; and gesture: kinesics, proxemics, and facial mime). The different notatory systems for gesture or facial mime are all far from perfect. Furthermore, the actor's work involves a great deal of subjectivity, an element of invention that is difficult to describe in words.

A fundamental difficulty is the obsession with the character: as if all the signals transmitted by the actor had as their sole or principal purpose to signify a complex "human being," the character. Everything takes place, deceptively for the spectator, as if what is presented on stage were a reality, that of the specific character, in all his/her psychological and other richness.

(A) THE FUNCTIONS OF THE ACTOR

The essential functions of the actor are those of *enunciation* and *monstration*. S/he has to speak and show. And indeed, it is high time to reverse direction and show the actor first of all as a producer of discourse and stage actions, an enunciator and an "actor": the enunciator and "demonstrator" of complex realities, *her/himself*, but also the character, the theatre, ideas, feelings, the fiction, and the performance: s/he is the point of intersection of all these.

Analysis will first have to disentangle the different verbal and non-verbal codes and show how they interact. In regard to the actor, even more, perhaps, than in regard to other elements of the performance, the analyst must take care not to jump straight to the meaning, passing with all speed from the semiotic to the semantic, all the more so since the performance is not only read in accordance with a combination of codes, but in accordance with a combination of "actors."

Two methods should be used in succession:

(a) first an inventory of the actor's "resources," that is, the signs s/he produces;

(b) then a diachronic study of what s/he does in the performance.

The analyst will therefore have to note *how* the actor

(a) conveys a story;

(b) demonstrates the conditions of its (imaginary) enunciation;

(c) delivers a fictional discourse;

(d) demonstrates a stage performance.

What should therefore be attempted is a review of the resources brought into play in accordance with the various codes, never forgetting that the actor never shows only one thing but always at least *two,* and that s/he produces at the outset a certain number of "permanent" signs.

(B) PERMANENT SIGNS

1. Some of these pertain to the physical person of the actor: physique, facial features, vocal timbre. To this must be added the fact that s/he may have become associated with a certain acting code as a result of his/her previous performances in the theatre or cinema and that the audience may consequently recognize him/her by physical appearance.

2. The remainder are produced for a specific performance: gait, physical bearing, costume, constituting a kind of complex of signs which may convey the character s/he is playing, but which must be identified as what they are, as *signifiers.* However, it is not always easy to distinguish signs of the first group from those of the second.

(C) GESTURE

The modes of analysis of an actor's use of gesture are derived from a certain number of methods: kinesics (Jousse) which is concerned with sequences of body movements; *facial mime,* which studies facial expressions, a form of analysis which has long been the subject of attempts at codification, but without much success; and finally proxemics, initiated by T. E. Hall, which consists in the analysis of the postures assumed by people in one another's presence. We know that generally speaking, gesture

(a) is very difficult to note down;

(b) depends on the whole socio-cultural context. It is true that all gesture is potentially coded, otherwise gestures would not be noticed, but very often their coded character goes unnoticed: the gesture seems "natural," universal.

In certain far-Eastern theatrical forms (Indian theatre or the Peking Opera), the coded character of the gestures is perfectly clear to the spectator, who interprets the *mudras* (gestures of the hand in Indian theatre) as *utterances.* But even in Western theatre, gesture is somehow coded, and the relevant gestural code must be taken into account.

(D) DISCOURSE AND PARALINGUISTICS

The actor being the enunciator of the discourse, it is necessary for the analyst to note not only the permanent elements of the *paralinguistic dimension* (that is, everything that gives the utterance not solely its "signification" but its "sens"[7]), but also the mobile elements: pronunciation, rhythm, intonation, vocal intensity (to which can be added changes in permanent elements, such as timbre or accent).

The actor's use of the paralinguistic dimension thus allows him:

(a) to specify the *meaning* (sens) *of the utterance* (a "vague" utterance such as "I love you" can convey adoration or exasperation);

(b) to ensure the *perlocutionary effect* of the discourse (emotional or comic);

(c) to demonstrate the *illocutionary force* of the utterance, and show the word-act in action: commands, promises, curses, etc.

(Notice that it is the paralinguistic dimension which makes it possible to understand a theatrical performance in a foreign language, even though the paralinguistic aspects themselves are also coded.)

(E) PROCEDURE: STAGE ACTS

It will be understood that the essential procedure for noting and analyzing the work of an actor is the one that concerns *stage acts:* in each sequence there will be for each actor a number of stage acts composed of the speech acts and physical actions which s/he carries out in the course of the sequence in relation to the stage acts of the other actors.

The stage act:

(a) is a complex *text* which must be read in accordance with the various codes just mentioned;

(b) necessitates in principle, in order to be more clearly understood, a return to the written text (didascalia and discourse); even though this return is not indispensable, since it is sufficient to analyze the dialogue during the performance, it is nevertheless useful.

It is, then, a complex act for which, in the absence, at present, of any really scientific procedures, descriptions that are as accurate as possible will have to suffice, taking into account:

(a) the *paralinguistic-gestural* relation for each stage act, a relation quite complex in itself (redundancy or opposition);

(b) the relation that the stage act of a particular actor bears to the other stage acts of the same actor, and to those of other actors in the same sequence.

The fundamental question is how to determine the sequences, but the stage act, far from being determined by the sequence, in fact contributes to determining it. Examples of stage acts: King Lear tries to revive his daughter Cordelia; Hamlet kills Polonius; the emperor Auguste delivers a speech to his counselors; Hermione curses Oreste who has avenged her; in the *Don Juan* of Vitez, Don Juan caresses a dove while Elvire's brothers try to tear each other's guts out. In most simple cases, the stage act can be defined in a few words; its description will be done in accordance with the various paralinguistic and gestural codes and in relation to the utterances of the discourse; and since the description must necessarily take account of the semantic context of these utterances, it will be situated at the point of intersection of the semantic and the semiotic.

(F) STAGE ACTS AND CONSTRUCTION OF THE CHARACTER

If one takes a panoramic view of the stage acts and their sequence, one sees that it is possible to construct sets of gestural or vocal signs which will define not only the activity of a particular actor, but also the corresponding *character*. Study of the character should therefore be left until this stage of the investigation, when the actor can be seen constructing the character with the help not only of his/her permanent signs, but also of his/her successive stage acts. It can be seen that the character, provided the actor's work is well done, is understood not at the start of the analysis but at the close.

A few remarks:

1. The work of the actor and the construction of the character constitute *wholes* formed by the recurrence (Corvin 1985) of the same or similar[8] (gestural-vocal) signs and by differences progressively introduced by changes in the signs: the character develops, the actor's activity changes.

2. We do not distinguish at this stage between what pertains to the character and what to the actor, because at this point of the investigation we do not have the theoretical means to differentiate between them, except in obvious cases (the trembling of a character gripped by fear, for example); what enables the distinction to be made is comparison with the text and the fact that the signs peculiar to the actor form a recognizable whole which is also found in other performances by the same actor.

3. The presence of stage acts not prescribed by the text makes it possible to measure the *inventiveness* peculiar to a particular interpretation or production; thus the actor who played Don Juan in Vitez's production gave intermittent signs of chronic illness: coughing, fainting fits; this Don Juan was a condemned man.

4. Description does not suffice: it is indispensable to give meaning not only to a particular, isolated sign, but to semiotic wholes.

(G) DIACHRONY OF STAGE ACTS

The succession of stage acts produces not only a series of paradigmatic wholes but also a significant sequence, a syntax: it tells a story which may not be quite the same as the fable constructed by reference to the text, thus showing a *difference* between the textual fiction and the acted fiction. It may therefore yield a parallel story which will form a pair with the fictional content of the text.

E. *The production*

It is only at the end of his/her enquiry that the student can form an idea of the work done by the producer. It is therefore only *after* the preceding analyses that s/he can ask her/himself questions about this aspect. This is the opposite of the strictly "journalistic" approach, which consists of comparing two *signifieds:* the one deduced from the performance perceived as a whole, and the one which the reader has constructed for her/himself from the text.

(A) COMBINATION OF CODES

To "read" a production is to perceive how the different codes have been constituted, how the producer has constructed the *tabular* system of the performance. It is the comparison of the ways in which the codes are handled that makes it possible to understand the producer's work in regard to the continuity or rupture of codes—continuity and rupture which are naturally not total: the analyst investigates the *points of rupture* which s/he has managed to pick out in his/her preceding analyses.

(B) THE PRODUCER'S WORK

The producer carries out a double operation:
(a) s/he indicates the broad lines to be followed in the production of signs by the various practicians, and *judges* the signs which are in fact produced;
(b) s/he combines the signs to produce an *aesthetic effect* on the spectator; it is interesting to show how the producer gathers the different bodies of signs into *tableaux and movements.*

One can, since it is impossible to take into account every moment of the performance, choose a few of the sequences in order to analyze the convergence or distortion (the montage) of the different networks of signs produced by the scenographer, wardrobe master, and electrician, the final aesthetic result being the product of the choices made by the producer (of his/her *judgment*).

(C) REFERENCE TO THE REAL WORLD

From the outset the construction of signs has been directed by the producer in relation to the referent (or referents) s/he has chosen. The choice of referent involves, in particular, the choice of the historical moment and/or of reference to the present. In practical terms, however, whatever the choice, the reference is always at least double: however "archeological" it may be, the performance necessarily reflects the contemporary world, if only by the inescapable presence (even if transposed) of the prevailing fashion in clothing—a pregnant code.

Procedure: To look in the performance for the signs which refer to the *past* (which past, that of the writer or that of the fictional reference?), as well as those which refer to the *present of the performance,* noting the (more or less) subtle interplay between the references to the past and the references to the present.

(D) THE CONSTRUCTION OF MEANING (*SENS*)

It will be seen that in the final analysis, what is asked of the analyst is reflection on both the meaning *(sens)* of the performance and the mode of representation. S/he in turn must construct, with the aid of all the elements now at his/her disposal, a meta-discourse both on the meaning *(sens)* of the production (in general) and on the work done by the producer.

This constitutes a kind of conclusion to his/her research: it is only at this point that the meaning *(sens)* can appear: it cannot be sought at the level of isolatated signs (there is no "dream book" for signs) but only in a total context—it being understood, for the rest, that the meaning, the *meanings,* in their open-endedness and multiplicity

(a) cannot be compared to a hypothetical meaning of the dramatic text (a strictly meaningless comparison);

(b) are never more than *proposed meanings,* whose richness and, so to speak, "probability" depend at once on the richness of the performance and on the perseverance of the analyst and the appositeness of his/her work.

NOTES

1. A.-J. Greimas, *Sémantique structurale, Du Sens,* 'Actants, acteurs, rôles,' in *Sémiotique narrative et textuelle*; for its application to the theatre, A. Ubersfeld, *Lire le théâtre,* chap. 2.

2. Not forgetting that the textual space(s) thus defined cannot but reflect references to a world different from the original referent: in the theatre history modifies the meaning and the functioning of space (see below).

3. In fact, it is generally a matter of metonymy.

4. Segmentation which may be textually indicated or arrived at by analysis.

5. The changes in lighting produce a reviviscence of the signs emanating from the space occupied by the set, which are now perceived differently by the spectator.

6. Compare the famous example of Mother Courage's wagon (Brecht), which becomes bigger and bigger as the situation of its owner deteriorates.

7. See preceding discussion of the relation between signification and meaning *(sens)*.

8. Signs may be said to be similar when they have a majority of semes in common.

BIBLIOGRAPHY

J. L. Austin, 1970, *Quand dire c'est faire,* Paris, Seuil.

Michel Corvin, 1985, *Molière,* Lyon, Presses universitaires de Lyon.

Oswald Ducrot, 1972, *Dire et ne pas dire,* Paris, Hermann.

Umberto Eco, 1978, "Pour une reformulation du signe iconique," in *Communications,* 29, Paris, Seuil.

T. E. Hall, 1971, *La dimension cachée,* Paris, Seuil.

1973, *Le langage silencieux,* Paris, Mame.

1979, *Au-delà de la culture*, Paris, Seuil.

Marcel Jousse, 1974, *L'Anthropologie du geste*, I, Paris, 1975; *La manducation de la parole*, II, Paris.

Michel Pécheux, 1975, *Les vérités de la Palice: linguistique, sémantique, philosophie*, Paris, Maspero.

John R. Searle, 1972, *Les actes de langage*, Paris, Hermann.

Anne Ubersfeld, 1977, *Lire le théâtre*, Paris, Editions Sociales.

1981, "The space of Phèdre," in *Poetics Today*, 2, no. 3, Tel Aviv.

1982, *L'Ecole du spectateur*, Paris, Editions Sociales.

V.
How to note performance?
Reading questionnaires

Questionnaire 1

1. MATERIAL INDUCEMENT

a. How did you get acquainted with the performance: announcements, advertising, press reviews, devices, posters, season tickets, para-texts such as programs, etc.?

b. Where in the city is the theatre located? Does this localization have consequences as far as audience, spatial codes, architectural configuration, symbolic desire, relationship with social life are concerned?

c. Relationship with historicity? Are there specific references to traditions, rituals, historical styles?

2. ENTRANCE

a. Why/how did you choose this performance?

b. How/where did you get the tickets? Importance for your budget?

3. COMMUNICATION

a. Social function: production of the convention, construction of the illusion (rehearsals, activities during the interval and after the performance: dinner, meeting with the actors, etc.).

b. The performance contract: Are there cognitive or theatrical/technical presuppositions, other (emotional, libidinal, etc.) dimensions?

4. RECEPTION

a. How did you perceive/understand/interpret the performance project?

b. Has the audience been addressed as a whole? Have you been involved as an individual spectator or as a collective audience?

Questionnaire 2

1. SPACE OF STAGE PLACE

    a. Its form and the form of the theatre.
    b. Nature: mimetic, ludic/symbolic?
    c. Coordinates: closed/open, shallow/deep, vertical/horizontal, furnished/empty?
    d. Relation between theatrical space and the space of the world outside, between stage space and audience space, between playing area and extra-scenic space?
    e. Aesthetics: colors, forms, styles, cultural references?

2. OBJECTS

    a. Origin, material?
    b. Inventory: Are there many objects or only a few of them? Are they polyvalent?
    c. Utility?
    d. Rhetoric/symbolic functions?

3. THE ACTORS

    a. How many are there?
    b. Relation of actor/character, type/individualization?
    c. Appearance: age, sex, gesture, voice/diction, costume?
    d. Sociality: history, previous castings, membership of a company?

4. THE DRAMA

    a. Which genre?
    b. Which fable?
    c. Type of dialogue?
    d. Is there any improvisation? Part of the aleatory elements?

5. THE WORK OF THE DIRECTOR

    a. How does the director emphasize the fiction (fictionalization)?
    b. What kind of referential function (historical, contemporaneous, fantastic) does s/he emphasize?
    c. How does s/he segment the performance into units? Does s/he prefer a continuous or a broken construction?
    d. Are sounds (music, verbal utterances) or images predominant?

Questionnaire 3

1. GENERAL DISCUSSION OF PERFORMANCE

   a. What holds elements of performance together.
   b. Relationship between systems of staging.
   c. Coherence or incoherence.
   d. Aesthetic principles of the production.
   e. What do you find disturbing about the production? (strong moments or weak, boring moments)

2. SCENOGRAPHY

   a. Spatial forms: urban, architectural, scenic, gestural, etc.
   b. Relationship between audience space and acting space.
   c. System of colors and their connotations.
   d. Principles of organization of space
      • relationship between on-stage and off-stage
      • links between space utilized and fiction of the staged dramatic text
      • what is shown and what is implied.

3. LIGHTING SYSTEM

4. STAGE PROPERTIES: type, function, relationship to space and actors' bodies.

5. COSTUMES: how they work, relationship to actors' bodies.

6. ACTORS' PERFORMANCES

   a. Individual or conventional style of acting.
   b. Relation between actor and group.
   c. Relation between text and body, between actor and role.
   d. Quality of gestures and mime.
   e. Quality of voices.

7. FUNCTION OF MUSIC AND SOUND EFFECTS

8. PACE OF PERFORMANCE

   a. Overall pace.
   b. Pace of certain signifying systems (lighting, costumes, gestures, etc.).
   c. Steady or broken pace.

9. INTERPRETATION OF STORY-LINE IN PERFORMANCE

   a. What story is being told?

b. What kind of dramaturgical choices have been made?

c. What are ambiguities in performance, and what are points of explanation?

d. How is plot structured?

e. How is story constructed by actors and staging?

f. What is genre of dramatic text?

10. TEXT IN PERFORMANCE

a. Main features of translation.

b. What role is given to dramatic text in production?

c. Relationship between text and image.

11. AUDIENCE

a. Where does performance take place?

b. What expectations did you have for performance?

c. How did audience react?

d. Role of spectator in production of meaning.

12. HOW TO NOTATE (PHOTOGRAPH AND FILM) THIS PRODUCTION

a. How to notate performance technically.

b. Which images have you retained?

13. WHAT CANNOT BE PUT INTO SIGNS

a. What did not make sense in your interpretation of the production?

b. What was not reducible to signs and meaning (and why)?

14. a. Are there any special problems that need examining?

b. Any comments, suggestions for further categories for the question-naire and the production.

Questions about a questionnaire for theatre analysis

The main purpose of the questionnaires is to push and/or assist spectators toward writing down precise notes on a performance, several hours or days after having seen the show. Students are not instructed to take notes during a performance, but it is true that notes on technical details (particularly staging) or on acting style are very useful when writing up a full report. Seeing the show a second time is also extremely useful, even if it must be admitted that this is not a normal situation for the "average" spectator.

The questionnaires were compulsory and had to be completed as part of course assessment. Students reponded well, so far as we can judge. They were allowed absolute freedom in formulating their answers, but had to fill in those answers in the week immediately following the performance. At first this was difficult, because—in spite of our efforts to avoid technical jargon and obscure theorizing—there were some questions, particularly (8), (10c), and (13), that required acquaintance with semiology in order to be fully understood. Theoretical work is gradually introduced in classes, linked to specific questions raised by the type of performance being analyzed. This avoids a dull, unacceptable presentation of "fundamental concepts of theatre semiotics," and there are some excellent introductory handbooks in any case. This pragmatic way of looking at things is also determined by a desire to apply semiological theories to the analysis of texts and performances and to introduce semiological practice into the educational system "from the inside." There was also a certain sense of dissatisfaction with questionnaires aimed at a "normal" theatre-going public (people who are not theatre studies students), where the formulation of the questions is necessarily simplified and adapted to codes of aesthetic and ideological reception that have been distorted by the mass media and the image that the media create of *art theatre* (taking up Stanislawsky's term that Antoine Vitez is so fond of today). We felt a similar sense of mistrust toward statistical studies based on the psychology of the reception of a work of art and toward sociological investigations into the social origins and the taste of the theatre-going public. This kind of research is, of course, both valid and illuminating, but does not lead us toward the core of the problem: how meaning is produced for the spectator, starting with a dialectical theory of production and reception aesthetics (Pavis 1983).

To obtain the type of response required, the questionnaire stresses the importance of verbalizing the aesthetic experience and of considering the overall system of a production after seeing it. The spectator-witness is therefore led along a systematic, linear path following a particular order. The questions were chosen to facilitate the verbal, but also to suggest a way toward an overall perception of the performance. Finally, the details and the listing of the aesthetic problems allow the questionnaire to be used as a *checklist* (not to mention an "idiot's guide") for the study of performance, in spite of some unavoidable overlaps in formulating the answers.

Each questionnaire is based on an ideology and a point of view that is necessarily predetermined and distorts the object of analysis. Overall it could be suggested that this rests on a belief that performance can be analyzed (that is, taken apart) and that it functions as an entity, wherein all the parts join in shaping it and giving it meaning.

We will now draw the theory underlying certain points out into the limelight.

(1) *General discussion of performance*

The first group of questions invites students to sum up their impressions and to think through one or more general signifiers derived from repetition and patterning of partial signifiers. The dominant discourse has to be established, whether it is implicit or explicit in the performance.

(1a, b, c). What holds the different (diachronic) moments and the (synchronic) lines together in the stage materials used? An awareness of the fabric of performance does not hinder, indeed it implies a criticism of coherence or incoherence (1c). The construction of the staging lies in perceiving redundant elements, contradictions, dislocations in the structuring of performance.

(1d) raises the same kind of question in a non-semiological way, by inviting the spectator to order what s/he knows according to the most obvious aesthetic choices available.

(1e) is somewhat contentious and offers scope for students who feel unhappy or who have not understood the performance. Critical judgment on the production is important, but analysis of the signs is balanced against the spectator's pragmatic response.

(2)   *Scenography*
(2a)   The question of nonliterary visual aspects and situations in performance has been sufficiently emphasized for it to seem logical to begin with a description of spaces (Pavis 1980, 151–59).

(2b)   The production is a meeting point in one place between a spectator (who is constructed and constituted) and objects located in a spatial context. That meeting is experienced as a face-to-face encounter and as shared participation. Between the extreme positions of confrontation and compromise, of voyeurism and participation, the spectator-witness has to establish his/her own individual and collective relationship to the performance.

(2d) presupposes that in order to describe space the different functions have to be described, with the contradictions between what is seen and what is intuited, between what is concrete in space and what is constructed in the mind. This exercise of perception and perspicacity contributes toward shaping a perception of space in relation to its use in giving meaning to the production.

(3), (4), (5)   *Lighting system, stage properties, costumes*
In order to describe these systems adequately, their function in performance has to be discussed together with the contrasts running through them. So lighting is often set up in flat colors, white versus warm yellow tones.

Variations of intensity are linked to change of place, atmosphere, themes, and dialogues. Being able to describe the variations means, in principle, understanding the way in which they are integrated in the complete show and grasping the way in which other signifying systems are subordinated.

The same applies to properties and costumes. Rather than talking about props or decor, terms such as *object* and *scenography* are used. The traditional boundaries between the elements on stage—such as might have operated at the end of the nineteenth century, for example—are far more fluid today.

(6)   *Actors' performances* are very difficult to describe, especially without the help of videotaping or notes taken during the actual performance.

(6a) invites a consideration of playing techniques that belong to a particular historical or theatrical tradition. A consideration of several actors might show whether the director aimed for a generally similar acting style, or whether each individual actor is working in his/her own way without considering the group.

(6c) invites a consideration of the way in which the text and the voice are integrated with the actor's physical appearance, in the distance between what is said and how it is said, between utterance and uttering. This involves taking notes on the actors' use of intonation and on their attitude to the text they are delivering. Is an actor trying to make us believe that the text is the expression both of the situation and of his/her physicality or, at the opposite extreme, are those two systems being divorced from each other?

(6d) and (6e) are not asking for any value judgment on the quality of gestures, voice, or facial expression. The questions are aimed at disclosing the system and the paradigmatic and syntagmatic expression of certain units.

(6f) notes the development of these paralinguistic systems in relation to the delivery of the text. Does the discourse unfold in a continuous flow or in fits and starts? Are there any pauses, accelerations, or halts in the fragments of spoken discourse? What do the breaks mean?

(7) *Function of music and sound effects*
Without going into the separate question of the semiotics of music, points where music is used should be noted, together with the way that music is performed (on tape, produced on stage) and the effect it has on the rest of the performance.

(8) *The pace of the performance* is the result of the rhythms of the different signifying systems (8b). This notion is close to the ideas behind the staging. What remains to be established, theoretically in the particular case of the staging, is whether the pace is imposed on the text and performance by outside pressures or whether it derives from a reading of the text to be performed.

(9) *The interpretation of the story line in performance,* according to Brecht's concept of plot and the way it emerges in performance, shows that every production (where a written text exists) makes choices in telling the story. Therefore the director and the actors decide on a specific reading following a dramaturgical analysis. We the spectators have to reconstruct that dramaturgical reading (9b, 9e) and establish which ambiguities are emphasized in performance and which can be determined by a reading of text either before or after seeing it performed. A hermeneutic process of clarification or confusion (9c) characterizes these investigations of the text through its staging and then through a "reading" of the performance (cf. Pavis 1983). Through a study of the staging, the genre of dramatic text emphasized in the performance can be determined.

(10) *The text in performance* does not always have the same status. The staging can simply illustrate and exemplify what the text says by suggesting a systematic making visual of situations suggested by the text. On the other

hand, it can reduce the text to one system that does not dominate other systems, that only derives its meaning as rhythmic sound or rhetoric.

Testing the relationship between text and image (10c) consists of comparing the signifiers produced by both and establishing the way in which one system can base itself on the other, or the way in which each system has its own range of meaning.

(11)   *The audience* is the central component of reception and certain mechanisms of reception can be analyzed. By determining the identity and status of the theatrical institution in which the performance takes place, a whole range of traditions, techniques, and selection processes which influence both acting and audience responses, can be explained. It is also important to take into account the very different set of expectations of each member of the audience and the way in which these expectations are met during the performance (11b, 11c). (11d) aims at discovering whether the production is the result of collaborative work, compelling the spectator to provide information that is only implied and to read metaphors and metonymies of the disposition of the stage, to construct the plot line, etc.

(12)   Moving from one metalanguage (the written commentary) to another (photography and film), the point of view changes radically. The student is invited to select from the performance those moments which lend themselves to an understanding of the aims. A starting point for considering the methods of emphasizing a given production involves the possibility of adapting those methods to the type of performance being examined. The images that we retain (12b) are not necessarily the most important ones in the performance, but they make up the framework of our perception and of what we remember and therefore exert enormous influence on how we structure the plot (9d) and the production of meaning (11d).

(13)   In spite of all attempts to transpose performance into signs, there may be certain elements left out. Don't worry about this! Those elements that cannot be described in semiotic terms may well be used by the director in an indefinable way (in relation to the rest of the production) or may not be used in a reading of the general discourse of performance. The latter case does not imply that the reading is faulty or incomplete, merely that it is based on other lines. This can result in a reconsideration of the relevance and usefulness of a reading of signs.

(14)   This is a metaquestion about the questionnaire itself, a final possibility of noting what has escaped the previous lines of inquiry. It also suggests that the order and type of questions is not fixed in any way. It is also possible that the questionnaire leads to a way of seeing things that is almost as rigid as the theatre event—if questions are repeated too often and in the same way. Not to be taken without proper medical advice, in fact!

In reality (and students seem to tend most frequently toward this conclusion), this process of questioning has the aim of eliciting a productive response—one that is both varied and fruitful—to the performance, and of establishing a dialogue between the production as it "happens" and the production that the spectator sees. This is the only avenue left open, since nothing final can ever be said about a performance, or said in any definitive way. Does this mark an end to the "death" of semiotics and make its results and methods relative? This is yet another question that must remain without an answer.

BIBLIOGRAPHY

Patrice Pavis, 1983, "Production et réception au théâtre: la concrétisation du texte dramatique et spectaculaire," *Revue des sciences humaines,* 60, no. 189 (Jan.-Mar.).

1987, *Dictionnaire du théâtre: Termes et concepts de l'analyse théâtrale,* Paris, Editions Messidot.

VI.
From analysis to production
Dramaturgy

The various semiotic approaches to theatre have as their objective a highly refined, object-sensitive analysis. As long as dramatic texts or theatre productions are being analyzed, the results are rather convincing. The success of this analytical competence commends its application within a performance's genesis. Given such a task, the dramaturg, i.e., the intellectual at work within the theatre responsible for the repertoire, would truly earn the title of "production dramaturg." This is the title existing especially in Germany but whose content still wants a precise determination.

But errors are inevitable in this practice. For it is conceivable that the dramaturg beforehand, and probably collaborating with the director, elaborates so rigid a set of stage directions that rehearsals turn into mechanized obeisance to the prescribed model. In this way, an entirely new text will have been offered up as substitution for the original, and an unbearable hierarchy (re)imposed, which, if nothing else, completely detracts from the actors' creativity.

This is the manner in which many rehearsals still proceed, with or without models constructed from competent textual analysis. If, however, we determine that there is no single definitive solution but, on the contrary, that there are several possible interpretations and, likewise, that there is no one path into a recognition of the meaning of the text but, in fact, analytical as well as intuitive in-roads, then this approach to the dramatic text could be applied in the collective creation process. The dramaturg's analytical competence hereby assumes its essential place alongside that of the scenographer's image-reading and the actors' psychic and physical competence in true interplay with the text—which the rehearsal, ultimately, should be.

The rehearsal does of course have its boundaries. For the public to be able to relate to something, selection must occur, which means that in the final instance an interpretation of the totality must be rendered. Perhaps this is where the dramaturg acquires his/her most vital function by merit of the fact that in close interaction with the director s/he is at leisure to analyze and look upon the heterogeneous product. Capable, to a certain degree, of furnishing a pre-performance analysis (including suggestions for cuts, changes in scenic order, etc.). It is here we register the need of concrete semiotic competence for its ability to win a perspective over the comprehensive body of signs, to distance itself from the process, which, until the concluding phases, was directed on an open playfield and by endless patience in trying out even the most oblique proposals. Proposals which often in the end prove to have penetrated the performance's essential core. At least when the performance is successful: this is virtually the seal of quality for the creative process.

In the following we are going to concentrate on processes which have resulted in productions which the public and critics (some of them at least) found interesting, even ingenious. Starting with a few accounts of the rehearsals, we will attempt reconstruction of the creative process giving up these yields. The experiences are very diverse and any true conclusion would therefore also be incorrect. It should be possible along the way, however, to explicate some "rules of play" which are reproducible under other conditions.

I have selected three productions: Peter Brook's staging of *A Midsummer Night's Dream,* the Royal Shakespeare Company's dramatization of *Nicholas Nickleby,* and, finally, Pina Bausch's dance theatre production, *Tanzabend 2.*

1. Peter Brook's *A Midsummer Night's Dream*

I have not seen the performance; my knowledge of it stems from commentary and criticism. The general impression: this production was epoch-making. It is of such character that it has not been possible to stage Shakespeare since then without direct or indirect reference to it. After premiering in 1970, it toured for two years world-wide, with 535 productions in thirty-six cities. The result—the finished product—had an impact, but it was not until ten years later that the author David Selbourne published his diary-like record of the rehearsals in *The Making of* A Midsummer Night's Dream: *An Eye-Witness Account of Peter Brook's Production from First Rehearsal to First Night* (London, 1982).

Selbourne took part in all but a few of the rehearsals. Like a fly on the wall he saw, heard, and recorded partly the general occurrences, partly the things going on within himself. Therefore the prose form is virtually intact, and there is nothing reminiscent of an after-rationalization.

It is the encounter of the literary being with the theatre being, and Selbourne nurtures traditional expectations of the rehearsals. Where he anticipated a lengthy interpretational process marked by intellectual interaction, he instead encounters Brook's attempt, inspired by Artaud and Grotowski, to involve the actors in a totally contrary process:

An actor asks, "Is the whole play a dream?"
And Brooks replies: "Don't impose a theory on it. Don't take it literally either. Discover the truth of it." (9)

Brook discourages his actors from intellectualizing, from trying to derive meaning from a prior reading of the piece. Instead of exchanging proposals for different readings of Shakespeare's text, each single actor, albeit under Brook's guidance, *discovers* the play, finds individual pathways to what Brook refers to as *the truth*. "The rhythms of the play," he asserts, "are deeper than the words Shakespeare is able to use" (11).

Brook's method is one of infinite improvisation and, at first glance, one without a perspective. Selbourne says it is degrading to the actors and, in comparison to the text's precision and potential, unrefined. Brook progresses from the body, grimace, rhythm, play, emotional exercise, acrobatics, clowning, through the many layers of the Shakespearian convention of theatrical play, in realizing a version of *A Midsummer Night's Dream* which in the actuality of 1970 England is "true":

> Yet in the effort to find what Brook, a few days ago, had called a style which is "not-acting," where things happen as if "by themselves," was there not a tacit admission of the primacy of the written? Is he not saying to the actors that, with the sufficient sensitivity, a form can be found where the written word, in its simplest and truest evocation, will arouse and sustain all meaning? (165)

Brook has been recognized after this for his essence-searching versions of classics such as Chekhov's *The Cherry Orchard* and Bizet's *Carmen*. *A Midsummer Night's Dream* was perhaps his first success in this new tendency to shun theatrical mechanics. In one solitary white room he focuses completely on the actors' presence together with the few props (the trapeze!). Shakespeare's text went unaltered during the rehearsal, and a complete analysis of it was not at any point presented. Nor did Brook stick to it during rehearsals, and here and there misquoted. His work is non-literary but is guided by a crucial respect for the text as a totality. It is physical and technical, he moves outside and in, he is primarily anti-intellectual but, nonetheless, prompted by the unifying intention of a director:

> Nevertheless, much more important—as I have come to see during these unregarded, but carefully observed, weeks of rehearsal—is the overall consistency of Brook's pronouncements. (Even the contradictions and obscurities are consistent.) His intention, as well as his principles of interpretation and guidance, have held steady, and without undue repetition, from the outset. (139)

In the pictures from the production, the simplicity and physicality are the striking elements. The white room, the loud costume, the spectacular yet refined props. A "minimal" Shakespeare. A Shakespeare for actors and noninitiates. A shocking, straightforward story which even the schoolchildren before whom Brook performed a week prior to the premier could understand.

Up to now I have stressed something which those with a literary bent may find surprising because of the very physical approach. But this method seems bizarre to many in the theatre world as well.

It seems that each new rehearsal day begins at square one in a never-ending pursuit of the moment in which it is experienced that something "true" occurs:

> "There is something consistent," Brook (once more in his stride) continues, "which happens when a play bursts into life. Watch for this," he tells them. "After such a moment has passed, it can't be switched on again, or mechanically pieced together. What has to be recalled are the meanings which come out of a burst of life. This becomes the starting point for new invention." (101)

Brook bombards his actors relentlessly with new darts in order to call forth the so-called "free intuition" which emanates *"from a group sharing the same direction"* (101). Still, it would be an illusion to imagine the process without the "direction" of one particular person: this is, as in other institutional theatre, a well-prepared process. The roles are assigned. The scenography prepared. The fundamental idea hence prescribed. It was necessary for the director to preconceive an approximate result of the interaction with the actors. The vision of the collectivity's final product is necessarily conceived from one person's ideas about and specific experiences within theatre. So, though the scenario is individual, it cannot be completely overlooked that the production mode is largely in the hands of the process. Without a willing group of actors participating in the "excesses" in almost blind faith to the director, a boundary-breaking project is unrealizable:

> I have learned from these rehearsals that with one theatrical false step—which can sometimes not be traced, or even discovered—love can become sentiment, pathos bathos, and the tragic comic. Moreover, just as yesterday's jokes are today unfunny (especially if endlessly repeated), so today's realism is artifice tomorrow. In the theatre, relativity is all. (273)

All that remains, frustrating as it is, is the after-effect of a chemical process whose basic elements are identifiable but whose point of catalyzation can be surmised only very summarily. Thus the analytical point of view would deem this experience very negative: we can be certain that a detailed analysis of the text has not been *presented* to the actors. On the other hand, we cannot exclude the possibility of Brook having a conceptual background for his preparatory work with, for example, the scenography. It is more probable, however, that Brook, rather than by conceptualization, has been inspired by a formal idea which implies an ideological choice—simplification: strip the story down, recount it as if the company itself had thought of it.

Even if Brook knew of Jan Kott's penetrating criticism of the romantic version of *A Midsummer Night's Dream*, Kott's analysis is only one of the inspiration's sources. Judging from Selbourne's book, the genesis of the production is essentially evoked in the rehearsals' initiation-like mode of individual and collective recognition of epic and dramatic means and effects.

2. Royal Shakespeare Company's *Nicholas Nickleby*

Peter Brook's production of *A Midsummer Night's Dream* was set down within traditional frames: a text, a director, an assignment of roles to pre-chosen actors. Whereas for the RSC, once the decision was made to dramatize Charles Dickens's 900-page novel *Nicholas Nickleby*, it was wholly an institutional experiment.

Its novelty was the absence of a text. It was the author David Edgar's job to produce one during the production process. It was novel, too, that the actors could sign themselves up for the project. The approximately fifty who did so were not guaranteed a part. And it was innovative that the group, as a whole, had to produce the story, the play, the scenography—in a word, the scenic totality. They were, of course, under the direction of the directors—Trevor Nunn, John Caird, and Leon Rubin, the first having chief responsibility—and in professional collaboration with scenographers, componists, ateliers, but still more as a whole than as a part of an institution.

Preparation took eight months and resulted in one of the company's greatest successes. It lasted two days and played successfully in London and New York and, thanks to the televised version produced in conjunction with Channel 4 (in itself a masterpiece of televised theatre) reached a broad public. Leon Rubin describes the entire process in *The Nicholas Nickleby Story: The Making of the Historic Royal Shakespeare Company Production* (London, 1981). This gives a detailed and nuanced analysis of the creation process; it presents the analytical, practical, and organizational creativity which through a unified engagement came up with a scheme to solve a task fundamentally different from that usually tackled by the company.

The directors had already devised a work schedule which would structure the first phase into three subject areas: (1) the socio-historical, (2) the narrative, (3) the characters. The idea was that everyone started by gathering material on Dickens and his period. One should figure out a way to relate his or her part of the story to the rest of the company. Finally, everyone was to begin developing and performing individual characterizations from the novel.

The result was naturally all-encompassing. At once varied and chaotic. Rich in perspective and confusing. Engaging and frustrating. Some actors loved this new-found freedom; others experienced it as being enrolled in a seminar. Yet, in retrospect, it can all the same be stated that these tasks greatly influenced the final product. A great deal of the secondary literature contributed to the re-evaluation of the textual material. The involvement in the epic moment led to a decision early on not to discard the novel's less "dramatic" sections, which led to the production's special trademark: the unifying of the epic and the dramatic and the discovery, among other things, of original solutions to the various difficulties of addressing the public in the epic sequences.

Another important consequence of the reciprocal retelling of the novel chapter-by-chapter was the discovery that Dickens's text had "left some ends untied." That certain points in the action were obscure. That, in a word, the text suffered from a certain "blindness." In this context, the question of Ralph Nickleby's economic situation was central, which was one theme (the so-called financial plot), which David Edgar had already pointed to as being central to the performance. Combined with the filmed versions which the company also saw during the first working weeks—versions in which the script and the stage direction had tried to create cohesion precisely where this was impossible without secondary sources and re-editing—it can be concluded that the community effort had already contributed concrete and improved lines of direction.

One of the exercises of the greatest import for the production's "style" was the attempt by various groups at producing one of the novel's most fundamental descriptive sequences, that of Nicholas Nickleby's arrival by coach to London. This tableau's corporeal mimical evocation, where the characters can change 180 degrees, from persons of rank into proletarians, was a decisive sign that the grandiose scenes should be dealt with by the actors and only a minimum of stage props. So that, in the final production, the departure from London by coach occurs as a wonder of imaginative theatricality with a vehicle loaded down with suitcases, a commenting and acting choir, together with a cacophony of live sound provided by the characters on stage.

Certainly there were lengthy discussions during the long rehearsal, processes whose subject matter included the theoretical foundation of the actors in this process, which Nunn believed could gain more inspiration from Brecht than Stanislavsky; the general impression of this production is always that the great leaps, the moments where new insights are won and where everyone could perceive the excitement, occurred in connection with the concrete tests—bodily or verbal. Take, for example, the scene in Dotheboys Hall where the boys are to introduce themselves while they eat: Whom should they address? Of what consequence will it be for the addressing of the public in general?

> In David Edgar's production of the scene, the boys spoke as though they were speaking both to Mrs. Squeers and to the audience. Narrative technique was thus internal and external at the same time. In the discussion that followed, many thought the boys should speak directly, in an alienated manner. But when this was eventually tried, the scene lost its impact. We discovered in this way that narrative need not necessarily intrude and could, indeed, enhance the dramatic impact of the story. (56)

The processual barriers are overstepped through an open attitude toward testing all possibilities practically. Even the company's traditional Christmas luncheon right in the middle of a difficult period was a stimulus for their interaction. The theatre's process of artistic realization is as much intellectual as it is physical and emotional, which is hardly surprising to practicing theatre people, but perhaps can be for an academic dramaturg who must watch as his/her finely cogitated textual concepts are reduced to a few scarcely usable details in a production traveling headlong toward new horizons which were inconceivable from his/her initial assumptions. But this problem will be returned to. It could, however, be important to emphasize that *Nicholas Nickleby's* success—its theatrical originality, in short, the uniting of such different theatrical forms as represented by Meyerhold, Brecht, and the English music-hall tradition in an epic-dramatic combination, which were essentially intelligent and entertaining, historical and actual—cannot be imagined without a harmonious pre-planned collective process. A comparison to other productions, which are based upon the dramatization of other genres, emphasizes the particularly tough odds which were faced. One generally does not find such correct solutions to immanent narrative problems. Far more seldom do we find examples of simultaneously preserving the mood of the original (which is an essential part of the public's horizon) and justifying the translation into another medium. An example of a playwright's attempt at tackling the problem, indeed, almost of combatting an obsession, is given in Peter Weiss's two dramatizations of Kafka's *The Trial*. In the first version from the early 1970s, he reduces the story to a specific socio-political fable and thereby loses the mood of the novel completely. In the second version, which was to be his last work, he captures its nightmarish character to a far higher degree, but is unable to tell the story and thereby fails dramaturgically.

3. Pina Bausch's *Tanzabend 2*

Here the scenic space is a classical bourgeois sitting room done completely in white. The windows facing "the elements"—water, desert, forest—are closed. The final image is established. Eight dancers, paired in sitting position, holding each other by the hand, forming a sort of rhythmical snake, move themselves diagonally across the stage to the droning version of Ravel's "La Valse." In the background, a man in a smoking jacket tries frenetically to mount an immense pair of stilts. The music and movement are intensified. Just like the navigators of "Le Radeau de la Méduse" by Géricault, the group of waltzers desperately press themselves up against the walls. The man on the stilts abandons his preoccupation and dons an angelic robe, continuing to paint himself white so that in the end he becomes almost one with the backdrop against which he leans. Is the performance over? Mechthild Grossman, who has figured as a kind of narrator-commentator throughout the performance, now enters through a door in the wall at the back of the stage. The lights are dimmed to twilight. A blue neon light shines through the open door. Grossman appears in a dream of a 1950ish evening dress. Blue with a long train and a V-cut that amply reveals her breasts. With a cigarette in her mouth she holds in her long gloves a pitch-fork which she uses to pitch hay into a wheelbarrow. The music has changed. It is now Hugo Wolf's lament "Everything ends that is commenced," "We too were joyful and sorrowing beings just as you," "Now we are lifeless here." Thus setting the general mood on stage. This characteristic ephemeral quality, where the narrator begins calmly to stack coal briquets after having changed from business gloves into work gloves, and where the man in the background is now one with the wall, is suddenly interrupted by the rest of the company who, with an exaggerated friendliness in mimic and gesture, dance in to German-American swing music with the refrain "two cigarettes in the dark." The house lights come on. The macabre atmosphere is preserved as background for the finale's euphoric pulse. Is the play over? The company steadily surges back and forth in a seemingly infinite overture. Some spectators begin clapping sporadically. "Everything ends, but when?" Then after three and a half hours of sense bombardment with this duality, it ends: the biting sorrow (the piece starts with "Come right in, my husband is at war") and the manic joy. The final image is the piece's most successful. The most cohesive in its tension-packed disharmonies. It sums up the performance without harmonizing its contradictoriness.

The piece with the meaningless title has until then had the character of independent stories, each of which could have been experienced as more or less expressive, more or less narrative, more or less successful. The production's specific characteristic is the dissolution into individual recitations, not the flow of collective dance or the company's interplay in general. The recollection of the performance consists of moments, favorite stories, "pearls on a string" —a rough structure, which can be captured in a cross-network of general semantic units such as happy/unhappy, man/woman, oppression/liberation, culture/nature.

The scenography's duality expressed through the classical and bourgeois whiteness and the almost film-like presence of natural elements, is a manifest and constant framework of the piece's functional conditions. The characters proceed from this highly civilized space, to a more "original" space where, for example, a melodramatic murder of passion can occur or where one of the piece's maniacally active men can mellow out in the uterine warmth of the aquarium—complete with flippers!

The man-woman relation is a given thematic constant in the activity of the dance theatre. In this performance this is evidenced in Pina Bausch's costuming: an exaggerated femininity, in the 1950 dresses' low-cut tops and the macho smoking jackets. In the course of the production, this is often with a role-liberating effect changed into a transvestic utopian man-dance in high-heels, ballroom dresses revealing the hair on their chest. But also retained, for example, in the image of "girl" socialization, depicted materially and generally, as one of the female dancers "pairs" a whole sackful of shoes in chronologic order, creating a point of identification for the public, for a personal, sex-specific upbringing.

The production consists of an infinite number of small stories essentially of the same character. Their point of conjunction even in the individual sequences is ambiguity: women who, seemingly independent, dancing bare-footed to rapturous music in a free space, have a pot tied to their leg, and cannot escape. A woman who, tied to the man's leg, is used in loving embrace as a nutcracker! Totally instrumentalized she is lifted up and down so that her behind can efficiently crack the edibles for the guests. Harmony, but sheer disgust among the audience, whose senses on the whole are provoked all through the evening's morass of concurrent disharmonies and harmonies. Or by the violent tension between hysteria and serenity. Major and minor—concretely in the purposely forced cuts between the different musical genres—classic/modern, serious/popular, uplifting/depressing.

During the past ten years with her company in Wuppertal, Pina Bausch has earned a place in the international dance theatre scene. Her dance productions are both dance and theatre. In contrast to, first and foremost, Modern Dance from USA, her body-theatre is a mixture of language and body, and its expression an exponent of the narrative dance form, an epic-dramatic contrast to Modern Dance's corporeal abstraction. The consequences of Pina Bausch's influence of modern theatre are naturally quite extensive in a period when a trust in linguistic expression is questionable and the influence from visual media on theatre's practioners and public is so overwhelming. It can therefore be interesting to see how a production such as *Tanzabend 2* was created. The rehearsal is described in the program. Rehearsals were started with cues to the company, who should illustrate, practice, dramatize their respective memories and associations. Here are some of them:

> When does one say shit? / Sentences where God appears / To use the word mother / To do something with the belly / The small joy / Teaching somebody / Someone has gone astray / Children's play / Itch / Throw your own head away / Tuck the thumb / A Punch-like movement / Something in a waltz step / Swing / Exaggerated movement / The optimist / Cause-effect / To strike with body part / To motivate oneself / Something has gone to pieces / To snap one's fingers at someone / Something pleasing on the chest / Flee like Punch / To hide like Punch / To howl and be miserable like Punch / To search for help like Punch / A sign of rain / Something troubling / To stretch a body part to the extreme

Certain lines and basic themes obviously stick out in this seemingly impenetrable list of cue-words. These are the structures and topics which are re-identifiable in the final production and which are described above. Nonetheless, it seems nearly magical that this menagerie of imperatives could end in a three and a half hour long performance in just two months.

The dramatist Renate Klett, who had worked with another choreographer,

Reinhold Hoffman, on the latter's production *Föhn* for Bremer Tanztheater, in a very interesting article (in the weekly *Die Zeit*, 18–26 April 1985) described the genesis of this dance performance. Renate Klett, who is normally a theatre dramaturg asserts that, whereas a theatre production functions under prerequisites of a script- and role-distribution, a choreographed production begins simply by creating the piece. As we have seen with *Nicholas Nickleby* and what has gradually emerged from more and more improvised theatre, this is far from the usual case but still a veritable norm. Renate Klett describes the methodology:

> The content generates from the form, from the tension between whisper/ shout, horizontal/vertical, solo/tutti, from the relation between movement and space, movement and music, action and counter-action. It is a choreographic way of thinking foreign to me; it orients through pictures instead of through meaning, only with other means. The stories which are told in this way are secretive and complicated, interchanging in their ambiguity. The dramaturgic principle is intuitive, not intellectual. It endows the piece with the confusing fascination which causes the spectator to believe for a moment that he understands everything, and then, in the next, nothing.

As we have seen in connection with Brook, Nunn, and Bausch, it is perhaps too clear a distinction which Klett makes between intellectual and intuitive dramaturgy. The distinction, rather, lies on the one hand between the analytic and calculatory reduction and the interests in cause and effect, indeed, the exactitude of an ordered system, and, on the other, the multifarious facets of the creative production—intellectual, intuitive, but determined most of all by practice—the search for ambiguity, openness, contrasts.

Conclusion

Literary science, indeed, science in general, conceives of itself as being analytical. In its everyday pedagogical praxis it in fact functions excellently. It seems scientifically legitimate to analyze a text—for example, a dramatic text—by establishing a differentiated, detailed, and well-supported account of the text's semantic potential, and the one most correct and most convincing for the respective interpreter; however, every determination of this sort implies the death of a creative process which presupposes an active and imaginative participation of actors, dancers, musicians, scenographers, etc.

If one super-imposes an analysis a priori, the process withers on the spot. And if the dramaturg—or a highly analytically gifted director—attempts to intervene too early in the process, to summarize, in a word to *reduce,* then no new insight is brought forth, and new possibilities of new meanings are nullified. The role of the dramaturg is therefore different from that of the external critic. He must not completely immobilize the intellect but apply his analysis non-reductively, attempting to analyze actively, opening instead of stiffening, explosively and not implosively. Like Roland Barthes in *La Chambre claire,* as an intellectual who has the entire intellectual apparatus at hand, but who uses it in an excessive, inquisitively inspired self-transcendence.

Of course there are very concrete tasks which a dramaturg can carry out during a rehearsal. His/her knowledge of the text's complexity will be utilizable for the director and the actor, in that many rehearsals are wrongly preoccupied with a genuine striving toward coherence and harmony, where the text—perhaps conceived of as an artistic whole—upon closer examination proves to be riddled with ambiguity and blind spots. Inasmuch as the texts appear dramatic and coherent, or fragmentary and contradictory, the work of the dramaturg is a new one each time. From his/her analytical assumptions about the text, the dramaturg is challenged to go into (but also against) the text in order to make room first for the participants' and thereafter the public's imagination. Hermeneutics' most important task as active participant in the creative process lies in an opening of the hermetic texts (e.g., Ibsen) and in a non-simplified selection of the non-streamlined texts (e.g., Shakespeare). This fundamental conception of the text as a score ought to have a liberating effect for the analytically schooled dramaturg, who with this sort of background will have ample opportunity to introduce apparently academic but relevant points into the process.

VII.
Three applications

1. Minetti[1]
Directed by Philippe Sireuil

The Varia, a former music-hall theatre built in 1904 and subsequently used as a palais de dance and then a garage, has now become a center for innovative and experimental Belgian theatre. It is situated in a working-class district without any particular cultural pretensions and began by offering a working space to young practitioners (Sireuil, Delval, Dezoteux) before they gained official endorsement from the funding authorities. It now receives a direct subsidy from the government and provides a home for a range of performance practices that developed particularly during the 1970s. That period saw the flowering of a multi-focused exploration: so-called poor theatre, experiments inspired by the work of Grotowski, attracting a wide range of different spectator groups, and modifying the physical arrangement of the space to suit the needs of each production. In March 1985, Philippe Sireuil put on *Minetti (Portrait of an Artist as an Old Man)*, adapted from the play by Thomas Bernhard. The dramaturgical project was intended in the first place as part of a collective exploration of the work of the actor:

> Following the superproduction of Brecht's *In the Jungle of the City* in which the set and staging had been very well received, the actors complained of the frustration they had felt, the physical constraints under which they had worked prevented them, they felt, from freely expressing themselves. For me this problem had to be considered in connection with the often discussed question of the role of director in my kind of theatre where the dominance of the director can make him a kind of automaton or god figure. I felt the need to pay hommage to the actors, to their work and to the risks it involves.

The Bernhard play is furthermore well known as a kind of thesis play which raises the whole question of the nature of art and role of the artist. A heavily loaded choice of play on the part of a young playwright who has on more than one occasion found himself in conflict with the cultural authorities of his country. The play is doubly significant in that it concerns the theatre itself and presents the anguish of an actor who is still alive. As Minetti himself says in his monologue: "You have to be cruel to the audience. And if they aren't prepared to acknowledge the cruelty of life or of their own situation, then you just have to play against them, even to the extent of provoking anger. But this doesn't mean that you can't also, without hypocritically pandering to them, stir them erotically so that they will finally feel the emotion you are communicating."

Both the choice of performance venue and the statements made by Sireuil indicate an intention to reinvent theatre space and desire and thus to marginalize the production in relation to the mainstream theatre of the day. The very idea of a production centered on a single actor confirms this impression for those familiar with the development to date of the work of Sireuil, hitherto preoccupied with highly visual effects and boldly experimenting even with opera production (*Katia Kabanova* at the Brussels Opera).

1. The lead-in

Advertising for the show placed great emphasis on its innovative features and the commitment to certain aesthetic premises. The posters brought out this somewhat didactic approach, but it was above all the press commentaries which stressed the almost narcissistic "readability" of the production: "Sireuil produces Minetti: theatre is an act of faith."[2] A simple dual isotopy was apparent in the organization of space and place: in accordance with normal practice at The Varia, all the identifying markers were concerned exclusively with the production in question. On the outside of the theatre only the poster advertising the show indicated the function of the building. Once inside the door, the spectator was immediately plunged into the world of the play: pleasant interior design, display of books by Bernhard, photographs of the production, newspaper articles and reviews. The overall effect was somewhat precarious, and this was reinforced by the actual conditions of reception: once seated in the theatre the spectator was encouraged to wrap himself in a rug which had been carefully rolled up and placed under the seat. The lack of heating in the theatre was one factor, but the blankets served also as a means of drawing attention to the discomfort and the difficulties involved in obtaining modern luxuries. A further important function was as a sign of a more fundamental ambiguity: throughout the show the spectators were encouraged to immerse themselves in a universe where the real and the theatrical were continually merged. Outside The Varia, an empty street, freezing temperatures; inside, an arctic chill, a simulated snowstorm produced by gusts of wind, a set representing a deserted beach, and the rugs in which the shivering spectators wrapped themselves.

2. The performance contract

The entrance into the theatre building served as a reminder of the functionalism of the space: neutrality, initial chill evoking the mobile historicity of the piece, the operative elements constituting a kind of montage made up of the blocking of the action, the acting, the signs of the text, objects, sounds, and spectators. The major compositional features can be defined as follows:

a) The proximity/distance relationship: as soon as he came on stage, Minetti gave out his visiting cards to members of the audience, thus involving them in the fictional story; furthermore, for all entrances and exits the actors utilized the same doorways used by the audience to gain access to the auditorium. The communal use of the space effectively blurred the distinction between participants in the theatrical event.

b) The use of spatial relations, in particular horizontal and vertical dimensions: the first three scenes took place in front of a red curtain, and the staging of the epilogue opened up new spaces; three different spatial planes were activated one after the other by Minetti after he had torn the curtains which initially barred access to them:

• on the fore stage, a narrow strip traversed laterally by the masked characters (first space)

• an intermediate space occupied by Minetti and his interlocutors (second space)

• finally, beyond the curtain, a wider space (third space) to which Minetti allowed himself to be drawn, and where he discoverd depth (the vertical dimension).

c) The exploitation of distance and crossed perspectives; each of the three spaces mentioned above involves specific modes of movement: lateral (1), crisscross (2) (the movement of Minetti around his suit case), transversal (3). A triple focalization on the surface, on mobility, and on depth to which correspond three symbolic spatializations: illusion of life, moment of conscious awareness, the profound truth of theatricality and death; this development was marked by the passage from exteriority to interiority.

3. Space and design

Bernhard's didascalia are virtually ignored in this production: the play is supposed to take place in a large hotel in Ostend, and numerous visual features evoked in the play text (antique English lift, reception desk, bar) here reflect the performance locale (former garage) and are symbolic of a threadbare past which is conjured up during the time of the performance. Access to the stage necessarily involves passing through the foyer, that intermediary space where the audience, awaiting the beginning of the show, regains its narcissistic function. The intrusion of this into the performance proper is activated by signals and symbols: it is from the foyer that the classical music is played which heralds the opening of the performance; this remains audible even in the auditorium (a transition from real to theatrical space), and it incites the audience to begin to move. They must first pass through a closed chamber strewn with dead leaves, the dream connotations of this space are reinforced by the walls made of canvas painted with skyscapes, and they then pass through double doors leading into the auditorium. The somatic experience enshrined in this itinerary is repeated on stage during the production: lighting effects, sound of footsteps, music and set elements open the way and establish the necessary convention.

4. The set and staging

If, at first sight, the acting space and audience space (five tiers of twenty seats in each row) seem to be clearly separate, a number of signs function to blur the distinction: the same half-light dimly illuminates the total space, the set glimpsed in the shadows seems itself to represent an auditorium, the stage within the stage is closed by a red curtain, the prompt box is visible, the same red dominates the on-stage theatre design (seats, carpet) and the auditorium proper. A dwarf servant is silently folding up a pile of towels on the stage within the stage as the audience files in: for the actors as for the spectators the beginning of the performance is indistinct, the demarcation between performance and reality has become blurred.

Sireuil's purpose is double: the virtual absence of stage design and the transfer of responsibility to the audience. As he explained it himself: "I wanted to work in a less restricting space, with a less intrusive set. I tried to take personal responsibility for the space (doing without a set designer) and to create an ambiguous space in which the distinction between reality and fiction would be unclear."

The resulting staging was composed of absent references, made up of a variety of quotations: pictural (Ensor), literary (Shakespeare), mythological (Acteon and *King Lear*). Mimesis functioned primarily through the imagination. The unbridled fantasy that prevailed at the end marked the final lurch into the world of play; the progressive elimination of reminders of everyday reality (despite a proliferation of these at the figurative level in both set and sound effects) revealed the function of the actor in the construction of space: it was through the blocking of the actors' movements and positions that the spatial relationships were endowed with both metaphorical and topographical power.

5. Lighting

A uniform filtered light united both stage and auditorium in a single statement. Focalization was nevertheless made possible by a row of spotlights along the front of the stage at floor level, a follow spot was focused on Minetti and two quartz halogens were recessed in the large up-stage auditorium: the three spaces thus each had their particular form of lighting.

6. The soundscape

Sound effects were used to reinforce the set. Variations in volume (the classical music, the gusts of wind), a more or less obsessive use of music (records

Minetti by Thomas Bernhard at Théâtre Varia,
mise en scène by Philippe Sireuil, 1985.
Photos by Daniele Pierre, © Théâtre Varia

of songs by Piaf, Delille, the Rolling Stones) rhythmically punctuated the imaginary level of the play and provided the narrative tempo.

7. The use of objects

Objects were sparsely used and both in their sparsity and in their readability accentuated their rhetorical and symbolic function. Sometimes references from the text (e.g., the mask of Ensor, referred to in the story, was shown only at the end of the epilogue at the death/deliverance of Minetti); more often they functioned rather to evoke mood and atmosphere through their general connotations. A typology of props would reveal the following functions:

• assistance in creation of fictional word—the dishes brought on by the hotel waiter and used as rhythmical chronological markers in the development of the story

• symbols of theatricality—masks, red velvet couch, the head of the stag—king in the epilogue

• props having an actantial function, which serve the characters as partners in discourse (Minetti's suitcase and its contents—metaphor of the journey; the "proof" of his past)

• period images—the old-fashioned gramophone, the piano, wireless, slot machine, beach cabin.

8. Costume

Minetti's costume was a veritable metaphor of the text: his hat connoted Britishness, his umbrella indicated mobility, discarded clothes underscored his deterioration; most of the other costumes were social stereotypes, apart from that of the dwarf which, changing scene by scene, finally presented the figure of Harlequin leading Minetti toward his death.

9. Acting style

Performance was the center of the discourse. Nothing surprising about this in a play about an actor, one who is moreover simultaneously a fictional character and a reference to one of Germany's finest postwar actors. The words of Minetti, through the monologue, constitute the vocal pivot of the play. The performer utilized an internalized tone of controlled mastery, and the words shine out, as in the original German, without there being any true exchanges between characters. The girl and the intoxicated older woman, images of departure and arrival, fixed signs representing purity and madness, seemed to function as witnesses rather than active participants. It is paradoxically language itself that is at the heart of this lack of communication, and this was emphasized by the way certain phrases were left in German or even translated into Dutch.

10. The production

The production was not obviously referential but focused the spectator's attention on the work of the imagination. "We were not trying to present old age so much as the traces it leaves behind, to make this felt without overemphasizing it. The major problem posed by the play for the main actor is that he has to perform certain scenes very close to the spectators without any physical barrier or separation between them. His task is to ensure that it is all there but without drawing attention to it, making it all seem perfectly natural."

The dominance of the aural component in no way diminished the power of the visual; on the contrary, the continual alternation of focus on linear and tabular perceptions was an indication of the homogeneity of all the means used to translate the imaginary world of this production. The objective was that of a continuous flow rhythmically structured by numerous techniques, accentuated by the lack of an interval. The production plunged the spectator into a world of illusion and never released its hold.

It should moreover be noted that in this production Sireuil reversed the normal spaces of The Varia: the stage was situated in the auditorium and vice versa. This permutation developed the reflection on illusion that is central to the work, and the end of the show provided a reminder of one of the key statements of the code: the curtains of the false theatre, constantly present at the back of the hotel lobby, opened onto a deserted beach flanked by two rows of beach cabins. Minetti, led by the servant/dwarf, now disguised as a clown, crossed over to the other side, to be swallowed up irrevocably in the world of pretence. A reminder of Lear being guided through the storm by the Fool.

11. *The story*

Bernhard's play presents an allegorical fable whose constant references to King Lear are apparent from the initial dedication of the work. The basic story line is as follows: Minetti, an elderly retired actor who has not performed for thirty years, thrown out of Lübeck due to his refusal to perform the classical repertoire, has been living in exile in Dikensbühl and comes to Ostend to sign a contract with the manager of the Flensburg theatre. It is New Year's Eve. The action takes place in a run-down hotel that has seen better days. Minetti is at last going to play Lear and finally to assume the role he has hitherto been able to play only to his reflection in the mirror. While he waits (fruitlessly) for the theatre manager to arrive, he delivers a long monologue: the old man sums up his life, tirelessly repeating the same story to uninterested characters, usually silent, disintegrating, locked in their own solitude. Only the girl listens with a degree of attention to Minetti's soliloquy. As he becomes increasingly aware of his isolation, he moves slowly toward suicide while the noise of the storm outside becomes more and more piercing.

The monologue is also a reflection on duplicity: the separation between actor and character is progressively diminished as Minetti's madness consists precisely in taking over the identity of his double; the ambiguous connections between Bernhard's drama and Shakespeare's tragedy go further: Minetti dies wearing Lear's mask and on three occasions recites passages from Shakespeare.

It is necessary to stress the extent to which Sireuil's adaptation transformed the dramatic text provided by Bernhard. The ideological content of the original story, for example, reflections on the oppression of the actor in Nazi Germany, was here resituated in a democratic society and took on metaphysical connotations. Similarly, the inversion of Minetti's madness which echoes that of Lear, had a more general applicability: it was as if the death of Minetti revealed the extent to which madness affects all the "others," those who refuse to hear, even those who led Minetti to his death.

The text was very precisely segmented into three scenes and an epilogue.

Activating the play's content depends crucially on the work of the actor's voice, in particular that of the actor Minetti.

Sireuil's dramaturgical concept functioned on two levels: the "visible" and the "readable":

a) a sequential rhetoric working essentially through visual elements—immediately accessible symbols (water, torn curtain); the discovery of new spaces marked each stage in the process with the hope of a rebirth, a return to the beginning.

b) the dynamic presentation of recurring figures which have to be read globally rather than within each sequence: variations in volume impose a rhythm on the monologue, the presence of the dwarf, obsessive signs, redundant signifiers which constitute the markers of the actor's imaginary.

The central focus of the play is the voice of the main character which not only relates the story through the monologue but physically places everything. Words set up veritable spatial matrices in the text, and movement within the space, facial expression, gesture illustrate the inner conflict presented through the story.

12. The production's mode of readability.

The spectator was struck by the way the production harmoniously integrated redundant elements. The pleasure for the spectator was in the perception of allusions which open up reflection on the essence of theatricality and on its readable and visible modes. The dramaturgical signs were simultaneously clear and connotative to the point of raising through the fictional story the whole problematic of the reverberations of the actual place, of theatricality, of the nature of performance pleasure, and of the fate of the artist. A drama of destruction and salvation by theatre, performed in a proliferating space which emerges from historical time in order to construct a continuous present in which all periods merge.

The spectator is forced by the production to ponder this wealth of contradictions—one of the reasons, incidentally, that the actors mix with the audience after the show.

The production constitutes a mockery of totalizing visual stage art and stylized symbolic theatre; it presents a fleeting glimpse of a reading that the actors themselves encourage each spectator to continue outside the theatre.

NOTES

1. *Minetti (Portrait of the Artist as an Old Man)* by Thomas Bernhard was published by L'Arche, Paris, 1977. The production described was put on at the Varia Theatre in Brussels in 1985.
French translation by Claude Porcell
Director: Philippe Sireuil
Cast: François Beukelaers, Amid Chakir, Florence Madec, Janine Patrick, Louis Vervoort
Assistant director: Alexis Poelmans
Set and costume design: Philippe Sireuil
Masks: Jean-Claude De Bemels
Makeup: Jean-Pierre Finotto
2. *Le Soir* (7 March 1985).

2. *The Seagull*
Directed by Antoine Vitez[1]

1. *Global stage discourse*

A) ALL THE FEATURES OF THE PERFORMANCE ARE "HELD TOGETHER". . .

first and mainly by the identification of the *plot*—term that Vitez prefers to *fable* (Vitez and Copferman 1981, 168)—the possibility of following Treplev's fate and the clarity of the story that is told, even though the exact motivations of characters (in Chekhov's drama as well as in this production) are never given once for all. On the stage, the performance's features are also held together by their spatial relationship in which, as in a fresco or a collage, each feature remains autonomous, without integration and reduction to a whole. Features signify by their contiguity, by their coexistence, and by echoes they create among them.

B) THE RELATIONSHIP BETWEEN STAGE SYSTEMS . . .

is based therefore both on convergence and coexistence. For example, gestures and intonations produce the same effect of artificiality and falseness as does the cardboard scenography. Yet the various stage systems never cancel each other in a common signified, in an ultimate meaning.

C) COHERENCE OR INCOHERENCE

The staging purposefully seeks a certain incoherence as it refuses to homogenize and bring together the stage systems, and notably stresses the falseness of acting, situations, locations. It takes care not to let the various signifieds converge on a common signified and thus create a general atmosphere that would eventually give a meaning to each separate feature.

The reading of the text lays no claims to an internal dramatic coherence, all the more because Vitez does not carry out, and in fact rejects, a dramatic analysis that would clarify the meaning of characters and their projects (cf. (9)). Better, the staging almost always reveals contradictions and diverging aims of the characters; it does not reserve the part of the hero for anyone and never fully condemns an action. In that sense, the staging testifies to an extreme coherence in the choice of its forms of incoherence.

D) AESTHETIC PRINCIPLES OF STAGING

The staging not only deliberately applies incoherence as a sign that conflicts are not solved, it also avoids creating a Slavic or Russian atmosphere where silences, cultural allusions, a slow rhythm, or the historical nature of costumes and sets could play a dominant part. The historical and geographical aspects of Chekhov's play are suggested by only a few marks (women's costumes referring to Parisian fashion very popular in Russia at that time, the cap and boots of the intendant Chamraiev). The translation also erases overly explicit allusions to Russia. The presence of the samovar, inevitable in all Chekhov's stagings, is played down: it is barely visible in the interior scene in Act III, appearing like an ironic quotation from the type of symbolic staging that Vitez is rejecting, though with some filial feeling of respect. As a result, giving up the easy clichés of the "Russian soul," Vitez runs the risk of focusing on universal values and abstract human relations. The *non-dit* ("that which is not stated")—which, in the so-called "atmosphere" staging, supplies the performance with an aura of mystery and potential discourse that calls for clarification—is replaced by Vitez with a *trop-dit* ("that which is overstated"), notably in the acting (cf. (6)). The actors indeed seem to express and show so many feelings, attitudes, and contradictory behaviors that they greatly increase their expressivity, but one can no longer see what the results of this interaction are.

The staging's aesthetics brings together two principles usually considered to be mutually exclusive: the principle of realist representation (the sets represent trees, a house, a garden) and the principle of abstraction (sets and acting openly display their falseness, theatricality, and artificiality). The staging thus creates a new relation between realism and symbolism, representational reality and theatricality, illusion and denial, proximity and remoteness. One could claim that Vitez here frames a polemic with Stanislavsky, supports the position of Meyerhold and his theatre based on conventions, and grants the convention a similar basic function as a necessary feature of realism (see also (10b)).[2]

E) WHAT DISTURBS YOU IN THIS STAGING? WHAT ARE ITS STRONG, WEAK, OR BORING FEATURES?

The disturbing feature is precisely that uncertainty concerning the fictional status of the performance: the uneasy acknowledgment that the staging, simultaneously and successively, aims at a realist illusion and/or at an illustration of artificiality and falseness. This uncertainty is very uncomfortable because the spectator is not accustomed to changing his/her system of perception in the middle of a performance. The staging oscillates between the principle of minimal atmospheric realism (and hence illusion) and the principle of maximal deconstruction of discourses, gestures, and characters. It is not always easy to understand why these changes occur at one moment rather than at another. In other terms, acting and sets/props retain many features of realism and psychology that, because of the stress on conventions, appear to be false or mishandled; and, inversely, deconstruction processes are insufficiently developed and systematized, and thus fail to prevent spectators from getting the impression of a reconstructed psychology and atmosphere that want to be credible. Vitez refuses to solve conflicts, to judge verbal debates; he is trying to convey on the stage the absence both of totality and center that marks Chekhov's writings (Pavis 1985). He transcends the choice between a naturalist and symbolist staging. The question is whether spectators can also resist the temptation to redirect the staging so it would point only to one direction, i.e., whether they can stand to be torn apart between psychological identification and the deconstruction of lines and intonations. The malaise caused by the staging is no doubt generated by moments when the deconstruction is too overt, for example by Treplev's or Arkadina's crises, Trigorin's "manifestoes," the impact of Macha's breaking voice, or Chamraiev's "transgressions." The spectator attributes to a dramatic analysis those considerable divergences between gestures and intonations of actors (cf. (6e)) that, in fact, are not contrasted at all in terms of any total conscious pattern.

2. Scenography

A) SPATIAL FORMS: URBAN, ARCHITECTURAL, AND STAGE SPACES, MOVEMENTS, ETC.

The T.N.P. is located on the Trocadero Square in one of the vast buildings that housed the League of Nations, then NATO, but it occupies its basement, cut in the Chaillot hill, "a territory that Jean Vilar separated from the XVIth *arrondissement*" (Vitez 1981, 11). On the Trocadero esplanade, sort of a roof over this bunker-theatre, children skateboard and rollerskate, unaware that they are playing on the roof of a Parisian intellectual center. Appointed director of the Chaillot National Theatre in 1981, Vitez wanted to draw to it a larger number of theatre spectators: "Beyond the professional public, beyond the four thousand people who make up the public of a show that fails, there are at Chaillot eight thousand people who form the public of a semi-*succès d'estime*. Then, without any transition, thirty thousand people show up: these are spectators who materialize when a performance really works well" (Vitez and Copferman 1981, 21) (cf. (11a)).

The space of the auditorium has been rebuilt. The public faces the stage, sitting in rows of comfortable seats set along a rather steep and long gradient. The stage has a frontal line, in the Italian style. The stage space is very large, especially very long. The huge stage floor is structured in depth by parallel panels that represent, on each side, rows of trees with the sky behind them. The back of the stage represents a vast sky with a setting sun and the façade of Sorin's house. In Act II, the house seems to have moved forward, and in Act III the façade and the terrace are now quite close to the footlights. Act IV takes place inside the house which is perceived from the reverse perspective as a very vast space with a relatively short depth. In order to animate the large stage space, especially during the first two acts, actors must move around quite a bit and draw harmonious patterns on the floor. The space properly devoted to movements—changes in positions, mutual spatial relations, and voice projections—fulfills thus an indispensable function in filling out the oversized architectural space of the stage.

The sequence of set arrangements, which first brings nearer and then inverts the vision of the central panel representing the house's façade, suggests a zoom-like movement, a close-up view of the inner existence of characters, an investigation of a life's itinerary, a spatial and temporal trap where Treplev is boxed in.

The space of the lake is not shown on the stage. One realizes that it corresponds exactly to the space of the public since the stage of Treplev's little theatre is tied to the footlights, like a landing stage, and that actors look at the public when they are located on the lake or on the small theatre. This space inversion (that Meyerhold might have called a *paradoxical composition*) turns the Chaillot public into a double voyeur who simultaneously watches the actors/characters, their observation of the little theatre, and the latter's backstage (where Nina gets dressed up and ready for the show). This strategy calls for a response from the contemporary public, associated in this manner with the symbolic and enigmatic function of the lake, the space of all desires and all questioning. The relation to Chekhov's stage directions and the dramatic space he suggests is marked by a move back to representation, but a representation of reality (house, trees, garden) that displays its own falseness and theatricality, as if Vitez were once again presenting a polemic with Stanislavsky, who "in theatre, hated the 'theatre,' i.e., the theatrical effects, the cardboard sets and the cardboard feelings" (Vitez and Copferman 1981, 44). The lines of trees on both sides of the stage, the house seen at a distance, everything indeed is made out of cardboard which, by contrast, increases the reality of actors and the rare objects. The only truly spatial effect occurs after Treplev's gunshots, when the wall panel is lifted and the lake becomes visible in the back. Most of the time, actors take charge of a large part of the huge stage space. Sometimes they generate a focusing effect, for example when they move to the foreground of the stage, as Macha and Dorn do at the end of the first act.

c) RELATION BETWEEN AUDIENCE AND PERFORMANCE SPACES

A heavy red velvet curtain separates the stage from the audience. It moves sideways with a very theatrical noise of its rings, breaking up the illusion of a realistic *tableau* (an illusion has just been created) and thus, especially at the end of an act, bringing back to mind the great days of theatricality—the very naïve theatricality enjoyed by the people, notably in plays staged for the young—and achieving an ironic contrast with the sophistication of the *tableau*.

d) SYSTEM OF COLORS AND THEIR CONNOTATIONS

The dominant colors of trees (brown, black) and the façade (grey spots), their texture (pointillist effect, impression of a rather dirty "camouflage," without clear lines or hues), their relative immobility, all that creates a rather gloomy and heavy climate that the representation of spaces and objects never dissolves into a definite feeling or atmosphere. Scenography operates like a mainly inflexible constraint, precluding both aesthetic plays on colors and the already mentioned naturalist realism; no relation to Strehler's style (as in his use of white in *The Cherry Orchard*) or to Stanislavsky's (as in his evocation of a heavy and homogeneous *milieu* by the means of real objects). This scenography refers to a dominant prosaic reality, which however cannot sustain its illusion and rapidly reveals its falseness and theatricality. Thus it does not even try to give the impression that the stage is extending backstage into a space beyond the stage, that the stage is an integral part of a larger reality. Everything that is shown on the stage always conceals something else, without ever providing a definite explanation for the motivations, gestures, and symbols (the lake, the seagull). That which is concealed is buried at the "heart" of the stage, "behind" that which is shown; it is never made definitely explicit.

3. Lighting system

Light constitutes a capital feature of the story because the action takes place at sundown (Act I), at noon (Act II), in daylight (Act III), in the evening (Act IV). The movement of the sun, visible in the sky shown in the back of the stage by the means of a *cyclorama*, marks the passage of time. Variations in light intensity illuminate the stage "from within," providing each *tableau* with a specific emotional coloring: contrasted, romantic, and agitated in Act I, sensual in Act II, humdrum and tragic in Act III, uncanny and morbid in Act IV. Light projects color on the tree panels and the ground; it fully animates a scenography that would not come alive without its constant variations.

4. Objects: nature, function, relation to space and body

Objects seem to be lost in the vast stage space. They basically are furniture pieces: wicker chairs (I) and a bench, croquet hoops (II), a table set for breakfast, suitcases (III), a sofa-bed, a card table, a desk (IV). In a rather vague and artificial scenographic environment, they appear to be the only real objects inserted in the story; however, the scenography does not attempt to turn them into realistic manifestations of a specific society. Instead, they are used as acting aids, supporting the actors' performance; their function rarely deviates from their normal utilitarian role. They always retain their realistic character, even when they serve, concurrently, as potential starting points for a symbolic reading (see, for example, the seagull which looks like a stuffed bird, the theatre stage that is imperfectly tied to the lake shore, the croquet game that Nina transforms into a slalom and a balancing act, etc.). In the last act, the space surrounding Treplev is considerably reduced; the routine of his existence inside the house during the bad season is heavily weighing upon him but, in contrast with Nina, he doesn't manage to "escape through the glass door." At the beginning of the play, the curtain of Treplev's little theatre is lowered all the way down, inverting the perspective (one sees Nina backstage, getting ready to get on the stage). The curtain operates like a wall that prevents any communication between Nina and Treplev, located on the opposite sides of this artificial separation.

5. *Costumes: system and relation to body*

Among all the stage systems displayed in this performance, the costume system best relates the play to a historical context that could be nineteenth-century Russia. But Yannis Kokkos, the costume designer, limits references to Russian fashion to only a few details: the cap and boots of the intendant Chamraiev. The "handyman" Iakov does not wear the traditional muzhik blouse. Women—Arkadina, Paulina, Macha—wear long, elegant black or white dresses. Their colors are clear and contrasted on the basis of a rather simple characterization: a simple white dress for Nina (I, II) and a dressier black dress for Arkadina. Dorn wears a white jacket that refers to him as an "experienced man," the vacationer and the traveler rather than the physician.

6. *Performance of actors*

A) INDIVIDUALIZED OR TYPE ACTING

Whereas most actors are "Vitez actors"—his former students or actors accustomed to acting for him—there is no typical Vitez acting style, or rather that style consists of preserving the individual contribution of each actor (personal accent, delivery, gestures, image), exploiting the performers' diversity and heterogeneity. Each one has a special personality that is stressed in acting: the quavering intonations and always-changing body tension of Edith Scob (Arkadina), the deep and solemn voice of Jean-Marie Winling (Medvedenko) and Bruno Sermonne (Dorn), the ability to move from dejection to over-excitement displayed by Jean-Yves Dubois (Treplev) and Dominique Reymond (Nina).

B) RELATION BETWEEN AN ACTOR AND THE GROUP

The space is animated by the entire set of actors. No attempts are made to highlight one or several characters, but a classical technique is used to focus on those who hold the central role in the dialogue. Movements follow the logic of the situation, without stressing any moves, pauses, or glances.

C) TEXT/BODY

The staging does not try to suggest any identity between a character, his/her psychology, voice, or gestures; it stresses contrasting impressions created by these features. Arkadina, who looks fragile and unsure of herself, has exceptionally violent intonations and outcries. When he comforts Macha at the end of Act I, Dorn uses an intonation which has little reference to the situation at hand. His words "O enchanted lake! But what can I do my child? What? What?" are said with a detachment that might seem to imply a separation between the words and the body. It does not simply express the coldness, intellectual outlook, and remoteness of the character; it also demonstrates that Vitez wants to carry out a rhetorical deconstruction of Chekhov's text, to lay bare its mechanism, to underline its alarming strangeness.

The actor remains at a distance from the role, but without a real effect of alienation. Several actors have character roles and almost seem miscast: Jean-Claude Jay plays an ill and irritable old man, Bruno Sermonne seems too young and vigorous for his part as a fifty-five year old physician. Both adjust to their roles (through makeup and body posture), but only up to a point: they do not attempt to have the audience believe in the age or situation of their characters.

D) GESTURES, MIMICRY, MAKEUP

Body, voice, and text are never harmonized or synchronized. No one seems to have a well-integrated personality, except perhaps for Dorn, despite his resigned slowness. One sees how time wears out the body (Macha deteriorates from act to act, but so does Arkadina, who, trying to show that she remains young, gets winded when she dances and has trouble reading without glasses). The malaise of bodies is general and shown with comical effects (Sorin who gesticulates in his wheelchair) or through allusions (missed "meeting" of Nina and Trigorin: Nina waits for a kiss that does not materialize, etc.). In contrast, the friendship betwen Treplev and his uncle is conveyed through a complicity of bodies: they are both similarly juvenile, awkward, clumsy. They understand each other through the language of eyes and attitudes.

Makeup is used mainly to age the actors. In the last act, one barely recognizes Treplev because his face has become extremely pale and his hair has been plastered down. The daily gloom, routine, and sacrifices have marked his face. He offers the only example of a very marked use of makeup.

7. Function of music, noise, and silence

Music has a diegetic function, i.e., it originates and is produced on the stage, and is justified by the situation. In Act IV, Treplev is heard playing the piano in another room: it is a melancholy tune that corresponds to the twilight atmosphere and the character's despair. The insistent noise of the wind howling from the lake doubles the feeling of strangeness—a disturbing strangeness (the Freudian *Unheimlich*) and weirdness that seem to invade the living room and the house; but this effect is limited to only a few occurrences and never lasts very long.

Dialogue relies a lot on silences, when what is not said weighs heavily on the characters (Nina and Treplev in Act II, Nina and Trigorin at the end of

Act III). Each character has a different attitude toward the "holes" in the dialogue: Nina uses them as means of expression, Arkadina cannot stand them, Trigorin does not dare to "hear" them or to create them; he fills them with small talk ("It's nice here"). After Treplev's gunshots in the wings, the play ends with a general silence underlined by the futile moves of lotto tokens that clatter on their board and pace the time as if nothing happened, as if everything would keep going on. Music, noise, and silence form the stage systems that best contribute to the creation of an atmosphere of anxiety and mystery, even though other stage signs, such as intonation and gestures, immediately undermine that atmosphere and disturb its droning harmony.

8. *Rhythm of the performance*

A) RHYTHM OF SOME SEMIOTIC SYSTEMS

B) GLOBAL RHYTHM

Some systems follow a regular and continuous rhythm: for instance, variations in light intensity. Others, such as gestures or intonations, testify to broken rhythms and extreme variations. As a result, systems are markedly desynchronized, so that no global rhythm can unify their totality (cf. above, (1c)).

Vitez intended neither to slow down the delivery of lines, which would have produced a melodramatic and depressing tonality, nor to speed up their tempo, which would have evoked a tragi-comical vaudeville. He created a series of strong and weak measures, successive accelerations and braking. Thus when Nina gives the locket to Trigorin (Act III), she recites her text at full speed: "I beg you to accept . . .". And Treplev moves without transition from tenderness to physical aggression when dealing with Arkadina. (For the problem of rhythm in performances of Chekhov's plays, see Pavis 1985).

9. *How this staging reads the fable*

A) WHAT STORY IS TOLD?

It is not easy to reduce a staging to a linear story, i.e., to a series of actions that bring about a single result. It is impossible to read this performance as the story of Treplev's tragedy or Nina's agony, etc. Besides, Vitez is known to be suspicious of the fable: "I rejected this notion of the fable such as it had been used, and now I have come to question the very word itself. I no longer feel like fighting against the fable, but I wonder what that term really means. I am afraid the use of this type of vocabulary (which Brecht took over from Aristotle) traps us in an obligation to move in one or another direction" (1981, 168). This *Seagull* can neither be summed up nor reduced to a story, a thesis, a moral.

B) WHAT DRAMATIC CHOICES?

The rejection of the fable as the organizing narrative structure explains the absence of choices intended to clarify actions and motivations of characters. However, some "choices" have been made concerning major temperamental determinations of characters: Arkadina's hysteria, Treplev's cyclothymia, etc.

C) WHAT ARE THE STORY'S AMBIGUITIES, WHAT CLARIFICATIONS ARE OFFERED BY THE STAGING?

The ambiguity of motivations, action, and conclusion of the play is as high as possible. Yet a certain number of major temperamental and unconscious figures seem to be outlined: Oedipal relation between Treplev and his mother, connection between neurosis and Hamlet's situation (cf "The Daily Life and Mythical Figures" in Pavis 1985).

Obviously, the determination not to conclude does not preclude some rather clear judgments: Treplev is portrayed like a temperamental juvenile who is both ridiculous and moving. Nina delivers the monologue in a very modern style, almost like words in a contemporary musical piece. Vitez thus seems to offer the parody of "fashionable" art. In fact, it is almost a self-parody, when related to the way in which he used to direct his actors in the cast.

D) E) NOT APPLICABLE: cf (9a)

F) WHAT GENRE OF DRAMATIC TEXT DOES THIS STAGING IMPLY?

A black comedy rather than a vaudeville or a melodrama. The method of "ups and downs," alternating comic and tragic moments, slow and fervent moods, deviated and hidden meanings, makes it difficult to propose a homogeneous reading that would follow the canon of a particular genre. The staging suggests several possible readings, favoring none of them and thus promoting a generic uncertainty.

10. The text in the staging

A) ASPECTS OF THE TRANSLATION

Vitez had the special opportunity of himself translating the text from Russian (a language he knows well, having studied it and translated from it for many years) and then doing its staging. Thus, at the time he is producing the French text, he is already thinking like a director, very much aware of the syntactical rhythm, stylistic impacts of words grouped together, modern tonalities of certain expressions ("Please!"). His translation does not try to simplify the Russian text or to remove its ambiguities, neither does it attempt to convey a "Russian flavor" by a forced reproduction of diminutive forms or verbal plays on names. However, it retains the Russian terms for units of measure (*poud, kopeck, verste*). Its rhythmic scheme is close to the scheme in the original version, readily sacrificing the "gallicization" of the text in order to preserve the rhythmic rhetoric of the Russian text.

B) HOW DOES THE STAGING TREAT THE DRAMATIC TEXT?

The text and the fable (at least as it can be reconstituted) are not "forced" or "buried" by an omnipotent visual display (as Chéreau does, for example). They remain autonomous and are marked by a "visualization" of their phonic, rhythmic, and rhetorical architecture. Voice, intonation, and silence remain the essential "structuring" systems. The text is raised to the level of high tension in its verbal expression: it is, so to speak, "forced up to its breaking point," as if it were to generate a *super-text* instead of a *sub-text à la* Stanislavsky. Here again Vitez clearly shows his preference for Meyerhold over Stanislavsky. He writes about the latter: "His [Stanislavsky's] famous 'system,' which owes much to the encounter between Moscow's Art Theatre and Chekhov, is based on the notion that the actor's work is as creative as that of the composer and the designer, and that the actor must discover, beneath the author's text, an underground flow, the *sub-text,* which accounts for the real life of the character and is only imperfectly manifested in the text" (1981, 45). Nothing testifies to that *sub-text* in the staging of *The Seagull.* Vitez is much more concerned with artificiality and conventions, as Meyerhold was in his time: "We must acknowledge that everything in theatre is a convention, that everything is conventional in theatre. Using the same word to refer to a good and a bad convention is quite legitimate. The bad convention is the routine convention, which has become *normal* to the point that it is no longer noticed. Meyerhold tells us that we must reject that type of convention; instead, he promotes a conscious convention: the artist must create his own convention, i.e., his own system of signs, and have the public understand it" (1981, 45).

C) RELATION BETWEEN TEXT AND IMAGE

Since the image plays no role, or very seldom, as a support or justification of the staging, the actor must continuously draw everything from his/her own resources. S/he is thrown into an empty space, difficult to fill out, and uncomfortable. The actor's voice, gestures, and movements insert him/her within the performance.

11.

A) WITHIN WHAT THEATRE INSTITUTION DOES THIS STAGING TAKE PLACE?

The *Théâtre National de Chaillot* is an institution that, under Vitez, has become known as a quality theatre for the people, an institution that manages, in a critical spirit, the theatrical heritage. This theatre is subsidized by the

State, and it appeals to a middle-class public, students, professors, and theatre enthusiasts who follow all Vitez productions (cf. (2a)).

B) WHAT DID YOU EXPECT FROM THIS PERFORMANCE?

Finding out how Vitez would reconcile Chekhov's atmosphere and his own experimental style, sober, hyper-intellectual, overall distrustful of sensuality. This contradiction has been neither resolved nor highlighted in the staging. Hence the impression of a middle-of-the-road direction, contradictory and disappointing on all accounts. Such is both the wager of that staging and the source of its predictable failure, for its aesthetic principles are totally antithetical.

C) HOW DID THE PUBLIC REACT?

The show was followed with sustained attention. No overwhelming enthusiasm, no romantic emotion. It seemed that people were saying: "This is not the usual Chekhov, nor the experimental Vitez."

The spectator's role is fundamental because s/he must complete and reconstitute the puzzle of diverging signs, rhythms out of phase, unresolved contradictions, and closely follow all sorts of echoes, intonations, and quotes during the entire performance. Vitez states that he is "against the illusion that one first has an idea and then illustrates it" (1981, 173). He sees no point in trying to reorder the signs on the basis of a preconceived idea (i.e., conceived before the contribution of actors). Instead of reordering perceptions on the basis of a fable or a dramatic analysis, one should read the performance in its horizontal pattern, its "mythological system": "One must not rely on the fable but show the succession of associations of ideas developed by the director and the team of actors. Staging is the assembly or collage of all these associations of ideas one after another. This collage leads to a global reading of the work, even to a meaning, but a global meaning. This meaning seemed to me to be richer than the meaning one gets by simply following the fable" (1981, 2).

12. How to record (or photograph or film) this performance

A) HOW TO RECORD

It might be important to record the movements of actors, to keep track of their movements as traces of stage business. And, at the same time, one ought to mark "explosions" of gestures and intonations, as well as their ties to the text and to the global system of such marks. There is an original relation between continuity and breaks that occurs only in this type of staging and hence should be grasped.

A film (for example the video made by the T.N.C. for its archives[3]) does not convey successfully the impact of an empty stage or abrupt changes. Also lost, almost totally, are the strange locations of Arkadina's and Nina's voices, the original relation between the concrete scenography and the abstract acting, especially evidenced by intonations and movements.

B) WHAT IMAGES DO YOU REMEMBER?

• The cyclorama and the setting sun;
• The landing stage in the foreground;
• The line of trees against the sky;
• The house wall panel that is lifted up and discloses the view of the lake already used in the staging of *The Heron.*

13. What cannot be semiotized

A) B) WHAT PART OF YOUR READING OF THE STAGING IS LEFT WITHOUT A MEANING? WHAT CANNOT BE REDUCED TO SIGNS AND MEANING?

Some outbursts of gestures or voices occur at unexpected times. As a general rule, any sequence of signs seems to have at least a fragmentary meaning, an incomplete meaning, as if the staging rejected a final and unequivocal solution. "Theatre," Vitez states, "is the very flow of time. It is inequality, imperfection, incompletion" (1981, 139).

14.

A) WHAT SPECIAL PROBLEMS SHOULD BE EXAMINED?

• How the translator and director are working together.
• How this staging differs from Vitez's first staging of *The Seagull*
• What is Vitez's place in the tradition of interpretations of Chekhov?
How this staging relates to his other stagings, notably that of *Hamlet* (produced the previous year with many of the same actors) and especially that of Axionov's *The Heron*? Thus one would see that Vitez's directing activity always keeps very close intertextual relations with other productions performed by the same actors.

BIBLIOGRAPHY

Patrice Pavis, 1985, "Commentaires à l'édition au Livre de Poche de *La Mouette* de Tchékov."

Anton Tchekov, 1985, *La Mouette*, Paris, Le Livre de Poche.

Antoine Vitez and George Banu, 1980, "Entretien," *Silex*, 16.

Antoine Vitez and Emile Copferman, 1981, *De Chaillot à Chaillot*, Paris, Hachette.

NOTES

1. *The Seagull,* translated into French by Antoine Vitez *(La Mouette),* was published by *Actes Sud* in 1984, and by Livre de Poche in 1985. The production described was put on at the Théâtre National de Chaillot in Paris the 9th February 1984.
Director: Antoine Vitez
Set and costume design: Yannis Kokkos
Music: Bernard Cavanna
Choreography: Milko Sparemblek
Lighting system: Patrice Trottier
Director Assistant: Kasia Skansberg
Set and costume design assistant: Nicolas Sire
Cast: Jean Allain, Joël Denicourt, Jean-Yves Dubois, Jean-Claude Jay, Patrice Kerbrat, Dominique Reymond, Edith Scob, Bruno Sermonne, Boguslawa Schubert, Claudia Stavisky, Dominique Valadié, Agnès Van Molder, Pierre Vial, Jean-Marie Winling.

2. Vitez points out his relationship with Meyerhold and insists upon the fact that every theatrical fact belongs to conventions; rejecting the bad usual convention, Meyerhold prefers the intentional convention and the realistic genre is only one of the conventional games theatre provides (p. 45).

3. T.N.C. document. Thanks to Jacques Roulet and Françoise Peyronnet who gave me the opportunity to see it.

3. *As You Like It:*
A dramaturgic analysis of Shakespeare's *As You Like It*

1. *Prologue*

Whether we regard the old Duke's, Rosalind's, or Orlando's story as being the play's principal line of action, the result will be exactly the same: the former intrigue in its intertwinement with the two others is, from a dramatic point of view, absolutely hopeless. It is not playable. The Duke's banishment is a fact from the outset but any potential action which might have otherwise been extracted from it (through his brother's attempt to do away with him in the forest of Arden) is substituted by a brief communiqué telling that he has repented, will live as a hermit and place his brother in the position of which he has robbed him! And Rosalind's story is just as unlikely: well arrived (despite sore feet) to Arden, she meets not only her father but her lover as well, only to retain her disguise to the great confusion of both, duping them until she guilefully acts *dea ex machina,* shifting from masculine into feminine clothing in order to marry someone whose betrothal she could have secured without all the fuss! Actually, most of the action lies in Orlando's story, but this is the stuff of which folk tales or Dostoevsky novels are made: Old Sir Rowland de Boys has three sons when he dies. . . . The folk tale structure is in fact identifiable in the very trials he undergoes: (1) the confrontation with the brother: qualification test; (2) the vanquishing of the usurping duke's wrestler: principal trial; (3) the overcoming of himself in helping the brother with the snake and the lioness: the glorifying test.

Despite this absolutely impossible scenario, *As You Like It (AYLI)* is one of the most often-staged comedies and—just like the bumblebee who will not heed wizened opinions telling that its flight runs contrary to natural law— it challenges dramaturgs and literary scholars to identify the sustaining force clearly keeping the piece alive. The problem is in itself quite simple: all the provisory consequences of the intrigue are retired at the conclusion of the first act, none of which again come into play until the fifth act. This means that *AYLI*'s incontestable power of fascination must derive from sources outside of the intrigues and, seen negatively, that every staging which necessarily builds upon an accentuation of the drama's narrative core is foredoomed to miscarry.

2. *All the world's a stage*

The Hymen masque is but one aspect of *AYLI*'s formal and stylized ending: first Hymen, then a dance, and finally Rosalind's epilogue. But why now this plural construction? What does this say about the play as a whole?

A refined dialectic finale serving which aim? Or rather, of which necessity? Indeed, by necessity of the fact that up until then the play has as a whole been unsuccessful in convincing us of its essential kernel of reality. The obvious

staging of the final scene as a play accentuates the rest of the piece's construc-
tional and play-making character. That which is left in the public consciousness
is perhaps the feelings, the experiences, the possibilities which are only present-
able via the interaction between framing and patterning which might receive
existential meaning when given the chance to live on in the memory freed
from the cool logic of experience:

> Ros.: O come, let us remove.
> The sight of lovers feedeth those in love.
> Bring us to this sight, and you shall say
> I'll prove a busy actor in their play.
>   (III, v, 53f)

Corin has interrupted a conversation between Celia and Rosalind, and has
promised them "a pageant truly played." The actors are here Phebe and Silvius
who together constitute the parodic pair. At first, Rosalind and Celia keep
hidden from these two who, through the voyeurs, are revealed to us as they
behave when they are—or when they believe they are—alone. The voyeurs
allow us the possibility of looking into the private sphere as private sphere.
Not as something which must be pretended as a private universe (like that
imposed upon us in illusionism by naturalistic theatre, where we must abstract
from the fourth wall), but as a first-hand reportage from the play revealing
the delusions of private life and reality set in opposition to each other. At
a certain point Rosalind breaks in and gives instructions, becomes the active
actor and transforms the scene. Now the play has lost its character of genuine
play, of being an extension of the actors' sincere and insincere feelings and
strategies. They must from now on meet a public demand: they must bring
those standing outside into their play. In this scene, then, we must have observed the significance which the existence of outsiders has for our perspective
on the stage, namely as a visualized reference point for the action's premises:
the actors are alone, are understood as being alone precisely through the presence of hidden observers visible only to the public. Shakespeare uses the soliloquy in the tragedies and the historic plays in order to communicate the characters' inner thoughts. In the fundamental dialogic form of the comedy, however,
other roads must be found leading to the center of the contrapuntal structure
of mistaken identity, transformation, role-play, satire, irony, and even ambiguity, which gives anchorage for uprightness, harmony, intention, that is,
for situations where the mask has fallen away and the character is revealed.
The hidden observer of this genuine masque is the audience's touchstone.
Here we can be assured that what happens is what the centrifugal force
on stage wishes to happen through his or her artistic means. Thus the
structure of *AYLI* can be seen as alternating between the theatre and theatre-
within-theatre. It is only through a melding of the two forms of presentation
that a comprehensive picture of the play's action and characters can be formulated.

There is no theatre-within-theatre in the somber universe of the first act. Role play here is something envisaged self-consciously: "what think you of falling in love?" (I, ii, 23) or a pretentious mask of loyalty (as exemplified in the courtesan Le Beau), concealing critical attitudes and somber feelings.

It is not until the second act, where Rosalind dons the essential mask in her shift of gender, that the scenes increase in which the public, through a hidden observer, has the possibility of receiving edited information about the characters who are otherwise seen only on their own conditions.

Jacques is the primary observer, but even he is spied upon. We meet him through a second-hand account of his encounter with a wounded deer. A story in which no embarrassing detail is spared for the delivery of the sentimental kitsch in the melancholic's response (II, i, 30f.). But, as noted, Jacques is otherwise basically a looker-on. He serves as our on-the-spot commentator (II, ii, 290ff) for Touchstone and Audrey's "mock-marriage," allowing us a peek into the lifestyle and aspirations of the more congenial folk.

But we are also given audience to the principal character, Rosalind, from an outsider's point of view, though perhaps on different conditions: Ros.: "I will speak to him like a saucy lackey and under that habit play the knave with him—Do you hear, forester?" In Rosalind's reply to Celia, the framework of Rosalind and Orlando's meeting is determined simultaneously for the public, even though Celia is on stage during the entire meeting (III, ii, 422: "Come sister will you go?") and the director must stage her presence while sufficiently distancing her from Orlando. Thus it is by way of Rosalind's ceremonial-like introduction to the anticipated content of the scene that we are forewarned that even if it appears to be a peek into the relationship between two lovers, it is actually no more than a consciously governed role-play.

Nor can Rosalind be closely observed in this kind of scene: she is imbued with a role-consciousness here as well. Nor does Shakespeare allow her to perform on the slackrope for a third party in a sort of involuntary peep-show. Our sole formal point of view is the *confidante* Celia. This is again the case in IV, i, 35f., where Rosalind puts on the second "mock-marriage" with Celia being the implicated, unwilling procuress (Celia: "You have simply misused our sex in your love-prate"). Celia's presence has only formal significance—she constitutes the fourth wall—in a conscientious role-acting on the part of Rosalind: "By this hand, it will not kill a fly. But come, now I will be your Rosalind in a more coming-on disposition; and ask me what you will, I will grant it."

The final and absolute proof of Rosalind's true love for Orlando—if ever we doubted—evinces in Act IV, iii, where, maintaining her Ganymed identity, she must endure the impassioned story of Orlando and the lioness, and where —even though it is out of role—she topples over at the sight of the blood-spot, whereby she must affirm for the stage's doubting public—Oliver and Celia —and the audience, that she merely *acted*. Oliver: "This was not counterfeit, there is too great testimony in your complexion that it was a passion of earnest." In this way, the true director of the theatre-within-theatre must in the last instance function as a simple element in the company and allow itself to be espied from the outside.

The public, directly and indirectly, has received a glimpse into the characters' natures: Jacques, who despite social possibilities to the contrary, has been bound to one special line, the eternal voyeur. Touchstone who, because of his social status, can only play out his vision of the world in the form of verbal word-play. Silvius, in an emotionally stiffened, period-specific role of "the sad shepherd" plays a predictable sado-masochistic role in relation to Phebe who, due to social constraints, cannot realize her dreams of another love relationship. This lies in contrast to the happy-go-lucky Rosalind, who acquires everything through her role and through Celia who receives her wages for faith's servitude as a by-product of her friend's efficient organization. All the world may be a stage, but even in the forest social status forces a distinction between the star players and the water boys.

However, what is common to the assembly in the forest is the possibility of feigned insanity without fatal consequences. The action and the forms of dialogue are endowed with the freedom of experimental and non-commitant action. The meeting as such between people in the forest is a play where normal —sometimes fatal—consequences are suspended.

The formal manifestation of the conclusion and the inserted "genuine scenes" with the built-in witness guarantee all serve to shed a glimmer of reality over the life in the forest. But why are such occasions at all necessary? This necessity stems from the structure and thematic of the piece itself.

3. A motley coat

The general structure of the play is quite clear and simple. The first act presents an infernal civilization under an omnipotent and fear-inspiring sovereign along with the victims of an arbitrary and inexplicable oppression. The silent and tacit acceptance of injustice is by no means a guarantee against sudden attack and menace of destruction. Orlando's activeness and Rosalind's passiveness are equally life threatening.

Life conditions in the forest are diametrically opposed. Despite the rigid framework dictating the development of the action, nature's meteorological caprices, and the animals' demonic behavior being potential adjuvants, we can still speak of a free stage for everyone who must be content with playing a part in the ordinary development of human feelings and aspirations. And naturally there are differences between people here as well: we cannot refer to a paradisic frame where civilization's social and economic ranks do not come into play. Even a mechanized tick-tocking clock accompanies the forest sojourners. Yet it is not these structural forms so restrictive in civilization that are the essential factors determining the interaction in the forest of Arden. It is rather the diverse forms of emotional life and sex roles which dominate in the intrigues of high and low plot.

The differences of rank and order are quickly resolved as the forest sojourn concludes and the return to civilization commences. Through happenstance everything falls into place so that the social foundations of the emotionally based alliances are also held intact. Here the realist in Shakespeare manifests itself in a couple of brief lines. However, without allowing these conditions (evident to any spectator with just a trace of common cynicism) to destroy the overall joy which, as we know, we receive in spite of everything. For even though Jacques will not return home with the others, preferring to hold on to his role as the hermit, and even though Phebe will not accept another offering, and even though we can anticipate difficult communication problems between Audrey and Touchstone, when we abstract from the carnal intercourse, the general impression we get—at least from the principal actors carrying the main action—is that one goes on to meet better times ahead, understood as better conditions for those people who receive their due (the Duke, Rosalind, Orlando), and for those who find one another (Oliver and Celia). At a lower level the situation is more confused.

Life in the forest is more vegetative. There is time to escape. Indeed, the structure of the play is at its initial stage purely escapist. The plot is extremely unmarked. The moments of tension are practically non-existent. This is why the interest in a possible reconciliation of Ganymed's true identity in the relationship to Orlando and the aged Duke serves as the focal point of the audience's attention. Nor is it this which is at question. Rosalind's shift in gender on the other hand provides the centrifugal force, the actor, the possibility of becoming a woman, with the added advantage for the dramatist that language can be placed at the center, in opposition to the stone-faced tragic hero who does not use the language master's lapidary linguistic forms and who adheres to the action-marked approach to existence: Rosalind: "Do you not know I am a woman? When I think, I must speak" (III, ii, 249). But, in the forest, the men themselves become speakers. Touchstone continues right where he left off. Silvius can simply not resist a page-by-page recitation from the poetry book. Jacques has personally affirmed his message and the old Duke in his exile has become a bit of a bittersweet commentator. Together they comprise a complete orchestra of voices crying for admission on stage to present a little number. And this they are granted!

The design of the forest scenes resembles a patchwork quilt—or the Harlequin's suit sewn from patches which harmonize or oppose, deepen, prolong, contrast, or neutralize each other. When one pageant is rolled out with a team of actors, another is rolled in. Just as in a series of skits from a variety show. The forest is a supermarket of attitudes. A therapy forum for the needy. A theatre piece for us—about us.

The danger of completely distancing the public from the events on stage has already been identified as a structural element: nonetheless Shakespeare tests our ability to effect a participatory synthesis of, and identification with, the general fable (the love story of Orlando and Rosalind, including the subsequent family activity) to the utmost in Orlando's poetics in the form of love poems tottering on poesy's unsteady feet. The pastiche of adventurous romance recounting the virtuous brother's selfless struggle with snakes and lionesses. Touchstone's and Audrey's marriage by the preacher Oliver Martext. Touchstone's underdog status and *repetitive,* vain, and unsuccessful tirades. Jacques's melancholic lectures. The authentic ritual as contrasting actions.

4. *Music and dialogue*

During the time in which *Four Quartets* was written, T. S. Eliot wrote an essay, "The Music of Poetry" (1942), in which he describes the relationship between poetry and music thus:

> The use of recurrent themes is as natural to poetry as to music. There are possibilities for verse which bear some analogy to the development of a theme by different groups of instruments; there are possibilities of transitions in a poem comparable to the different movements of a symphony or a quartet; there are possibilities of contrapuntal arrangement of subject-matter. It is in the concert room rather than in the opera house, that the germ of a poem may be quickened.

This description of course corresponds precisely to Eliot's undertaking in his writing of the *Four Quartets,* but what he presents in this essay are general principles for a gestaltization of poetic texts, and this could just as well be a description of the construction of *AYLI.*

That his parallel with music is fruitful and particularly amendable to the dramatic piece can be seen in a remarkable instance from the fifth act, where Phebe asks Silvius to explain to Ganymed (Rosalind) what love is. This is developed in the following exchange:

Phebe:	Good Shepard, tell this youth what 'tis to love.
Sil.:	It is to be all made of sighs and tears,
	And so am I for Phebe.
Phebe:	And I for Ganymed.
Orl.:	And I for Rosalind.
Ros.:	And I for no woman.
Sil.:	It is to be all made of faith and service,
	And so am I for Phebe.
Phebe:	And I for Rosalind.
Ros.:	And I for no woman.
Sil.:	It is to be all made of fantasy,
	All made of passion and all made of wishes,
	All adoration, duty and observance,
	All humbleness, all patience and impatience,
	All purity, all trial, all observance;
	And so am I for Phebe.

Phebe: And so am I for Ganymed.
Orl.:   And so am I for Rosalind.
Ros.:   And so am I for no woman.

(V, ii, 82–100)

This dialogue, which continues a little further in the same vein, closely resembles a song with a chorus and individualized voices in a sort of refrain; at the same time, it illustrates what Roman Jakobson would call language's metalinguistic and poetic function and their concrete interlacing in the textual process. We have discussed themes and their orchestration, and the play contains many themes. An example of this can be noted in the developments in the traditional pastoral conflict between agricultural and city life (especially among the older Duke, Jacques, and Touchstone). *AYLI* however, is characterized by one principal theme, love between man and woman, and through this very specific orchestration the play must—and can—be held in sway. The above quotation from the fifth act is also illustrative of the classical method of theatre where counterparts, a series of independent voices, are often bound pair-wise in an attempt to define the nature of love: they advance hypotheses, give examples, raise questions seriously and in jest, mischievously or in despair. The voices enter into a dialogue with one another. They argue, quarrel, tease, entrap, supplicate, refuse, confess, etc., and out of this polyphony emerges a kaleidoscope vision of love and particularly that of being in love. This multiplicity and rupture and reflection of the main theme in the individual dialogue situations almost always possesses the autonomy of the sketch and is so to say the centrifugal principle of the drama which orders the voices in relation to one another, assigning them different importance and meaning and finishes by establishing a hierarchy, an order of precedence between them.

5. Your if is the only peacemaker: much virtue in if

Without generalizing on the dramatic piece as such, we will contend that there is a marked difference in the way in which the discourse functions in Shakespeare's tragedies and comedies. Often, the major difference between tragedy and comedy is defined as the difference between *alienation* and *integration,* so that at the end of the play the tragedy's hero stands alone, isolated from society, a society which in some cases is itself disintegrated, whereas the protagonist or protagonists in the comedy are integrated in the society, most often recognized in a celebration having an affinity to a fertility rite (e.g., wedding, as contrasted to the tragedy's traditional execution or another form of the body's destruction).

It is in relation to this decisive difference in the fable's peripety and dénouement that the function of discourse must be understood. It is characteristic of Shakespearian tragedy that *discourse is fatal. King Lear* is a good example because the drama's point of departure is Lear's wish that his daughters, through utterance, give a formal, almost ritualized expression of their love for him. He subsequently regards the discourse as an action and bondable, and this is the arbiter of his fate.

Another trait of the tragedy's discourse is its monologic and declamatory nature. Although Shakespeare's tragedies are naturally comprised of dialogues, it is characteristic that these do not lead to understanding or agreement; discourse serves neither to create a common existential conception nor an agreement on the justification for social norms. It is often true that in the tragedy the action or deliberation is central, but the modalities of discourse themselves prohibit a reconciliation, either because it is declamatory (e.g., imperative utterance) or *strategic*, i.e., because they pursue their own ends without regard to truth or ethical validity. This affects the relation between discourse, identity, and self-recognition: the declamatory nature of the discourse is a rigid confrontation of an identity where the force of this confirmation and the spectacular demonstration of this identity are frequently proportional to a lack of self-understanding. This does not mean that the tragedy cannot result in a process of consciousness, for example, in Lear's wandering through the countryside toward Dover he worked a way through insanity to consciousness; but, in tragedy, recognition (anagnorisis), whether the manifest change in destiny (peripety) happens before, after, or simultaneously; it always occurs too late, because the powers which initiate the destruction of the tragic hero have worked silently and unrecognized.

The experimental action (action as play) is the representation or the delimitation of a situation and a series of actions (Freud for example defines thought as a sort of experimental action in the mind). In characterizing the tragedy, we have spoken of the restrictive relation between discourse and action and not of the experimental action for the good reason that it is practically nonexistent since the cards have already been laid on the table. Even when theatre-within-theatre is utilized in the tragedy as, for example, in the staging of Gonzago's murder in *Hamlet,* we speak of an *irreversible event,* a fatal revelation, whereas the simple gestural indication, the role-play, on the contrary, is *reversible.* This is why, in the tragedy, discourse is identical with binding and consequential action. However, the discourse may only incite the action; it cannot govern it. Thus tragedy's discourse is characterized by a duality of *omnipotence* and *impotence,* command confronting supplication, proclamation confronting doubt's plaintive dirge.

The relation between discourse and body differs in the two genres as well. This of course has to do with thematization of the body where, at the mythical level, the opposition is between the broken body expressed emblematically by Lear when the blinded Glouster would kiss his hand:

> Glou.: O! let me kiss that hand.
> Lear: Let me wipe it first; it smells of mortality.
>   (IV, vi, 134–35)

and between the comedy's double body, that of man and woman unified in the act of love:

> Ros.: I would thou couldst stammer, that thou mightst pour this con-
> cealed man out of thy mouth, as wine comes out of a narrow-
> mouthed bottle; either too much at once or none at all. I prithee
> take the cork out of the mouth, that I may drink thy tidings.
> Celia: So you may put a man in your belly.
>
> (III, ii, 195–207)

Although Celia's and Rosalind's brazen indecencies (which here almost elude Touchstone) thematize sexuality, a performance will also demonstrate that in Shakespearian comedy, discourse as an action is eroticized to such a point that often (as above) it takes on the character of a pleasurable physical blossoming. Hence discourse becomes the physical manifestation of a mental excess. Tragedy's discourse, on the contrary, is correlated with the statuary or martyred body, so that the material realization of the linguistic expression becomes either an indicator of social worth and power or of tragic isolation; the pompous or laconic voice of the author on the one hand and the eruption or oppression and inhibition in the intonation on the other. In both cases, the language's concrete materiality is semanticized and refers to something stringent, to a non-freedom.

By sole virtue of its being a comedy, *AYLI*'s discourse is diametrically opposed to that which has been said about the tragedy's and, what's more, Touchstone, near the end of the play, delivers a digression on the rules for the duel and his own quasi-duel, a discourse which at first glance appears irrelevant filler material but which upon closer inspection appears to embody the poetic of the Shakespearian comedy:

> Jacques: Can you nominate in order now the degrees of the lie?
> Touch.: The first, the Retort Courteous; the second, the Quib Modest;
> the third, the Reply Churlish; the fourth, the Reproof Valiant;
> the fifth, the Countercheck Quarrelsome; the sixth, the Lie with
> Circumstance; the seventh, the Lie Direct. All these you may avoid
> but the Lie Direct; and you may avoid that too, with an If. I
> knew when seven justices could not make up a quarrel, but when
> the parties were met themselves, one of them thought but of an
> If, as, "If you said so, then I said so." And they shook hands
> and swore brothers. Your If is the only peacemaker; much virtue
> in If.

The consequences of an utterance can be avoided six times and the seventh can be shuffled off by rendering it hypothetical; hence, a form of fictionizing it. Confronted with the irreversibility of the tragedy's discourse, Touchstone advocates the reversibility, or better, perhaps, in biblical terminology, the reconciliation which characterizes the comedy's discourse. Touchstone's reply also gives notice of the fact that the comedy contains the possibility of true dialogue; discourse is of course used strategically in the comedy as well and deception and trickery are employed almost willfully, but in the final instance, this does not keep its dénouement from resting on an accepted consensus on what is considered *pleasurable, reasonable,* and *allowable.*

6. This is the Forest of Arden

In the preceding we have been occupied primarily with the role-play and staging of the thematization of theatre-within-theatre and what seems to be the essential characteristic of the Shakespearian comedy as an extension of these reflections:

> Celia: Therefore, my sweet Rose, my dear Rose,
> be merry.
> Ros.: From henceforth I will, coz, and device sports.
> Let me see, what think you of falling in love?
> (I, ii, 21–24)

As we have noted, this is a good example of the will to stage existence as a play, and this play has the character of self-dramatizing an arrangement of the outside world in such a way as to contribute to the protagonists' *con amore* presentation. In the dialogues between Rosalind and Celia, particularly in the first act, this self-made reality is primarily linguistic, the young women create a conversation space into which only Touchstone gains entrance, and which becomes an imaginary refuge in the oppressive reality of the nobility. But what happens? Rosalind has barely suggested infatuation as a pastime in their common, exclusively discursive universe before Orlando makes his physical entrance on stage and she falls hopelessly in love (just as Phebe has barely refuted love, before she becomes its prisoner). This points to a *magical* relationship between imagination and reality, between the discursive universe and the action universe. This magic is a well-known psychological and anthropological phenomenon: *thought's omnipotence.* A humoristic-realistic version of this is found in the folk tale in which the realization of three wishes leaves the protagonist exactly where s/he started. From this point of view, *AYLI* can be seen as the representation of a *wish-fulfilment,* where the stage's fictive, but simultaneously physically present space, serves as a material base for Rosalind's performance.

Thus, in connection to its mythical function as a natural regenerative space, Arden also becomes a landscape of consciousness, a foil for the playing out of a wish fulfilment. Shakespeare, however, is far too great a poet simply to make do with this, and complicates and orchestrates love's thematic as it is described above. However, the concrete passage from the imagination to concretion contains two aspects which lie latent in the answer to the question of why Rosalind does not immediately reveal herself to her father and her lover. For, at first glance, this seems unreasonable: in revealing her identity she could enjoy both her father's loving protection and the betrothal of her noble lover, but chooses instead vulnerability under another identity, indeed, under another sex. The explanation of this can be attempted in a few key words, namely the concepts of *liberation* and *individuation*. Because of their status as nubile virgins, Rosalind and Celia find themselves in a biologically and socially determined phase of transition, marked by departure from—and often revolt against—the family and particularly the father figure (authority). This phase concludes with the establishing of an individual, personal, sexual, and social identity. In the comedy of intrigue having its roots in neo-Attic comedy, the son's revolt against and refusal of the father figure is the fable's central element. This is why Frye, among others, can define the comedy as a comic resolving of the Oedipal conflict. In *AYLI*, there are traces of this tendency in the girl's flight from the Duke Frederic; a flight that frees them from the evil father image (so say the psychoanalysts), and this relationship, seen in connection with the phase in which Rosalind and Celia find themselves, makes their actions logical, something which Rosalind also expresses quite clearly: "But what talk we of fathers, when there is such a man as Orlando?" (III, iv, 34–35).

But if *AYLI* is not a comedy of intrigue with the revolt against authority as its central theme, then what is it and why does Rosalind not reveal her identity to Orlando? One possible answer which contains a grain of truth is that she will be certain of his love before allowing herself to be recognized, but this explanation does not go very far, for in fact she has no reason whatsoever to doubt this. The real reason is that she enjoys the freedom which role play gives her. Early in the piece Rosalind and Celia distinguish between working-day world and holiday foolery (I, iii, 12 and 14), and the transition to a holiday world occurs in the flight to Arden, to a world in which young women are not bound to a socially restrictive identity. Even though Rosalind is truly and deeply in love with Orlando ("O coz, coz, coz, my pretty little coz, that thou didst know how many fathom deep I am in love!", IV, i, 195–96), she grants herself the few days' liberty where the world is exactly As You Like It. This transitional phase in which Rosalind and Celia find themselves is characterized by a search for self-identity and a search and waiting for the beloved but, in the play's magical world, the partner is present as soon as the possibility of being in love is mentioned, and Arden's function therefore becomes not primarily that of a hunting ground or mating place for Rosalind (but just that for the others); its function is another, that of a space of freedom where Rosalind's individuation takes place.

7. *According to the measure of their states*

With Rosalind's final choice of a personal, sexual, and social identity, Arden has fulfilled its intended purpose of a play-ground yet, in compliance with the piece's phantasmal logic, proves its magical uniqueness to the very end as, entering into the forest, the Duke Frederic is converted. The forest of Arden, however, both as a regenerative natural space and as a landscape of the consciousness, is a *transformation space* and not a static place, both because it is an unreal, imaginary universe and because the pastoral idyll is not Shakespeare's ideal. The transformation does not, as mentioned above, consist in change but in evolution, insofar as the reality is brought into harmony through the protagonist's nature and desires—except for Phebe, who serves to remind us that this is not possible all the time.

8. As You Like It

Rosalind's epilogue, in spite of its being unfortunately excluded in many productions, is absolutely essential for the piece. In the first place, it echoes Touchstone's If, an if that first appears in Rosalind's and Celia's oath: "By our beards, if we had them. . ." (I, ii, 68), in the mouths of the young male actors it becomes "If I were a Woman" (V, iv, 214–15), and the fiction of the entire piece is characterized by this. This thematization of the redoubling of the problem of sexual identity, of a young boy playing a woman playing a young man, but who, masked as a woman, remarks that "she" is a boy is important too because the freedom to assume another (sexual) identity, something that is an utopic extension of the individual's potential within the euphoric universe of Arden, is again revealed, but which at the same time shows that this is possible only in the world of theatre. The presentation of this difference between fiction and reality indicates that the universe of the play is an illusion sectioned off from the public's reality. The epilogue, however, contains at the same time an opening between fiction and public; consider Rosalind's formulation of the traditional *plaudite*, the applause:

> My way is to conjure you, and I'll begin with the women. I charge you, O women, for the love you bear to men, to like as much of this play as please you. And I charge you, O men, for the love you bear to women —as I perceive by your simpering none of you hates them—that between you and the women the play may please. (V, iv, 208–14)

The adjuration of Rosalind / the boy actor which accords perfectly with the magical spirit at work throughout the drama, places the play's fate in the public's hands. The epilogue is in this respect quite traditional; but the essential is that the fate of the piece is determined by the love which the actual women in the audience show for the men and vice versa. Something is thereby said about which conditions the drama can satisfy, on the condition that the public feels attracted by, is in love with persons of the opposite sex. The fictive concretization of wish-fulfillment in this way takes on a psychic reality, as long as it is not accepted as a true rendition of reality but as a convincing interpretation of ordinary dreams of the realization of love between man and woman.

We have postulated that whereas the tragic discourse was monologic and fatal, the comic discourse was a dialogue and discussion on the conditions of desire. *AYLI*'s epilogue correlates three different dialogues: the mutual dialogue between fictive characters, the dialogue between stage and audience, and the dialogue among the public. In all three, dialogue's pleasure and happiness is the order of the day. When Rosalind conjures the men "that between you and the women the play may you please," she makes the play an object of common desire and for a mediation of that desire which men and women feel for one another, and in doing so relates the telos of the piece and that of our own existence, or at least the telos for a decisive part of it.

9. Epilogue

The insightful and creative reading of a dramatic piece evokes an immense wealth of nuanced experiences and detailed images. Every possible variant can be tested, possible interpretations weighed against each other. In respect to the reader's inner world, the play is limitless if the conditions for the interaction with the text are otherwise present. And perhaps it is precisely in relation to a dramatic piece that the freedom is particularly greatest, especially when we meet a playwright such as Shakespeare, who has no desire to produce excessive stage instruction. Thus, the reader is his/her own director in a way that the director of the theatre can never be, indeed the reader is an enviable person. The director must choose *one* interpretation in order to tell his/her story to a public which cannot be expected to have the same predispositions as those which the director has judged fitting for the piece. Understood in this way, a concrete realization of a Shakespearian work is in principle always a limited realization, from which other possible interpretations had to be excluded for the concrete interpretation which s/he has chosen to present to the public.

A literary approach to the dramatic text can assume different forms. These may extend from the philological, word-by-word unraveling of the partial variants with their possible consequences for the texts as a totality, to theory-governed analyses issuing from a holistic view of man, language, period, and which choose to accentuate fundamentally different elements in the text. The footnotes will interpret hard-to-understand lines. The basic analyses will be possible conceptual sketches, even if more often than not they will prove too abstract for their realization.

A proficient dramaturgic analysis must combine the competence of literary analysis with the faculty of scenic representation founded in part on an attentiveness to direct and indirect scenic instructions in the dramatic text, in part on a synthesis between the plan and the fundamental texture of the realization (fable, play, universe). The dramaturgical analysis surpasses the literary analysis without in any way rendering the latter superfluous. One might instead speak of the dramaturgic analysis which is partially preoccupied with concrete interests: How to play this scene? Which stage props? What shall they do when speaking? Why are three people on stage when only two are in dialogue? —i.e., with establishing some relevant criteria for the literary analyses's wealth of inspiration which can result in revision, development, or simply in a new insight into the text's potential that might escape literary analysis, which so often is fixed on the meaning of a written text.

From the literary and dramaturgical intercourse with the dramatic text one must hazard an approach, a concept, or, quite simply, a good idea; but mark well, an idea which is more a form than it is a content. This is created ideally in a rehearsal where everyone—the dramatist, director, actor, scenographer —offers suggestions, discusses, and executes trial runs. The essential function of this basic sketch consists, in the first instance, in an eventual translation and elaboration of the scenography and the costumes, and at this stage much is already set in motion. A circumstance whose effect is that theatre often opts for the certain, i.e., the traditional (a known director with the performance of the concrete piece behind him), or an anti-traditional representation which can be foreseen as a general opposition against the tradition but which often will eschew its cultural-political objectives in relation to a public who cannot be expected to have any knowledge of the tradition; the best result in these instances is a sort of backstairs revolution within the limits of the cultural institutions.

Perhaps Schaubühne's version of *AYLI* from 1977 (which the authors of this essay have seen only in a truncated version on video) suffers this pitfall in that the director, Peter Stein, in an anti-romantic zealousness, succeeds in giving more an anti-traditional *AYLI* than a coherent and convincing interpretation in its entirety or even a good story based on its own premises.

In allowing the life in the forest to appear as a sort of junkyard adventure land for alien interaction and communication among the fragments of citations from culture and nature (cf. Eliot's "heap of broken images") where decadence and artifice dominate, he can only tell his story to an initiated audience who, remembering singular, earlier, perhaps too idyllic romanticizings of nature in Arden, are capable of establishing an intertextual meta-play consciously based on the different versions of *AYLI*. In this way the theatre becomes something of an intellectual enterprise. Stein's version is exciting but one-eyed. Provoking but unsuccessful as spontaneous comedy for a so-called ordinary public.

The televised BBC version is the exact contrary to Schaubühne's. It is common and servile, naturalistic and anti-theatrical. True to the genre in its dominant tone of gaiety but fundamentally rigid in its incompetence of nuance and contrast. The sketch, the theme, the dynamic, and the contrast, that is, all the pertinent and provocative modernity of the fable disappears in lyrical musical flights and the blooming frivolities of the English park.

Where Schaubühne kills Shakespeare's fundamental story in his attempt at a new rendition, the BBC loses its audience—except for the true-blue subscribers—by recounting a story so that the words exist in the localities which correspond with the stage instruction. Neither expressionism nor naturalism, originality nor conventionality ought to account for a lucky result in an encounter with *AYLI*. The originality must be grounded as much in the text as in the demands of the genre.

A possible theatrical version, in continuance of the above reflections, must maintain two facets of the story: on the one hand, the fairy-tale quality of the plot and the imaginary nature of time and places and, on the other, the fable's reality and the will to strive for and realize these utopias.

In the initial scenography, it ought only to be minor changes creating a new world before our eyes. It is in the middle of a whirlwind of delayed excess that the fable should unfold both as the point of identification and as the dynamic element. In spite of visible evidence of the pollution in the pastoral's idyllic environment, the vision of a more beautiful life should shine through. The re-establishment of the initial scenography's civilized development must not resemble that of the first act. Also the second version of civilization is an imaginary product of the character's aspiration, not a cold reality existing outside the theatre.

Note on the contributors

Contributions

Marvin Carlson (City University of New York), chapter 3 (part 1)
Marco De Marinis (Macerata University / Bologne University), chapter 3 (part 2)
André Helbo (University of Brussels), chapters 1, 5, and 7
J. Dines Johansen (Odense University), chapters 3 (part 4) and 7
Svend Erik Larsen (Odense University), chapter 3 (part 4)
Ane Grethe Østergaard (Odense University), chapter 3 (part 4)
Patrice Pavis (University of Paris VIII/III), chapters 2, 5, and 7
Franco Ruffini (Bologne University), chapter 3 (part 3)
Lars Seeberg (Odense University), chapters 6 and 7
Anne Ubersfeld (University of Paris III), chapters 4 and 5

Coordination/editing

André Helbo (University of Brussels)

Translation

Jean Alter (Pennsylvania University), **Susan Bassnett** (Warwick University), **Susana Epstein, Jeanette Ferreira-Ross, Firenza Guidi, Loren Kruger** (University of Chicago), **Gay Mac Auley** (University of Sidney), **Raymond Nault, Mitchell Shackelton**

ANDRÉ HELBO is a professor at the University of Brussels and president of the International Association for Semiotics of Performing Arts. He is the author of *Sémiologie de la représentation, Les mots et les gestes: Essai sur le théâtre, Approches de l'opéra,* and *Theory of Performing Arts.*